LEGAL CANNABIS

The Great Social Experiment

PETER M. BIRKELAND

Peter M. Birkeland

CONTENTS

INTRODUCTION

As I was leaving a meeting with Scott, the owner of an athletic club, I walked past the reception desk and he shouted out after me, "Hey, Pete, do you smoke?"

I must have looked startled by the question and he clarified his point.

"I mean, do you smoke pot?"

"I'm not opposed to it," I replied, "but I haven't used any marijuana in over 30 years."

"You should try it when you're writing. It's like, just incredible." I must have kept that startled look because he said, "Pete, I'm telling you, you'll be unbelievably productive if you smoke first. I do it all the time and the pages just fly off my computer."

He looked over at his receptionist, nodded, and said, "Me and Carrie, we're smoking buddies. We smoke all the time, don't we Carrie?"

"Well," responded Carrie, a woman in her early twenties, "I used to smoke but I'm not doing that anymore."

Scott turned back to me, "You know, I should hook you up with my brother-in-law. He and his partners are in the black market now but they're going legal. They're looking at some grow space and they want to wholesale that. You could probably interview them for your book, or maybe help them with their business plan."

"Yeah, sure thing" I said as I headed out the door, reflecting on the conversation with Scott. It was not a remarkable conversation in any way other than the public nature of the exchange. And in that respect, it was quite remarkable. I have been asked the question "do you smoke?" multiple times throughout my life, but it has always been during a private moment. The hushed whisper at a party, a question asked while walking down a deserted and empty street, or within the anonymity of a throng of people at a concert. But in the entryway of an athletic club, in suburban America, with moms and children walking past? In front of other people waiting to get a towel or to check in? I could not have imagined several years ago that the question of whether or not I use marijuana would be asked so casually in a public place, asked so nonchalantly, and that no one within earshot — about 15 people — would seem to care.

The casual conversation on marijuana use in a public place highlights one effect of the revolutionary decision by Colorado voters in November of 2012 to legalize possession and sale of recreational marijuana: an openness and acceptance in talking about a drug that has been illegal since 1937. By a 55 to 45 percent margin, Colorado voters passed State Constitutional Amendment 64, which allows any resident twenty-one years of age or older to possess one ounce of cannabis and provides for the regulation of recreational marijuana sold through privately owned marijuana dispensaries.[1] Amendment 64 also allows any person over age twenty-one to grow six cannabis plants in their home or apartment, if allowed by the landlord or home owner's association. Colorado's historic constitutional amendment has not gone unnoticed, and what Colorado Governor John Hickenlooper refers to as the "Colorado Experiment" has generated intense interest throughout the United States and the world. A Pew Research Report (2015) states "Attitudes about marijuana have undergone a rapid shift in public opinion, paralleled by few other trends in the U.S." [2]

That's an understatement. Since Colorado legalized marijuana in 2012, eight states have followed including Alaska, California, Maine, Massachusetts, Nevada, Oregon, Washington, Vermont, and the District of Columbia. Today, over 21 percent of residents in the United States have access to legal cannabis. And the legalization movement is not just limited to the contiguous states: the U.S. Territory of Guam and Uruguay legalize cannabis similar to Colorado's regulatory framework, with a few minor differences in amount that can be possessed, and the number of plants a citizen is allowed to grow. [3]

The upheaval, discussions, thinking, and the debate on cannabis policy reform has consumed the American public since Colorado passed Amendment 64. For example:

- The *Denver Post* created the first ever "cannabis editor" for an online newspaper called, *"The Cannabist,"* which provides daily breaking stories on the cannabis industry, political developments, feature stories, trends, reviews of cannabis strains, and profiles of cannabis entrepreneurs, among others.

- The website, marijuana.com, sends out numerous emails a day on breaking marijuana-related stories.

- Features about cannabis *by NPR, 60 Minutes, CNN, New York Times, Huffington Post, Fortune, Forbes, The Economist, Time, National Geographic,* and a host of media conglomerates are commonplace.

- The television documentary, "Pot Barons of Colorado" features a number of cannabis entrepreneurs, the problems they face, and their determination to overcome them. It is the first reality television show exploring the cannabis industry, and prior to passage of Amendment 64 the publics' understanding of the cannabis industry came primarily from fictionalized accounts.

- During past presidential election campaigns candidates were asked, "Have you smoked marijuana?" In the 2016 presidential election candidates were asked about the Tenth Amendment of the United States Constitution and whether states have the right to legalize marijuana, which is still illegal under Federal law. The issue of marijuana for a Presidential candidate in previous elections was a personal one; for current candidates it's a Constitutional one.

- During the 114th Congress (2015-2016) more bills regarding marijuana were introduced than during any previous Congress in the history of the United States. And unlike previous Congresses, the bills were not punitive in nature, but progressive. There are several bills to allow easier access to medical marijuana for patients and for medical marijuana research; bills to allow marijuana businesses to access banking; and bills to allow tax deductions for marijuana businesses. [4] Bills introduced into Congress to regulate marijuana in the past typically didn't get very far in the process and few bills had more than one co-sponsor. The current bills have multiple co-sponsors and cross both state and party lines.

It is a watershed moment for both proponents and opponents of cannabis legalization, and a particularly ripe area for sociological and economic study. In this book I explore the transformation of Colorado's cannabis industry from black market to legitimate market, a transition that is unique since there is a definitive starting point, a "Day One," which happened on January 1, 2014. Of course, there is an economic impact when an illegal market becomes legal and although I analyze the economic impact of the newly legal cannabis industry, the social impact is far more significant and interesting and has broader repercussions than the economic consequences. To be sure, the economic impact of the cannabis industry has altered the fortune of the actual participants in the cannabis industry as well as the people that supply services to the industry. And it has altered communities and the state of Colorado, in both positive and negative ways.

But the social consequences of cannabis legalization are far-reaching. For example, my discussion with Scott at the beginning of this chapter, on whether I smoked pot, highlights one social impact of cannabis legalization. That conversation took place in a public space, and that's evidence of a social transformation, of a cultural shift in attitudes about cannabis that are subtle, but significant. Looking through the sociological lens forced me to ask a host of questions about the other changes that Colorado has experienced since legalizing marijuana. For instance:

- What has happened to crime rates, to teenage use of marijuana, to rates of driving while impaired? Are those rates all up as opponents argued, or down as economists predicted?

- Who are the people that own cultivation, processing, and dispensary operations in the industry? Are the business owners the high-school dropout who grew marijuana in his mother's basement and decided to "go legal," or is it a person who graduated from college with an MBA?

- Who are the customers? Are they the twenty-something, tattooed, pierced, dreadlocked guys, aimless and possibly homeless, or are the customers a slice of the American populace?

- What are the profit margins, the sales, and the numbers at the dispensary level, the city level, and the state level?

- How much money is involved in the so-called "green rush" and who's making the money?

- What about cartels and the black market? Opponents say that cartel involvement and the black market will increase dramatically after legalization, while proponents argue just the opposite, that the black market will disappear and the cartels along with that.

These were some of the policy-level, economic, and social-impact questions I started with when I began this research, but I came to realize that the micro-level data, the interactions among people, the conflict on perspectives, the differing opinions on cannabis, the clashing of cultural worlds – those social constructions were (and are) the fruitful area to study from a theoretical perspective as well as from a purely descriptive perspective. I spent eighteen months working with cannabis entrepreneurs, including growers who were vertically integrated—that is, had both growing operations and retail dispensaries—as well as with dispensary owners and marijuana infused manufacturers, the people who make edibles. In this book I share what I learned about the industry, the people in it, the growing pains, the conflict, and the significance of the social transformation we are witnessing, not just in Colorado, but in other parts of the United States and the world. I not only worked with cannabis entrepreneurs, but I spoke with marijuana enforcement regulators, with the lawmakers who pieced together the first regulatory system, and I interviewed Colorado Governor John Hickenlooper.

I also attended cannabis meetings and symposiums to learn about developments in the industry and to meet with the people who attended. I was curious to know, who attends a cannabis symposium, and why? I broadened my research to understand the cannabis industry from the perspective of the people who supply goods and services to the cannabis industry, like real estate developers, investors, attorneys, accountants, and others. And finally, I also spoke with people who are adamantly opposed to cannabis legalization to better understand their perspective. The end result is a first-hand account of the challenges faced by the cannabis industry, by the regulatory system, and by enforcement agencies, in creating a legitimate industry at the state level while at the federal level the industry remains strictly illegal.

During my final days of field work I met with Zander, a black market operator who was putting together a business plan to enter the legal medical and recreational cannabis markets in

Oregon. We met at a micro-brewery in Niwot, Colorado, on a Sunday afternoon and as he walked into the pub I thought to myself, *it would be really difficult to place Zander as a black market cannabis operator.* He's 30 years old, has short hair and a trim beard, and was wearing a button-down shirt, khaki pants, and tennis shoes. He looks like any other 30-year-old in Colorado.

"Wow," he stated as he sat down, "an Irish band? Did you know about this?"

"No," I replied, "I'm as surprised as you."

Actually, neither one of us should have been surprised. This part of Colorado, north of Denver and on the outskirts of Boulder, has a vibrant live-band scene and nearly every micro-brewery has live music, seven days a week.

"Are you going to have a beer?" I asked.

"No," Zander replied, "I had a puff on the way over."

"Ok. So I wanted to run some ideas past you on some of the major findings for my book."

"Yeah, sure. I'm interested to see what you came up with."

"One of the things that really surprises me is how little of an impact legalization has made in my life. I mean, it has made virtually no difference, no impact in any way. We don't have police coming to our neighborhood to arrest people for using marijuana, no one smokes in the parks, there aren't big busts of marijuana operations, the drug cartels have disappeared, there's no uptick in crime. Kids aren't using marijuana any more frequently than in the past. I don't see a big change in my experience. Living here with marijuana legal is exactly the same as living here with it illegal."

Zander sat up straight and looked at me with utter shock and disbelief. He thought about my comments for a moment and then waved his hand at me and said, "For you…yeah. Ha," he laughed and sat back in his chair.

It's an insightful comment by Zander. He knows that I'm not a participant in the cannabis culture. I moved to Boulder County in July 2011 and have witnessed the transformation from an illegal to legal cannabis market, but I didn't pay close attention to it and, as I mentioned to Zander, there's no discernable change to my life. I have asked other people about their experience since legalization—neighbors, colleagues, random people I sit next to on the bus—and if they're not a user of cannabis, their experience is much like mine.

For example, I spoke with my neighbor, Pierre, about legalization of marijuana and life in Colorado. He's 82 years old and a retired rancher from South Dakota and I asked him what his experience has been since Colorado legalized marijuana. He looked at me for a moment, thinking, and shook his head. "It hasn't made any difference at all. But we have a friend that has a sore back and he uses marijuana for that and it has made a big difference for him. But for us? It hasn't changed anything."

ACADEMIC RESEARCH

The casual observer might conclude that the cannabis craze in the media and at the Congressional level signals a new interest in cannabis—and it does for much of the general public. But there is a decades-long history of scholarly work on prohibition and drug policy and that body of work is useful in understanding how cannabis legalization is framed and how it impacts current legalization efforts. However, by necessity the majority of research on cannabis will be left for the reader to discover. Hazekamp (2007) noted that the cannabis plant, *Cannabis sativa L.* is the most researched plant in the world with over 10,000 scientific, medical, and academic works, and Abel (1980) stopped counting references for his manuscript, *Marihuana, The First Twelve Thousand Years*, when he reached 8,000, "most of which were published after 1965" (Abel, 1980). I will briefly present theoretical ideas on prohibition and drug policy research to help orient the reader to this larger context impacting legalization, and to place *Cannabis Colorado* within this context as well.

There are three basic streams of research in the drug policy and prohibition areas and they fall roughly into what I will term a sociological perspective, a neoclassical economic perspective, and an empirical perspective. Sociologists have a rich and long-standing interest in, and inquiry of, subcultures and of people who are marginalized in society. The relevant body of work is largely ethnographic and focuses generally on social deviance, and drug use in particular, covering nearly every aspect of drugs, illicit markets, and consequences of prohibition. Scholars have analyzed the college drug scene, women in prison and drug culture, drug dealing, and have specifically focused on marijuana.[5] The seminal and classic discussion of social deviance with respect to marijuana and culture is found in the works of Becker (1963) and Goffman (1963) and provides a comparative perspective covering over 50 years of deviant and subculture activity with respect to marijuana use. The sociological approach is vibrant today and is influential in immersive journalism and investigative reporting. My approach is ethnographic and fits within the sociological tradition, but differs from earlier work since it is not a case study of a segment of the cannabis industry nor of a particular subculture, but covers a wide range of participants from the "manufacturers" (i.e. cultivators), to retailers, regulators, vendors, financiers, and the illegal (black) market.

The most influential body of work, in terms of drug policy, stems from neoclassical economics and in particular, the path-breaking work of Becker (1968). Within this framework economists argue that prohibition raises the costs of supplying drugs, leading to higher prices under prohibition than what one would expect under a regulated free market.[6] Black market prices for marijuana are not hard to come by and the leading publication in the industry, *High Times,* lists retail prices for several strains of marijuana. Anderson, Hansen, & Rees (2013) analyzed prices from *High Times* in states before and after legalizing medical marijuana and found that after legalization, prices for high-quality strains of marijuana declined by 10 to 26 percent, "suggesting the supply response to legalizing medical marijuana is larger than the demand response" (2013). In Colorado, where recreational sales of marijuana are legal, prices per ounce for marijuana dropped from $350 to $280, or a 20 percent decline, confirming economic theory on prices and illegal markets.

Beyond prices, economists have studied illegal markets from a policy perspective with the intent of understanding, what the optimal allocation of resources is, given societal goals, with respect to illicit behavior. The overall conclusion is that society is better off with legal markets versus illegal markets and that "virtually all the effects of prohibition are undesirable, with the possible exception of reduced consumption" (Miron, 2003:72). Miron further states that "if reduced drug consumption is an appropriate goal for policy, prohibition is almost certainly the wrong approach" (Miron, 2003:72).

I spoke with Jeffrey Miron, a Professor of Economics at Harvard University and one of the leading scholars on drug policy, to understand his perspective since the publication of his book in 2003, *Drug War Crimes*.

"I really enjoyed *Drug War Crimes* and I was wondering what your thoughts are on Colorado's legalization effort, and how that might play out," I stated in a conversation in January 2015.

"Yes," he responded, "it's very interesting what Colorado has done. I'm focused exclusively on policy-level questions, like the effects of legalization on crime, on health, on traffic safety. I'm not interested in the industry *per se* but I expect the marijuana industry to become like any other legal industry. For all practical purposes it ought to be the same as...the bubble gum industry. Prices will come down and quality will go up."

"Yeah," I responded, "that's happened already at the retail level, and somewhat at the wholesale level. I just can't believe how high the prices are for a pound of marijuana, $2,000 a pound."

"If you think about it," he ruminated, "marijuana is like hay, and should probably be priced at, like, $10 a pound."

"Wow," I stated, "that would put a lot of people out of business."

"Well, prohibition raises prices and there's an assumption that if you make it legal you'll see huge declines in prices, like a thousand to one, but that's unlikely to happen. You can compare marijuana to coffee beans, which are a tiny fraction of the cost of a cup of coffee. If you're in the coffee business you have transportation costs, distribution costs, taxes, marketing, retail costs. So, the prices will fall for marijuana, but I would expect them to be modest."

"Plus the legal risk," I added.

"Yes, that is still a big risk until there is a change in policy at the federal level. It's possible that a Republican president could enforce federal law, so the legal risk is very real. But there are zillions of reasons why the effect of legalizing will not be a big boon to the economy and thinking otherwise is a recipe for disappointment, I think."

The conversation with Professor Miron sums up nicely the neoclassical economics perspective on prohibition and legal markets: prices will fall and quality will improve in a legalized market versus a prohibited one.

But what about the other effects of legalization, beyond prices and quality, what might one expect to happen? The third stream of research, and by far the largest, is what I term an empirical perspective and scholars in this vein tackle exactly those types of questions. These researchers look to see the effects of drug use on various individual and social outcomes. For instance, researchers have studied the effects of drugs on infants and small children, in youth, and in the health arena in terms of long-term effects of marijuana use and the effectiveness of marijuana in pain alleviation.[7] There is intense interest and numerous studies in the developmental aspects of drug use especially with respect to teen and youth use. And, there is a large literature on the effects of marijuana on driving, an area of particular interest for both proponents and opponents to cannabis legalization.[8]

For example, Initiative 502, the state of Washington's legalization amendment, is 65 pages long, with 18 of those pages devoted exclusively to the issue of driving under the influence of marijuana. [9] Colorado's Amendment 64, in contrast, is twelve pages long and only one paragraph is devoted to driving under the influence of marijuana. Did Washington go too far, or Colorado not far enough, in stipulating penalties, tests, and procedures for people who drive under the influence of marijuana? Laboratory studies have shown, for example, that while cannabis use impairs driving-related functions such as distance perception, reaction time, and hand-eye coordination, neither simulator nor driving course experiments provide consistent evidence that these impairments to driving-related functions lead to an increased risk of collision.[10] Studies on the effect of alcohol on drivers, however, is more consistent. As Anderson and colleagues note, "Even at low doses drivers under the influence of alcohol tend to underestimate the degree to which they are impaired, drive at faster speeds, and take more risks" (2013:5).

In fact, analyzing traffic fatalities in states that have legalized medical marijuana, Anderson found that "traffic fatalities fall by nearly 9 percent after legalization of medical marijuana," (2012:2), and further, that there is a 19 percent decline in traffic fatalities for 20- through 29-year-olds in states that have legalized medical marijuana. Anderson provides evidence that the mechanism responsible for reduced traffic fatalities in medical marijuana states may be marijuana itself. Where medical marijuana is available, people choose that over alcohol. In neoclassical economic theory, the term for choosing one thing over another is "substitute," and marijuana and alcohol appear to be substitutes: consumption of one reduces the consumption of the other. Anderson et. al. found that beer sales—the alcoholic beverage of choice for younger people—fell by 5.3 percent in states with medical marijuana. So, with fewer people drinking alcohol, traffic fatalities were reduced.

These three streams of research, the sociological, neoclassical economic, and empirical, dominate the ideas, policy-making, and research agendas of contemporary research in drug policy.

However, there is another way to analyze the emergent cannabis industry that could prove to be fruitful and interesting, and this is by asking, as a thought experiment, how would the great social theorists—Marx, Weber, and Durkheim—analyze the cannabis industry? What questions might they ask? What conclusions would they draw if they immersed themselves in the data as I have done? Wikipedia is fine in providing the casual reader with a general overview of each theorist, but for now I will provide a very general description of what they might find intriguing about the cannabis industry. Marx, I believe, would be interested in who has power within the industry—who makes the money? Who controls production? Who writes the industry rules? Weber would most likely be interested in the changing structure of cannabis businesses and relationships moving from an illegal market to a legal one. What are the management practices in these two regimes, and how have cannabis businesses adapted to the new reality? Durkheim would be interested in the coherence and differentiation of the cannabis industry in illegal and legal markets, including rates of innovation and diffusion of innovations. I will circle back at the conclusion with some thoughts on how these three theorists could possibly answer the questions I posed and how they might analyze the cannabis industry.

ORGANIZATION OF THE BOOK

This book can be read from start to finish like any book, but it does not have to be read in a linear fashion. I expected some readers to have their own interests and to pick and choose the chapters and topics of most interest to them. Having said that, however, if you are unfamiliar with the cannabis industry, or if you have preconceived notions about cannabis, then Chapter 1 would be a good place to start because it provides a perspective of the industry from a vertically integrated cannabis owner and looks at the challenges he faces. And if you are not familiar with the cannabis plant and its varieties, how it is grown, and what the pharmacological properties and effects are, then Chapter 2 would be interesting because that lays down the basics of the plant. Other than those two chapters, the book can be read in pretty much any order.

One final note, and I think this is telling: in all of my interviews with people in the industry, including people regulating the industry and people providing services to the industry, I asked the question, *"What do you know to be absolutely true about cannabis?"* Naively, I thought that would be an easy question to answer. It wasn't, and not one person provided an answer. Maybe there's nothing definitive that can be said about cannabis. Maybe it's an ideological fight between proponents and opponents, and the winner gets to determine public policy, gets to determine access to the plant for medical, recreational, research, or other purposes. Maybe the winner gets to create propaganda and a strategy for disseminating that to write a new future, or to reestablish the status quo. Regardless of the future societal framing of cannabis, the cannabis industry is an interesting vehicle to understand the transition from illegal to legal markets and to understand the varied interests that are battling to write that future.

Notes to Introduction

[1] The full text of Amendment 64 can be found here: http://www.fcgov.com/mmj/pdf/amendment64.pdf

[2] The Pew Research on cannabis attitudes in the United States can be found here:

http://www.pewresearch.org/fact-tank/2015/04/14/6-facts-about-marijuana/

[3] For a current listing of legal cannabis by country, go to https://en.wikipedia.org/wiki/Legality_of_cannabis_by_country

[4] The Library of Congress lists all bills, sponsors, co-sponsors, and voting details. See http://thomas.loc.gov/home/bills_res.html. Specific bills include H.R.1635, H.R. 1538, S. 683, S. 133, S. 683, H.R. 1538, S. 1726, H.R. 2076, S. 987, H.R. 1855.

[5] For work on the college drug scene see (Carey 1968); women in prison and drug culture (Denton 2001); drug dealing (Adler 1993, Fields 1984, Venkatesh 2008); and see (Goode 1970, Johnson 1973) for specifics on marijuana.

[6] For background on drug markets from an economics perspective see Miron 2004, Earlywine 2007, Becker et. al. 2006, Friedman 1972, Mishan 2001.

[7] For the effects of drug use on infants and children see (Richardson 1993, LaGasse 1999, Inciardi 1997); in youth see (DiNardo & Lemieux 2001, Dawkins 1997, Fagan 1993); and for pain alleviation see (Hall 1994, Hill 1993, British Medical Association 1997, Institute of Medicine 1999).

[8] See, for example, (Crancer 1969, Smiley 1986, US Department of Transportation 1993, Liguori 2007).

[9] The original text of Initiative 502 can be accessed here: http://lcb.wa.gov/publications/Marijuana/I-502/i502.pdf

[10] For cannabis effects on vehicle operation see Kelly, Darke, and Ross 2004, or Sewell, Poling, and Sofuoglu 2009.

CHAPTER 1.

THE ESTABLISHED CANNABIS OPERATOR

I first started working in the cannabis industry in June 2014 after I was contacted by Eric J. through a website that connects people looking for services with people offering services. The website sent me the following email:

"Eric J. is looking to hire a business consultant. Here are the details of Eric's business consulting needs. Dispensary group needs a professional, polished business plan."

I responded to that email with a quote and short description of expected outcomes, and a few moments later Eric J. called me.

"Yeah," he started in a long-drawn tone, "I'm trying to get a license to open a recreational dispensary in Aurora and I need a business plan for the application. Do you have a problem with that?"

"With what," I responded, "with writing a business plan for you?"

"No, in writing a business plan for a dispensary," he replied.

"Naw," I stated, "I don't have any problem with the type of business you're in."

"You'd be surprised," he stated, "A lot of people have strong opinions about the marijuana industry. *A-lot-of-people,*" he emphasized. "Anyway, we have a chain of dispensaries in Denver, but we want to go to Aurora and it's a requirement for their application process to have a business plan. This is not the type of business plan that you would write for investors, but my understanding is that it will be scored and graded by the city of Aurora for limited licenses."

I am vaguely familiar with Aurora as Eric continues to speak. It is the third largest city in Colorado, at 350,000 residents, and lies adjacent to and on the southeast side of Denver.

"Ok. I don't know anything about the marijuana industry, but I know a lot about writing business plans."

"Well, basically you need to take what I know and put it into the plan," Eric responded.

"And how about my price," I asked, "are you ok with that?"

"Yeah, that seems fair. One guy wanted $12,000 and another said he'd do it for $500. You're in the middle, so that's fine."

"Ok, well, that sounds good to me. What is your timeline?"

"It's pretty quick, I think. We should meet tomorrow. Can you come to Denver to meet?"

"Yeah, that's not a problem."

"Ok, let's meet at my lawyer's office," he stated, "You don't want to come here to our growing operations. It's dirty, your clothes will end up smelling like marijuana, and we would be constantly interrupted."

So, I met Eric at his lawyer's office in downtown Denver. Eric was a few minutes late and when he arrived he was talking on his phone. I later learned that he has two partners, Jason and Ryan, and that all three of them are constantly on the move, shifting from one task to another, speaking to different people, solving a number of problems. They deal with a daily barrage of emails, phone calls, and on-site visitors, and not just a few people, but hundreds.

"I get over 200 emails a day from people I don't know," Eric told me during our first meeting. "They're from all over the country."

"Two hundred emails from people you don't know?" I asked. "What do they want?"

He looked at me with a sense of disgust. "Money. That's what they want. They say they want to get into the cannabis business but what they really want is money."

"Who are these people? And how do they find you?"

Eric shrugged his shoulders and looked at me with a bewildered look. "I have no idea how they find me. I'm not listed anywhere. But they do. They find me. And it's everybody. They're from investor groups, from Fortune 500 companies, they're real estate guys. It's crazy how much interest there is and how many people want to get into this."

Eric is in his late-40's, well over six feet tall, thin, and has a Midwestern accent. I learned later that he grew up in a suburb of Omaha. He is wearing jeans and a faded T-shirt, but I'd seen him drive up for our meeting in a new black Mercedes Benz, a $100,000 car.

"Wow," I said, "nice car."

Eric turned red, shook his head and rolled his eyes. "I hate it. I'm embarrassed to be driving it, but my accountant told me I needed to spend the money. I have a Ford truck and that's good enough. I don't need a new car and I don't need a Mercedes Benz."

As we walked to an empty conference room Eric took several more calls. "It's nonstop," he said, "sorry about that." We entered and sat down. The room was empty except for the two of us and Eric began to tell me about his business and what he's looking for in a business plan.

"The city of Aurora is opening up the recreational marijuana market and they are taking applications for 24 licenses. They have six wards and each ward will have four retail stores. Originally you needed a million bucks in cash or liquid assets to apply, but I guess they didn't get enough people, so they dropped it to $500,000. They have a competitive application process," he stated as he slid a document across the table towards me.

It is the criteria and scoring system for the City of Aurora retail marijuana store application, and includes the following:

1. Experience in operating a licensed marijuana business

    1. 3 years (1 point)
    2. 4 years (1 point)
    3. 5 years (1 point)

2. No administrative penalties or license revoked related to the operation

    1. 3 years (1 point)
    2. 4 years (1 point)
    3. 5 years (1 point)

3. Tax compliant with all state and local tax laws for the last 12 months (2 points)
4. Applicant, principal officers, directors and owners have not ever had the following:

    1. No felony convictions (2 points)
    2. No drug related misdemeanor convictions (2 points)
    3. No pending criminal charges of any type (2 points)

5. Certifies the business will not hire a manager, employee or any person with a felony conviction in the last 10 years or a drug related misdemeanor conviction in the last five years, or a drug related felony conviction ever (4 points)
6. Prior to opening, the building contains air filtration systems that filter out marijuana odor (3 points)
7. Provides a security plan that exceeds the State requirements (2 points)
8. Provides an operating plan to be evaluated by a third party (1-10 points)
9. Provides a business plan to be evaluated by a third party (1-10 points)

Studying the document in Eric's conference room, I can clearly see that the application process by the city of Aurora is straightforward and mostly hedging the risk of felons or persons with criminal backgrounds in drugs from pursuing a license. It is also biased in favor of the established entrepreneur, like Eric, since people with less than three years of operating experience would get zero points for two of the questions while people operating five years could get six points. Plus, the fact that an applicant would need $500,000 in cash or liquid assets almost assures that no start-ups will be applying. There are three wildcards in the application, a security plan, an operational plan, and a business plan.

I note that Eric has optimistically penciled in 10 points for both the operating plan and the business plan, the two parts of the application that are unique, require a lot of thought, and are judged by a "third party." This is the first time I've heard about any of this: the independent evaluation of the business plan; the significant impact of the plan on the overall application score, and the required operating plan. I'm regretting charging so little for the business plan.

"Ok," I said to Eric after reviewing the application, "I see you filled in 10 points for the business plan, and what's this about an operating plan?"

"Yeah, I forgot to mention that when we spoke. We need both plans but the operating plan will be easy to do after the business plan is done."

"Alright, well, let's start with the business plan first. You mentioned that you have a chain of dispensaries now. Why is the Aurora location so important? Are you losing money on the other stores?"

"No," he quickly responded, "you have to be incredibly stupid to lose money in the marijuana industry. I mean, there are people who go out of business, but they're stupid. No, we want to build a new concept in Aurora that we can showcase for our consulting business. We want to mirror what will work in other states that have approved medical marijuana, like Illinois, Massachusetts, Maryland, and we think Florida. The bar is real high and there are a lot of cannabis companies going that route."

"The consulting route?" I asked.

"Yeah," Eric replied. "So, what we're doing is, when a state passes medical marijuana laws, we work with a business in that state and we'll bring all their employees here to our growing facility and teach them everything we know about growing, and we'll have them work in the dispensary, so they'll know everything about that. And they'll spend six months here working with us, so they will really know everything and know it from a hand's-on perspective. And then what we'll do is create an LLC in that state and own it jointly with them, and they'll put money into the LLC which is our payment for the service."

"That's pretty clever," I stated.

"Well," Eric continued, "you don't know which state is going to legalize marijuana next and they all have a residency requirement of two years, so really, the only way to get in there is to partner with someone who's already there and who doesn't know as much about the business as us."

"How much do you charge for that?"

"Ten percent," he replied.

"For how long?"

"Forever," stated Eric.

"Holy smokes! You'll get ten percent of gross revenues forever?"

"That's nothing," he scoffed as he waved his hand. "Most guys doing this are charging 30 percent."

"I know people can find you, but how are you going to find the people who are serious about operating a marijuana business?"

"I wondered about that myself, and…so, you know that saying, 'you've got to dig a well before you need water?'"

"Yeah, I know that."

"Well, that's what we're doing in Florida. We're thinking that Florida might go for legalizing marijuana and they'll probably go all the way, fold medical and recreational together. Anyway, I organized a 'cannabis seminar' and we put together a little table and brochures and we also had a panel. You've been to these before, right? We just rented a meeting room at a hotel. Anyway, it was sold out…standing room only. And on the panel were my lawyer, some accountants, guys that know a lot about marijuana, and me. I have to tell you, every question—*every single question*—went to me, the operator. At first I was kinda happy, you know? Vindication of sorts. But then it continued for another 45 minutes and, to tell you the truth, I was surprised. I was actually stunned by the amount of interest. Every question about the industry went to me. So, there's a lot of interest out there…a lot."

Eric paused for a moment, thinking, and then remembered his next thought. "But I have to tell you, the politics in Florida? Crazy. I mean, it's so political there about marijuana…I don't know," he shook his head. "First off, they need to elect a Democrat as Governor. And that's only the start. But if they go through with it, it will be a huge market. It will change everything. No way can the federal government continue the way they have if Florida legalizes, not just medical, but everything. And that's the way they're going to go. But it's still up in the air."

Eric leaned back in his chair and said, "Well, that's the plan for the future, but right now we need to get this Aurora license, that's really the key to the whole thing. So anyway, right now there are only a handful of players in the marijuana industry. There are about ten big operators, ten in the second tier and then a bunch of little guys. We're in the second tier, but we want to use the Aurora location to put us into the top tier. And actually, we want two locations in Aurora. But I have to tell you, it's really hard to find an 'A' location — near impossible to find a freestanding location. Last month I spent a day driving around Aurora looking for spots and I found one that was perfect. It was a freestanding location, good parking, good visibility, busy street, and so I approached the owner about leasing the location to me. That guy had never considered a recreational marijuana store, I mean, he was totally clueless about it, and he tells me, 'Well, let me think about it for a bit.' And you know what he does? He goes out and finds another dispensary to lease it at a higher rate. Can you believe that?"

"Actually, and this is unfortunate, I can totally believe that. But that's brutal anyway."

"I know! But that's what this business is like. Everybody's trying to make a buck, but they're trying to make it off of me."

"Did you find another spot?"

Eric looked at me with disgust. "Yeah, we found another place. It's not freestanding but in a strip mall. I already put down $15,000 that's non-refundable, so if we don't get the license we just lose that money. But the city of Aurora wants you to have your retail space all lined up before you send in your application, so we had no choice."

"Ok, in terms of your business model, things that might differentiate you from others trying to get a license, what else do I need to know?"

"Well, our model is the five-dollar foot-long hotdog," he looked at me and noticed my blank stare, so he continued. "There's trash out there, there's premium, and we're in the middle, the five-dollar foot-long hotdog, you know, like at the state fair?"

"Yeah, I get it, I just haven't heard anyone describe their business as a five-dollar foot-long hotdog."

"We're completely vertically integrated. We have grow operations, we have medical dispensaries, and we have recreational dispensaries. But it's really capital intensive. We make a million dollars a month and we're breaking even."

"Wow," I stated, "that's a lot of cash—and you're just breaking even?"

"Yeah!" he exclaimed. "Just breaking even on a million bucks a month, can you believe that?"

"Anyway, we have about 35,000 square feet of growing space now and we never have any left over—I can sell all I can grow. I have another 17,000 square feet of growing capacity but I'm selling that because it doesn't solve our inventory problem. So now we're looking into getting another 70,000 square feet."

"So, in total you'll have a little over 100,000 square feet?" I asked.

"Well, right now we've got a little over 50,000 square feet, but we're close to getting the 70,000 square feet. Actually, it's kinda interesting how we made that happen. So I was with my real estate broker two months ago thinking about this 70,000 square foot space and I turned to him and said, 'I need $10 million bucks. Do you know anyone who has that kind of money?' And he looked at me with a blank stare, stunned, and said, 'I'll have to think about it.'"

"Later that afternoon my real estate guy calls me back and says, 'I found someone. It's a group of investors from California.' And then he tells me that they're not interested in the cannabis industry, that it's just a real estate play for them. I tell you, there is so much interest in this industry right now from all over the country you can put together any deal you want. We're paying these guys 11 percent per year and have an option to buy it back after two years."

"But," I stated, "backtrack a bit. Why do you have an inventory problem?"

"Let me ask you this: have you ever been to a dispensary?"

"No, I haven't."

"Who do you think buys marijuana?"

"Well, I'm guessing 21 to 30-year-old males."

"That's part of it, I mean, they buy more than others, but it's everyone, I mean *everyone*," and he emphasized the word, *everyone*. "On Saturday morning when we open the store, there is a line of 50 people waiting to come in and they are grandmas and grandpas, people of all different ages, men and women, Hispanics, white, black—it's everyone. It's crazy, and it's like that all day.

"The other reason that we have an inventory problem is because of the **Vertical Integration Rule.** I can only sell 70 percent of what I produce in my own retail units and I have to sell 30 percent wholesale. And like I said, I've never had any extra."

The vertical integration rule was one of two unique features in implementing recreational marijuana, the other was that for the first ten months of 2014, only existing medical marijuana operators could sell recreational marijuana in the industry. Presumably those two rules were tactics used to simplify oversight of the industry by the Marijuana Enforcement Division (MED), since there would be fewer operators, initially, and the medical marijuana operators were known to the MED. In reality, it gave entrepreneurs like Eric a head start in the industry, what economists call first-mover advantages. But the vertical integration rule only lasted until July 1, 2014 and then the requirement that recreational marijuana retailers have experience in the medical marijuana industry was phased out. At the time I was speaking with Eric in June 2014, neither one of those stringent regulations had been relaxed.

Eric continued, "We have a formidable competitor in this business. There's a very successful real estate developer in Denver and Daddy," he raised his hands to indicate quote marks, "Daddy put his kids into the cannabis business and they have access to Daddy's unlimited funds." He looked at me earnestly and said again, "unlimited. Us? We're doing totally organic growth—never taken any money from anyone."

"Well, that's something to be proud of, growing totally organically," I stated. "So this guy, or his kids, are your biggest competitors? I assume they're going after the Aurora licenses?"

"Yeah," Eric stated, "and even though we're not supposed to contact the Aurora City officials, I've heard that they have spent $200,000 in lobbying."

Eric reflected for a moment. "So last month there was a meeting in Aurora and I show up like this, you know, jeans and a t-shirt, and I'm thinking that this is a group meeting with all the applicants and the city of Aurora officials where they go over the details of the application process. I was wrong. I was the only one in the room who was applying for a license and we were in a big conference room with every official from the city of Aurora—council members, the marijuana regulatory folks, the police, people from the permits and building committee. There were probably 20 people all sitting around a large conference table and me. I was totally unprepared for that but I figured, well, I'm here. I might as well talk with them and figure out what they're looking for."

"And what were they looking for?"

"Well, they had a lot of operational questions, like 'What are you doing to control odor?' That's really a non-issue. I mean, it's important to them, but we're not doing any cultivation in Aurora, just retail, and there is literally no odor because everything is packaged from our growing facility."

He continued, "They had questions on security but that is also a non-issue. We have our own on-site security company and we also have video cameras at all our facilities—we watch everything, and we have cameras that pan out to the parking lot that can see in detail over one hundred feet in total blackness. So, it's really difficult to do something to our employees or our business without us knowing immediately what's going on.

"One question that came up was, 'How can you protect the community from deals in the parking lot?' I mean, that was an actual question! This is not some sort of black market operation. We're selling to just regular people, people who have jobs, who have families. I don't know where these people get their information, but we're not anything like what the movies portray us to be. We don't want to be a headshop. We are low-key. If you try to go to our store in Washington Square and you don't know the address, you can't find us. It's just a door, literally, a door. We don't have big signs, we don't have a picture of a marijuana leaf, it is literally just a door on the side of a building.

"And that's our strategy."

"What's the strategy?" I asked.

"To be different," Eric responded. "We went to one of the best marketing companies in the country–they did the marketing for Smashburger–and we said, 'Do something different. We don't want anything green and we don't want the marijuana leaf.' I can't emphasize this enough: We don't want to have a flashy sign and a marijuana leaf, we don't want to have the color green as prominent. Everybody has the color green and a marijuana leaf! We want something different. So, they came up with a totally different approach, more like a candy store motif. Bright colors, good lighting. It's more like a bank, with 5 or 6 tellers and offices for consultation. We have some apparel, some t-shirts and hats that promote our brand, but basically, it's all business, somewhat upscale. Like an Apple store. That's the look and feel we're going for."

"Well, was the city of Aurora receptive to that?"

"We'll find out. I think so, but we'll see. I've heard that they have over 200 applicants for the 24 licenses, so we're up against a lot."

"Anything else I should know?"

"Yeah. At the end they asked me if I had any questions and I turned to the two guys who were police officers and I asked them, 'What are your concerns?' and they said, 'We don't have any concerns at all. Quite frankly, marijuana is a small problem that we have to deal with and we have a lot of bigger problems that we have to deal with.' And one of the guys said, 'To be honest, we can't find any black market Mexican marijuana on the market. None. It's totally gone since marijuana has been legalized.'"

GROWING OPERATIONS

After several hours discussing the business plan for the Aurora license, Eric turned to me and asked, "Do you want to go see the growing operations?"

"Sure. That would be great."

"Ok. I'll give you the address and can meet you there or if it's easier you can just follow me."

"Yeah, why don't I just follow you."

Eric took me to an industrial district tucked between two major thoroughfares of Denver. The entire enclave was incredibly busy with semi-trucks, utility trucks, construction companies, delivery trucks, and lots of foot and car traffic. We pulled into a parking lot between two nondescript buildings.

I said, "Hey Eric, did you see that Maserati that drove past us a couple of blocks ago?"

"Yeah" Eric responded with much less enthusiasm than me. "There's all sorts of high-end cars around here. Every single building here is a growing operation. They're all over the place."

Eric walked to a dark-tinted door with the sign "Suite A" on the front, unlocked it and let me in.

"When we started a couple of years ago, this was the only space the landlord had, and there was a tenant that shared this building. When that tenant left we expanded to the whole building. Then the guy across the parking lot left and the landlord approached us about leasing that space too. So, we have these two buildings."

Eric walked me into the first room. It was about twelve by twenty feet and had two rows of small, 4-inch plants on a shelf along one wall, and two shelves, an upper and a lower, on the opposite wall with 12-inch plants. All told, there were over one hundred plants in the room, which had a white linoleum floor, white walls, and fluorescent lights.

Eric walked over to the smallest plants. "These are just starting out. When they get to about a foot, we move them to the other side of the room and cover them so that they always have moisture. All our plants are clones. We just cut a leaf from an existing mature plant, replant that, and we have an exact clone of the plant."

"An exact clone?"

"Yeah," stated Eric, "exact in every way."

We then moved to an adjacent room that was at least twice as big. Along the back wall were 1-foot plants on a shelf. On the floor, two-foot plants were on one side and three-foot plants on the other. As before, the room was stark and clean with florescent lighting and fans with hoods throughout.

"Do you ever worry about disease or mold or anything that could kill the plants?" I asked.

"Well, each plant is attended to twice a day, every day of the week. We have people who water by hand and it's their responsibility to look at the health of the plant. So if something does come up, we discover it quickly. We have never had a crop failure. If we did, it would probably wipe us out financially."

"How many plants do you have?" I asked.

"About three thousand," he replied.

We continued walking toward the back of the building. Eric turned to me, "When we finally got the rest of this space, I had to completely gut and re-build this area. All the walls, all the ventilation, the wiring, the hoods – everything was done from scratch. It took me about eight months."

"Well, I know that's a lot of work, but did you enjoy that? Did you like being able to create the space the way you wanted and to have the satisfaction of completing the work?"

"Why do you ask that?"

"Well, it just seems to me that the overall expense of doing the build-out isn't that great, and also that your time is scarce, so I wondered if you enjoyed it, that's all."

"Yeah, it's funny. I was a mechanical engineering major in college but dropped out after the first year. College just wasn't my thing and I moved on. Now, thirty years later, all I'm really doing is mechanical engineering on all our operations. It's crazy."

Eric continued with the tour and took me to another room, only this one was locked. Once inside, I saw that it was nearly twice as big as the last room, probably 40 feet wide by 80 feet long. The plants on the floor are five feet high. On the shelving along the wall, the plants are four feet tall and stacked in rows of three. There must be hundreds of plants in this space, and it is a jungle of green.

As we walked toward the back, Eric noticed some leaves on the floor.

"I'm going to have to chew somebody's ass about this," he said as he stooped to pick up the leaves. "There shouldn't be anything on the floor. This room should be spotless." He pointed his arm across the room and said, "The room right next to this is exactly the same, but we can't go in there because it's in total darkness. When the plants get to this final stage, they have to be in 12 hours of light and 12 hours of darkness."

"Well, how long does it take to get an actual crop?"

"Three months. So we get four crops a year, and if we lose a crop we lose 25 percent of our inventory," he stated matter-of-factly.

We walked across the parking lot to the second growing facility. There were only mature plants in this building and, once again, we walked through a large room with hundreds of plants on the floor and on the shelves the plants are stacked three or four deep. Before we exit out the door at the opposite end of the room, I turned to Eric and asked, "I've noticed these whiteboards in each growing room—is that how you're keeping track of all three thousand plants?"

"Yeah. So, we keep track of temperature and humidity, and watering, and who was in here last and what time they did anything. And, we keep track of any issues or problems."

"Have you ever thought about using some sort of technology to manage all that?"

"We did that already. We used to use iPads but nobody liked it and it wasn't any more effective than writing on the whiteboard. It was actually worse, more time-consuming and, ah, well here," he continued as he pointed to the whiteboard, "you get to see everything going on in the room and who wrote what and when. With the iPad we never had that, so we got rid of those and went back to a more basic approach."

He turned toward the door and then stopped and looked back at me. "We might be the only cultivating facility that's not using apps and technology, but it works for us. I can't tell you how many people email or call me every day to sell me something. Maybe it's an app like what we tried, or an automatic drip watering system, or adding CO2 to the grow rooms. Everybody wants to make this a high-tech, complicated process but it's not. You put the plants in soil, you water them and provide some nutrients, and then you harvest them. About the worst thing that can go wrong here is that we lose power in the winter, but we have backup generators for that. Unless something makes a big difference in our yields or quality, I'm not interested."

He turned away and we exited out a door at the other end of the room into a small, enclosed area where five employees were harvesting the crop. They were doing this by hand, but using a small clipper and working quickly to separate the buds from the leaves and other branches.

Eric picked up a bud about the size of a pinecone. "This is the final product, this is what everyone wants. But see all this chaff, leaves, and stems? That's called 'trim' and that part of the plant is more potent than the buds. But everyone is fixated on the buds, that's the whole criteria for judging the quality of your product."

"What do you do with all this leftover product, with this trim? Just throw it away?"

"No, we sell that to the edibles companies."

"So nothing is wasted?"

"No, we use the whole plant."

We walked around the corner to the final room. It's small, with shelves on two sides as tall as the 12-foot ceiling. Each shelf has a screen stretched within a wooden frame and each screen is filled with product. On the outside of each frame is a sticker with numbers.

This, Eric tells me, is the drying room.

"After we harvest the buds and trim we bring them in here to dry."

"What do all these numbers mean on the screens? Is it something to help you keep track of the date?"

"Oh," replied Eric, "that's MITS."

"What?"

Eric continued, "Yeah, MITS is a tracking system the State put in for all producers and retailers in the cannabis industry. From the minute we take a cutting and plant it, we have to put an RFID tag on it so they can track that plant until it's sold. Then, when we harvest it, we have to weigh the buds and all the trim and clippings and enter that into their database. Then, before we ship it, we have to weigh it again and record that on the shipping register. Then when it gets to the store, the manager has to weigh each product separately and enter that into the system and make sure the weights match our POS and also MITS. And at the end of the day, the manager weighs everything that has not been sold and enters it into MITS. Basically, the State wants to know the status of every single plant and the weight of everything until the customer walks out the door."

Eric's right about that. MITS (now called METRC—or Marijuana Enforcement Tracking Reporting Compliance) was created by the Colorado Department of Revenue to track every gram of cannabis produced and sold, whether those grams end up as flower (buds), in edibles, extractions, or in drinks. These strict regulations were devised in response to the 2009 Department of Justice memorandum called the "Ogden Memo" which clearly specifies the conditions under which the federal government will shut down State-sanctioned marijuana markets. [1]

Eric and I walked back across the parking lot and into his main office and as we do I noticed that Eric is not the only one with a new car. The employees park here, between the two buildings, and it's not like everyone has a new car, but there aren't any clunkers in the lot. Eric's office is shared with just about everybody in the company and it looks like it: there are several folding tables with chairs, papers and computer monitors and printers taking up most of the desk space, filing cabinets, a paper shredder, and a cash counting machine. Pretty routine for an office, but then I noticed 15 or so monitors on the wall.

Eric saw me looking at the monitors and said, "That's our surveillance system. We have cameras that cover every square foot of our operation here, including the parking lot, and our retail stores. We monitor 24 hours a day and we can change the camera to look at any aspect of the operations—front office, back office, surrounding environment outside our store, and we can zoom in to incredible detail. Also, and I don't know how this works, we can see everything in total darkness, including outside. It's crazy. I don't know how they do that."

Just then a person walked in through a back door leading to the growing room. "Hey," he said, "you must be the guy writing the business plan?"

"Yeah, I'm Pete."

"Pete, nice to meet you, I'm Jason. We sure are looking forward to getting this business plan done."

Jason is one of Eric's two partners, the other is Ryan. Jason is about ten years younger than Eric, probably in his mid- to late thirties. Unlike Eric, however, Jason is married, has two small children, earned his degree in accounting and his MBA from the University of Colorado. Ryan, who I eventually meet but who I have little interaction with, is about Jason's age and played Division I golf at an Ivy League school. I eventually figured out that Eric was primarily the CEO, Jason handled all the finances, and Ryan was in charge of operations, especially growing operations. They made decisions collectively, but they each had a separate role with unique responsibilities and were accountable to each other for that.

Eric broke in, "Where's Ryan? I wanted Pete to meet him."

"He's got some issues in the back, do you want me to get him?"

"No. Pete can meet him next time."

The interaction with Jason lasted less than fifteen seconds, and then Jason started walking out the front door. "I'm going over to Tejon to meet with the festival organizers," he said to Eric, "I'll be back in a couple of hours. But we want to do basically what we did last year, right?"

"Yeah," Eric replied, "let's stick with that."

Eric turned to me after Jason left and said, "We opened a new dispensary last year in a mostly Hispanic area of town and we were approached to be a sponsor at a festival they called the "taco festival." So we did that, but our brand name is similar to a popular drink and people would come to our tent and ask for the drink and we'd say, 'we're a dispensary. We sell marijuana.' And they'd be like, 'cool.' I mean, nobody had a problem with it. And we gave out over 6,000 T-shirts. So, we'll do it again this year."

I turned back to the monitors, "Have you ever had a security issue?"

"Not really, not one that required us to take action or call the police. We had two guys at one of our stores get into an argument in the parking lot and they started wrestling, but we just sent our security guard to break it up. We have a security guard in each retail location and we've never had a problem. It's funny, everybody thinks, or thought before recreational marijuana was legalized, that this would be a really dangerous business, that we would be burglarized or there would be strong-arm robberies, but that hasn't happened to us or to others that I know of.

"I mean, look at that monitor up there. That's the inside of one of our retail stores. Look at the guy at the teller window. What is he, maybe 65 years old and dressed in a suit? Like I said, the people who buy our product come from all walks of life."

Eric walked around the desk to the monitors and said to me, "Look at this." He then used a computer mouse to zoom in on the transaction between the 65-year-old customer and his retail clerk. The detail goes to the level of her hand opening up while the customer placed money into it. "It's incredible," said Eric, "we can look at every aspect of our operation at this level of detail."

"Well," I stated, "I think that's important for the business plan."

"Actually," Eric replied, "we'll put that in the security plan. There's a whole separate security plan."

"Ok," I stated as I start to gather my things to leave.

Eric said, "One other thing you should know about us is that we're really concerned about edibles, especially for first-time users. People think that edibles are safer than smoking, but they are actually way more potent."

"Like Maureen Dowd, the reporter from the *New York Times*, who figured that out when she ate a whole candy bar?"

Eric rolled his eyes. "Who would do that? Who would eat a whole candy bar? We're concerned about the public not knowing anything about edibles and assuming that a brownie or candy bar is less potent than smoking. We started an initiative, and our marketing company joined in, called 'First Time 5,' with the tagline 'Consume intelligently.' We train our retail employees to identify first-time buyers of edibles and we steer them to products that contain 5 milligrams or less of THC. We have posters and packaging so that customers will know what products are safe for them. So, for the business plan I just thought you should know that and put it in there somehow."

"Sure. It should probably be featured if that's something that separates you from your competitors."

"Yeah. Hey, what's your retainer? I should probably pay you something."

I told him the figure and Eric stepped out of the office for a few minutes. When he returned he had a stack of money—all $20-dollar bills—which he put into a money-counting machine, then placed it all into an envelope, sealed it, and handed it to me.

"We pay all our vendors in cash. We have a checking account, but once you get up past $25,000, banks start looking carefully at you and they won't take the money and they'll shut down your account. It's still a Federal offense to sell marijuana, even though it's legal in Colorado. It makes it tough. I've even gone into the bank with a copy of my W-2 and they still won't take the money.

It's tough to pay for anything in cash, above a certain level, like a car, and near impossible to get a mortgage. I've got like four different banks that I have accounts with, but I still end up paying almost everything with cash."

"Do you carry a gun, then, with all that cash?"

Eric looked at me in total surprise, stunned by my question. And then he gets it, then he understands that my knowledge of the cannabis industry is based on fiction, on a screenwriter's perception of the industry, based on movies and television shows. "No," he shook his head, "that's heroin and cocaine, and meth. Those guys carry guns. Us? We're just regular people selling, basically, an herb to other regular people. No, the real drug dealers are dealing heroin, cocaine, and meth."

DEALING WITH THE FEDERAL GOVERNMENT ON BANKING

Several days after that initial meeting with Eric and tour of his growing operations, the *Denver Post* published an article about the problems cannabis businesses face in securing banking services. Banks, of course, are regulated by the federal government, and the relationship between state and federal regulations come into sharp focus when a state has legalized something that the federal government prohibits. The *Denver Post* reported that not only do banks reject business from legal marijuana enterprises, but they are rejecting business of employees and suppliers to the cannabis industry. The article states, "The trail of problems includes rejected bank accounts and apartment applications, closed retirement and investment accounts, trouble getting mortgages, and closing accounts of clients with even a remote affiliation with the marijuana business" (*Denver Post*, July 5, 2014 Pg. 1).

The idea that banks would not loan, lend, or even do business with marijuana companies, their employees, and vendors is not all that surprising given the strict stipulation that the Federal government imposes on financial institutions through the Bank Secrecy Act (BSA), and through the "Suspicious Activity Report (SAR)." Since marijuana is a Schedule 1 drug and prohibited by the federal government, any financial institution that conducts transactions with money generated by a marijuana-related activity will be subject to criminal liability under the BSA. Moreover, a financial institution can be prosecuted even if the marijuana-generated money does not lead to a conviction of a person or business under federal or state law. That is, the bank is guilty whether the marijuana business is innocent or convicted. [2] However, since 29 states and the District of Columbia have legalized some form of marijuana-related activity, both the Department of Justice (through another memo, this time by Deputy Attorney General James Cole) and the Treasury Department provided guidance to financial institutions on how such entities can provide services to marijuana-related businesses and still uphold BSA obligations. [3]

This second memo from the Department of Justice (Feb, 2014), reiterates the key points from the earlier memo: federal resources will not be used to prosecute financial institutions conducting transactions with marijuana-related businesses as long as those institutions are confident that the marijuana businesses are not violating any of the eight important priorities—most significantly, distribution to minors, diversion to other states, and revenues to gangs, cartels, or criminal organizations. And the Treasury Department memo (Feb, 2014) sent in conjunction with the Cole memo, stresses that the Cole memo priorities are a first litmus test for whether or not a financial institution can service marijuana-related activity. If none of those priorities are violated, the Treasury Department states that financial institutions must conduct due diligence with any marijuana-related activity. The Treasury lists an additional seven items that must be met if these financial institutions wish to avoid prosecution. Two of those items require "ongoing monitoring" for 1) "adverse information" about the business and related parties and 2) "suspicious activity."

Since marijuana is illegal federally, all financial institutions are obligated to file a SAR and the legality of marijuana at the state level does not alter that obligation. The Treasury Department suggested that if the financial institution determines that the marijuana-related activity does not violate the eight priorities of the Cole memo, and if the due diligence does not violate any of the seven items from the Treasury Department memo, a financial institution can fill out a SAR for what it determines is a legal marijuana-related enterprise and state "MARIJUANA LIMITED" in the subject line. However, before doing that the financial institution would need to be able to state with the utmost confidence that the marijuana-related business does not present any *red flags,* and the Treasury Department lists twenty-three items that could indicate that the legal marijuana business (at the state level) may indeed be trafficking in illegal drugs. All told, between the Cole memo and the Treasury Department guidance, a financial institution would need to be absolutely confident about nearly forty different measures before allowing a marijuana-related business to open a checking account. Otherwise, the bank itself can be prosecuted for criminal liability. Because of these strict requirements by the DOJ and Treasury, no bank provides services to marijuana-related businesses—not in Colorado, and not in other states that have legalized medical or recreational marijuana.

One company is trying to offer banking services to the marijuana industry, Fourth Corner Credit Union. Fourth Corner was formed with the help of leading money laundering experts to provide a banking solution to the industry that would not run afoul of BSA, SAR, and other statutes. Additionally, Fourth Corner has the backing of the Governor and regulators in Colorado. But getting a "master account" with the Federal Reserve in Kansas City has been slow and difficult. The master account allows banks to carry out electronic transactions with other institutions, and to issue credit cards and debit cards. Typically, it takes several weeks to get approved for a master account, but for Fourth Corner it took months—from November of 2014 to July 2015—and when the credit union finally heard back, their application was denied. Fourth Corner sued in Federal court in Denver, but the U.S. Federal Reserve asked the judge to dismiss the lawsuit, claiming that Federal law preempts state law. Moreover, marijuana still remains illegal under Federal law and the Federal Reserve cannot allow illegal funds to enter the system. The Cole memo and the Treasury Department guidance, despite good intentions on clarifying the role of financial institutions in the marijuana industry, are irrelevant to the larger problem of banking in the marijuana industry. The solution will most likely have to come from Congress and until that happens, the cannabis entrepreneurs, employees, and vendors are left to their own devices on how to grapple with excess amounts of cash.

DEALING WITH THE FEDERAL GOVERNMENT ON TAXES

If the banking system puts up roadblocks for the cannabis industry, the Internal Revenue Service puts up the tolls. Payroll taxes, for example, are due monthly and the IRS requires all businesses to use the Electronic Federal Tax Payment System (EFTP). But, since cannabis industry participants cannot get bank accounts, they cannot transfer money to the IRS electronically and consequently, have to pay in cash, in person, and incur a ten percent penalty because they are paying in cash.

The ten percent penalty for paying in cash was challenged in U.S. Tax Court by attorney Rachel Gillette, hired by a marijuana company, Allgreens. "The taxpayer is unable to secure a bank account," she stated, "due to the nature of its business. With no bank account and no access to banking services, the taxpayer is simply incapable of making the payments electronically."[4]

Allgreens asked for a waiver since the company had complied with the law, paid their taxes on time, and were not intentionally avoiding the electronic payment system. The IRS responded that Allgreens had two alternatives, both of which required Allgreens to funnel the cash to a third party who could then make the tax payment on its behalf.

"It is the very definition of money laundering," said Gillette. "It's absurd. An alternative should not force a taxpayer to engage in a potentially unlawful activity under a Federal statute."

The IRS did offer a third alternative, in addition to the two money laundering schemes, in which the business could pay a single lump sum each quarter. Doing so still incurs the ten percent penalty for paying in cash, but also increases the cost to the business owner by tacking on an additional late payment penalty fee. The U.S. Tax Court never heard the case. The IRS worked out a settlement with Allgreens that refunded $25,000 in fees paid by the company and, additionally, the IRS will not penalize Allgreens in the future for not using EFTP. But because the case didn't go to court it won't set a precedent and the agreement between the IRS and Allgreens has no impact on other businesses in the industry. All other cannabis businesses pay the ten percent penalty.

Besides the ten percent penalty, industry participants have to make an appointment with the IRS office in Denver to pay their payroll taxes in person and for those producers or retailers in Grand Junction, Telluride, Durango, or anywhere outside of metropolitan Denver, it is an all-day ordeal. Persons from any one of those three locations would have to travel over several mountain passes and drive hours to get to Denver.

Sometimes, however, the IRS will come to the cannabis business. During my second meeting with Eric and Jason we were in their main office and there was a steady stream of people coming and going. The accountant stopped by for a moment, as did the lawyer, the real estate agent, and somebody from their marketing company. No one interrupted us, so when a woman walked in and came directly to where we were sitting, no one paid attention to her.

Jason looked up from a document he was reading, "Can I help you?" he asked.

"I'm from the IRS," the woman replied as she pulled out an identifying badge from her purse. "I'm here to get your tax payment." She stated her purpose with confidence, with a sense of righteousness—with arrogance, even—with the full knowledge that the IRS has every punitive measure at its disposal to deal with businesses that avoid tax payments, especially ones dealing with products that are federally illegal.

Jason looked at her quizzically. "This month? It's not due for a couple of weeks."

"No," she responded, "last month's payment. For $11,000."

"We paid that," Jason said, and immediately he turned away from her and started to rummage through a number of file folders. Finding what he was looking for he turned back around and said, "Here. Here's our cancelled check."

The IRS agent's confidence faltered a bit. She was perplexed, and her frustration showed. She looked at the cancelled check and asked, "Who are you working with at the IRS?"

"What?" asked Jason, surprised.

"Who are you dealing with?" she repeated, agitated.

"I don't know," Jason replied, "no one." Again, he turned away and pulled out a file folder, looked through several documents, and handed one to the agent.

"Oh," she stated, recognizing the name on the document. "He didn't tell me." And with that, she turned around and walked out the door. She didn't apologize, she didn't say, 'I'm sorry to interrupt you,' or 'I appreciate you keeping better records than us.' She just walked out the door. When she was gone Eric turned to me, shook his head, and said, "Like I say, everybody wants their money."

"You know," I said to Eric and Ryan in a meeting, "I never asked you this, but how did you guys get into this business?"

"We were caregivers," responded Eric. "We had over 800 patients and thousands of plants."

"Wow. That must have been lucrative."

"It can be," said Eric, "but you can't charge people money for their marijuana if you're a caregiver."

"What? Why not?"

"That's just the way the rules are written—you can't charge anybody for the marijuana because technically it's their marijuana and you're growing it for them."

"Then how do you make money?" I asked.

"People donate, most of them," he said with a shrug. "Some of them pay market rates, some less, and some nothing."

"And how about before becoming caregivers, what did you guys do?"

Both Eric and Jason turned several shades of red. "I don't think we can tell you that," Jason replied with a laugh.

After a moment Eric responded, "We just sold marijuana to whoever."

"Yeah," stated Jason. He was silent for a moment, then said, "We called ourselves the backpack boys." He looked at Eric and they both start laughing. "We would go to Home Depot or someplace like that and meet up with people, sell them the pot and collect the money. That was a lot of fun. This?" he said with disdain as he waved his arm across his desk and the office. "This is just business. But getting here was a lot of fun."

Eric, Jason, and Ryan have been involved in the legal medical marijuana industry since 2010 when they opened their first medical marijuana dispensary. Since then they have opened two additional medical dispensaries and in 2014, when recreational marijuana was legalized, opened two recreational dispensaries. Along with their 50,000 square feet of growing capacity, they have a large, vertically integrated operation that employs well over one hundred people. But the two main parts of their business, the cultivation and the retail sales, differ dramatically in skills required of employees and managers. The City of Aurora required all applicants to provide a detailed operational plan of dispensary operations, and Eric and I sat down in his office to go over the day-to-day operations.

"So to start," Eric began, "our managers start their day about two hours before the store opens when they get here, to our production facilities, to pick up the product and deliver it to the store."

"Wait a minute," I asked, "are you saying that the manager carries all the marijuana in their own car to the store?"

"Yeah. We've never had a problem and actually, an armored car is more of a telltale sign that something valuable is being driven around."

He continued. "So the manager opens and closes the store. Just the manager. And they take all the product, open it, weigh it, and verify it with the shipping list to the gram. Then, item by item, they enter all those weights into the retail MITS system. If there's a discrepancy that gets addressed on the spot. Then they put the product into jars and display cases, and the employees show up fifteen minutes before opening."

"And then it's just handling retail transactions?" I asked.

"Yeah, then it's just business as usual. And for the closing it's about the same process. We lock the doors fifteen minutes before closing and no customer can come in after that, and the last sale happens before 6:59 pm. Then the individual clerks verify the transactions and after they leave the manager takes the inventory into a secure area, weighs it, verifies that the inventory matches sales, and re-enters the data into MITS."

"That's a ton of work for the manager."

"Yeah," replied Eric, "and they end up putting in two hours before and two hours after our operating hours each day." He reflected for a moment. "All of our managers are women."

"Really?"

"Yeah. We've tried men as managers and they just don't do a very good job. The women are much more careful about following all of the procedures and if you don't follow the procedures it's a big problem."

"You mentioned all this weighing to the gram and reconciling with inventory and sales at the end of the day. Is there ever a discrepancy?"

"There's *always* a discrepancy," he said with emphasis. "It's always a little bit off. Usually it's that the retail clerk gives a little extra to the customer. The last thing we want is for a customer to go home and weigh their purchase and find that it's less than what they paid for and come back to us with a complaint. Actually, it would be worse if they post a review online that was negative. Anyway, we don't ever want that to happen, so the customer always leaves with more than they paid for. So, it never adds up, at the end of the day."

"Well, this seems pretty straightforward, in terms of operations. They only real difference is the security issue, but you've never had an issue at any store?"

"Right," Eric responded. "I don't know if this is worth putting into the operational plan or the business plan, but the retail workers get an hour off for lunch and two fifteen-minute breaks, and we buy lunch for everybody every day. It's really not worth it to have them leave the store and go find lunch, so we just buy it for them."

"Well," I stated, "that's a nice perk. And other than the food industry, almost nobody gets lunch every day for free. I guess we haven't talked about this yet, but what are the salaries and wages for employees? I have no idea what the numbers are in this industry."

"A budtender will make about $35,000 plus tips," he answered. "That's probably higher than others in the industry. For people in cultivation we pay them $50,000 a year as salaried employees, so they get benefits, vacation, paid time off. That's about $20,000 higher than anyone else in the industry, but we don't want turnover. And we haven't had any turnover. We've only had to let one person go and they didn't want to leave. That was back in 2010 but since then? Same people."

THE TOTAL CANNABIS OPERATION

I spent a number of months working with Eric, Jason, and Ryan understanding their business, from cultivation to retail sales, to their marketing strategy, and expansion plans. And even though Eric would tell me repeatedly that "this is a pretty easy business," I came to understand it as both complex and demanding, and to think of Eric and Jason as two of the best business operators I've ever met. Both cultivation and retail sales take place seven days a week and both parts of the business have highly advanced surveillance, monitoring, and security systems, adding a level of complexity unknown to most small business. Because all trans-actions are carried out with cash, the logistics of where to store the cash, how much to store, and how to transport it safely from one location to another are real challenges that the cannabis entrepreneur needs to think about. The sheer number of mea-surements (weight) of the plant places a lot of pressure on every-one who is part of the production chain—from the drying room, to shipping, to the store—and the number of measurements is daunting, requires precision, and takes a lot of time. The tight regulatory framework that Colorado has established is far more onerous than what other industries are required to do and it's a testament to Eric and his partners' management abilities that they can successfully operate disparate businesses like growing operations and retail, while also looking for more locations, expanding to other states, and looking for partners in those states.

Notes to Chapter One

[1] The Ogden memo, "Memorandum for Selected United States Attorneys on Investigations and Prosecutions in States Authorizing the Medical Use of Marijuana," can be accessed at: https://www.justice.gov/archives/opa/blog/memorandum-selected-united-state-attorneys-investigations-and-prosecutions-states

[2] The Cole memo, "Guidance Regarding Marijuana Related Financial Crimes," can be accessed here: https://www.justice.gov/sites/default/files/usao-wdwa/legacy/2014/02/14/DAG%20Memo%20-%20Guidance%20Regarding%20Marijuana%20Related%20Financial%20Crimes%202%2014%2014%20%282%29.pdf

[3]. The Treasury Department memo can be accessed here: https://www.fincen.gov/statutes_regs/guidance/pdf/FIN-2014-G001.pdf

[4] *Daily Camera*, July 3, 2014

CHAPTER 2.

CANNABIS SATIVA L.

Since cannabis has been illegal since 1937 to manufacture, distribute, consume, and to study, little is known about cannabis by people who are not cannabis consumers, and what is known is often disputed by people with an interest in promoting or eradicating the plant. I attended a number of seminars, trade shows, and symposiums during the research for this book and in all those it was assumed that the characteristics of cannabis were known, experienced by participants, and understood. The focus was clearly on the business and regulatory challenges facing the industry, product innovations, and best practices, but there was rarely an educational component and the person who doesn't already know about the characteristics of cannabis, the consequences of using it or the therapeutic value, are left to their own devices to figure it out. In this chapter I provide a brief history of cannabis including the components of the plant, the varieties, the research that has been completed to date, and the status of that research. I also focus on the agricultural aspects of the plant, including the growing conditions, the growing process, and include conversations with people who either grow professionally or are "home growers." I was curious about the yields a grower expected, the revenues (for the professional cultivator) they generated, and the cost-savings for the home grower.

CANNABIS SATIVA L.

Cannabis sativa L. was formally named by Swedish Botanist Carl Linnaeus in 1753, but it predates his classification by thousands of years. In fact, cannabis is one of the oldest plants known to humankind and, according to archeological evidence, most likely originated in Central Asia over 10,000 years ago. Over the next several millennia cannabis made its way to India, Persia, Africa, Europe, and all other inhabited parts of the world, including North America in the 1650's. Cannabis is one of the three most widely used psychoactive substances (along with coffee and tobacco) and the most popular illicit drug in the world. Estimates for worldwide cannabis use are 181.8 million regular users, and 19.2 million regular users in the United States.[1] Given its long history and importance to a multitude of cultures, it's not surprising that there are over 700 known varieties of cannabis, and most likely many more that are not known.

Originally classified as three separate plants, cannabis sativa, cannabis indica, and cannabis ruderalis, scientists have since determined that cannabis is not polytypic, but monotypic, and there is only one species, Cannabis sativa. The indica and ruderalis strains are merely derivatives of cannabis sativa based on ripening stages or stages of maturity. Cannabis belongs to the small family of cannabinacae, the only other member being hops (humulus), but only cannabis contains cannabinoids, the element within the plant that leads to both medicinal and psychoactive benefits. The cannabinoids are located on glandular hairs called trichomes that cover the whole plant but are most abundant on the flowers. Although there are over 100 cannabinoids that have been discovered to date, by far the most studied and analyzed cannabinoids are delta-9-tetrahydrocannibinoil (THC), the component that leads to a psychoactive response in individuals, and cannabinoil (CBD), which is non-psychoactive.

Cannabis sativa, indica, and ruderalis and all of the hybrids do not differ in qualitative characteristics—it is the same plant with the same constituent parts—but the various strains and hybrids can and do differ in the quantity of those characteristics. The most significant difference between the strains is the amount of THC present in the plant since THC is what leads to a "high." For example, if cannabis sativa contains 0.2 – 0.3 percent (dry weight) THC, it is called hemp or industrial hemp and historically has been grown to provide products such as rope, sails, paper, and others. [2] In fact, over 20,000 products can be derived from hemp.

One other important characteristic of cannabis is that it is a dioecious plant, which means that it is a plant with male and female reproductive organs in separate individuals. While both male and female plants produce flowers and a resin that contains the psychoactive THC, females produce vastly more flowers and THC. In fact, the amount of THC is highest in the flowers, then the leaves (which are called "trim" and are used to make concentrates for infusion into foods and liquids), very little in the stalk, and almost no THC in the roots or seeds. Because THC, with its psychoactive result, is highly prized by most cannabis consumers, only female plants are used by cultivators and they will clone the female plants by taking a cutting of a branch, and killing the males.

One interesting avenue for further research on the cannabis plant stems from the discovery that humans (and mammals, fish, and other organisms) have specific proteins in the brain, the immune system, and internal organs—the cannabinoid receptors, CB1 and CB2—to which THC binds. Scientists are just beginning to understand how these pathways work. CB1 is located in the central nervous system and also in the liver, lungs, and kidneys. CB2 is located in the immune system. THC relaxes the colon and may help people with irritable bowel syndrome or Crohn's disease; it can help people with multipole sclerosis, epilepsy, and patients suffering nausea and vomiting from chemotherapy. CBD, which is non-psychoactive, has been used effectively to treat a wide range of health disorders and helps as an anti-oxidant, in reducing anxiety and inflammatory conditions, in reducing the aggressiveness of metastatic breast cancers, inhibits cancer cell growth, and reduce seizures from epilepsy, among others.

Although all cannabis sativa contains THC, the THC is only activated if it is heated—by smoking it, by extracting it with chemicals such as butane, isopropyl alcohol, or supercritical carbon dioxide, or by cooking or baking it. Without heat THC will not be activated and instead the cannabis plant will have tetrahydrocannabinolic acid (THCA), a precursor to THC. THCA is non-psychoactive so if a person were to eat raw cannabis, in a salad for example, they would not have a psychoactive reaction. This result could be very important to people who use marijuana medically, who want the medical benefits of cannabis but don't want a psychoactive reaction.

I spoke to a leading expert in medical marijuana, Martha Montemayor, CNC, who has a clinic with over nine thousand medical marijuana patients, to understand her perspective on medical marijuana.

"90 percent of our patients don't want to get high," she stated. "They want the therapeutic benefits of marijuana, but they don't want to be high. We use THCA, which is a non-psychoactive precursor to THC that, until it's heated, will not activate the THC. It is the raw cannabis."

"Really! Do you mean that you can get the same benefits of THC with THCA, and not be susceptible to a psychoactive response?"

"Absolutely. One of the most significant innovations in the medical marijuana industry is a patch, like a nicotine patch, that you wear all day and it is composed of non-psychoactive THCA."

"So you could be totally coherent, able to operate a car, work in an office, or do any task you could normally do but by using THCA you'll still get the therapeutic benefits?"

"Yes, if you use THCA you'll get the benefits but won't get high."

"I think there might be a common misunderstanding about medical marijuana. So many people believe that medical marijuana gets a person high."

"It can," she stated, "if it is high in THC. But some people need only CBD for their condition and some people need only THC for their condition. The vast majority of people need the combination of the whole plant. If you isolate one component, like CBD or THC, it diminishes the healing ability of the plant."

"I read a research paper from 2007 and at that time the researcher concluded that hemp didn't have any medicinal value, but that's not true today, is it?"

"No, that's not true anymore. Things have changed quite a bit since 2007. We now know that hemp, with CBD, provides a lot of therapeutic value, and hemp has the upside that it contains such small traces of THC that it can't produce a psychoactive response in the individual. It's impossible to get high from hemp, but you can get the medicinal benefits."

I had never heard of the "patch" before speaking with Martha and I always thought the way to consume cannabis was through smoking it, but it turns out that there are multiple methods. Of course, smoking is one of the most common ways to consume cannabis and onset of a psychoactive response starts within fifteen minutes, peaks within an hour, and lasts about four hours. But by smoking cannabis it's possible to inhale toxic compounds. Vaporization avoids the problem of toxic compounds and with this method the cannabis is heated to a temperature where THC is released, but before the flower is burned. With vaporization there is no smoke and no toxic compounds are inhaled. However, there is debate among health researchers about whether or not "vaping" is much less harmful than smoking.

Concentrates are created through an extraction process that removes impurities and also increases THC levels from under 20 percent (on average) for cannabis flower, to above 90 percent THC. Concentrates are burned on a hot point, called a "nail," and breathed in. Oral ingestion—whether through eating food infused with marijuana or drinking liquids infused with marijuana—is the most unreliable method: onset is slow, it is difficult to gauge the dosage level, and sometimes there is no effect at all.

Martha Montemayer continued. "Edibles are now 45 percent of the marijuana market, in both the medical and recreational markets, but the onset times are fifteen minutes to an hour and a quarter...to never. In our practice, with 9,000 patients, we see that one in five people get no response after eating an edible. I have an assistant that is five feet tall and 80 pounds and edibles have no effect on her. The recommended dosage for edibles is 5 milligrams and I have seen her eat a 400 milligram bag of chocolate cookies and it has no impact on her."

There are scientific studies that prove her point. Hazekamp (2007) highlights a study in which subjects were given 10-15 milligrams of an edible and after two hours 84 percent of the subjects had no measurable THC in their blood; six hours later, 57 percent still had none. An edible is metabolized differently than if THC is inhaled and an edible must be processed by the stomach, the small intestine, and the liver before entering the blood stream and consequently, longer times to onset for a psychoactive response. Finally, it is possible to create a tincture of marijuana with cannabis flower, leaves, or trim as the starting material, or purchase a tincture of marijuana. An eye-dropper is used to administer several drops of the tincture sublingually (under the tongue) and the psychoactive effect (if using a high THC cannabis) or therapeutic effect (if using a high CBD cannabis) is nearly immediate. Alternatively, several drops can be placed into a hot drink and the psychoactive or therapeutic effect is similar to an edible.

GROWING CANNABIS

Cannabis is a fast-growing, resilient plant and thrives in nearly all environments and soils. It is found throughout the world growing at different elevations, temperatures, humidity levels, light levels, and in conditions with varying nutrients. And it is the dominant plant in all those conditions, blocking the sunlight from reaching other plants and taking all the nutrients its roots can reach. At maturity it can reach anywhere from four to twenty feet in height, but I had reports from a client who saw thirty-foot tall cannabis plants in California. In very hot climates, like Africa and India, cannabis develops more resin (where the THC is located) as a protective shield to prevent water evaporation; in more temperate environments there is less resin and lower levels of THC. In the nineteenth century Europeans were surprised to learn that hashish, imported from India and Arab countries, was actually cannabis since the European climate produced cannabis used as a fiber, to create sails, rope, parchment, and to use the seeds to make oil.

A cannabis farmer can grow the plant in ways that create more fiber or more THC, depending on his or her aspirations. If a farmer desires fiber they would plant the cannabis close together, forcing the plant to grow tall and maximizing the fiber from the stalks. Hemp, for example, is often planted at the rate of 35-50 plants per square foot and will reach heights of six to sixteen feet with very few leaves. If more THC is desired cannabis is planted far apart, providing more sunlight and creating a bush-like plant with more flowers, leaves, and more resin.

In Colorado, most of the cannabis is grown indoors under artificial lights and conditions, in part to allow the cultivator to better control the plant, to manage pests, mold and fungus, and to increase yields. Also, it's much easier to secure the plants—which is required by strict State regulations—if cannabis is grown indoors versus outdoors. And the plants are very valuable. The current price for wholesale cannabis is close to $2000 a pound, several-fold higher at retail, and assuming one plant can generate two pounds of cannabis flower, each plant is worth $12,000 (two pounds per plant, three growing cycles per year, and $2000 per pound at wholesale)—and that's a conservative estimate since under ideal growing conditions a plant could yield more than two pounds and the growing cycle could be shorter than ninety days.

I spoke with Zander, a client of mine, about how he does his indoor cultivation.

"Yeah, we grow indoors and one of the things we've found out is that the key thing is the lights. Some people will put really small plants under a light, say four plants, and try to keep them under several feet in height. And others will have one or two plants under the light and they'll use something called a 'scrog' which is like a net that you use to keep the branches apart. If you do that you get top nugs. But no matter whether you grow four small plants or one large one, you still end up with the same amount of flower, anywhere from 1.5 to 2.5 pounds."

"And how about the growing cycle," I asked, "can you do anything to speed that up?"

"Yeah, it depends on the soil and nutrients, and how much you water them, but a good rule of thumb is that you'll get three cycles of flower in a year. There's different ways to do it, though. You could take your entire space and grow all the plants, and you'd harvest them after four months. Or what we like to do is divide up our space into two-month sections, because it's easier to spread out the production, the harvest, but also it ensures that you have a steady flow of product. We call it 'perpetual flow.'"

An indoor facility with a thousand plants is worth well over one million dollars in potential sales revenues. Beyond control, yields, and security, cannabis grown indoors has higher levels of THC than plants grown outdoors and the goal of most cultivators is to provide the highest levels of THC since that is what consumers demand. It has been reported in the popular press that potency levels increased 10- to 30-fold since the 1970's, but researchers at the Potency Monitoring Program analyzed 46,211 samples of cannabis and found an increase from 3.4 percent in 1993 to 5.8 percent in 2008. The cannabis samples were obtained from United States Federal and State law enforcement seizures and the researchers used gas chromatography to determine THC and other cannabinoid levels in marijuana, sinsemilla, thai sticks, ditchweed (hemp), hashish, and hash oil. Determining average THC levels in cannabis is quite daunting and the researchers conclude, "The data collected in this and other programs have some scientific and statistical shortcomings" (2010:1216).

What might those shortcomings be? Just about everything that invalidates a statistical conclusion: "randomness of samples, correctly identifying the various cannabis products, sampling, natural degradation of delta-9 THC over time, and different analytical techniques" (pg. 1216). The only conclusive evidence from the Potency Monitoring program, which the researchers ignore, is that the THC levels of hemp are consistently between 0.3 and 0.5 percent every year from 1993 to 2008. Despite the admitted shortcomings the researchers conclude that their analysis "makes a strong case that cannabis is not only more potent than in the past but also that this high-potency product's market share is growing" (pg. 1216). [3]

Colorado requires significant testing procedures on cannabis products prior to retail sales and there are a number of testing facilities that conduct the analysis. Andy LaFrate, founder of the testing lab Charas Scientific, shared his insight on cannabis testing at a Boulder Cannabis Meetup.

"All retail products are tested for potency and for chemical and biological contaminants. This is a high stakes industry, and no one can afford to lose a crop. Growers and infused products manufacturers have to test a harvest batch or a production batch, but they have to test by strain (if a harvest) and they have to test each extract. For the growers with one hundred strains it becomes a business decision: If they test a big batch with a lot of strains they risk losing it all. Also, if they make a material change to their production process, if they change soil or fertilizers, they have to retest."

A basic question came up from a person in the audience, "What are you testing for?"

"We test for THC, THCA, CBD and CBDA, and for concentrates we test to make sure Butane levels are below 800 parts per million, and Heptane levels are below 500 parts per million. We're also testing for biological contaminants like E. coli, Salmonella, and Aspergillus."

"What about caregivers and the medical marijuana industry? Are they testing their products?" a person asked.

"Testing is not required for caregivers or medical marijuana growers," he responded. "But also, they can't test because the testing labs can only accept material from other licensed businesses."

"Do you mean that if I grow my own marijuana and I want to know if there are toxins in my soil, I can't use a testing service?"

"Yes, that's right. We can't test it. It has to come through METRC (Colorado's regulatory system, Marijuana Enforcement Tracking Reporting Compliance system)."

The results from Colorado's testing system are far more accurate than what the Potency Monitoring program conjured up: the strains are known, the time-frame between harvest and testing is known, the soils, nutrients and growing conditions are known, the degradation of THC from harvest to testing can be calculated, and the testing facilities use liquid chromatography which does not alter the sample. Based on over 600 testing samples LaFrate calculated the average THC levels in Colorado marijuana to be 18.7 percent. Is that significantly higher than the potency of marijuana in the 1970's? It's impossible to know, but it is a baseline for 2014. Whether THC levels will trend upwards is an empirical question that can be addressed in the future and addressed with confidence that the THC levels in 2014 were measured accurately.

One significant challenge of indoor cultivation for cannabis, and recognized within the industry, is the vast energy required to produce market-ready products. According to estimates by Mills (2012), indoor cannabis production consumes 1 percent of United States electricity demand, costing $6 billion each year and generating carbon dioxide emissions equivalent to an additional 3 million cars. Energy requirements for indoors cultivation include high-intensity lights (1,000 watts, 500 times greater than recommended reading light, and on par with hospital operating rooms), dehumidifying the air, heating and cooling to retain a narrow temperature range, pumping in 4-times the amount of natural carbon dioxide to increase yields, and recirculating air on the order of 30 times an hour, six times the rate of a high-tech data center. For the cannabis consumer, Mills estimates that consumption of one joint emits three pounds of carbon dioxide, equivalent to "driving a 44-mpg hybrid car 22 miles or running a 100-watt lightbulb for 25h," (2012:60).

But, the figure by Mills is most likely an overestimate if applied to Colorado indoor cultivation, especially with respect to carbon dioxide emissions. Mills' analysis makes estimates based on "grow houses," illegal grows in residential homes, and he includes estimates for transportation costs of people and products as well as fuel to run generators that help the grower avoid detection based on extraordinary electricity usage. Nearly all of the indoor growing of cannabis in Colorado is operated out of commercial warehouses, and while growers do have backup generators, the energy consumed is from the grid. Nevertheless, the amount of energy consumed in indoor growing is significant.

The city of Denver reported a 1.2 percent increase in electricity usage after marijuana legalization and 45 percent of that increase was due to indoor growing operations. In 2012 there were 351 growing facilities in Denver and they used 114 million kilowatt hours; in 2013 there were only three additional growing facilities, but electricity usage jumped 86 million kilowatt hours to 200 million kilowatt hours. Tim Cullen, owner of a growing operation with Colorado Harvest Company stated in a Colorado Public Radio interview that his monthly electricity bill is $12,000. And that's for a 10,000 square foot space; many growing operations are above 50,000 square feet. Another growing operation, River Rock, spends $21,500 per month in electricity and the owner of that company said he knows of a competitor that spends $100,000 per month.

Notes Mills, "Shifting cultivation outdoors can nearly eliminate energy use for the cultivation process," (pg. 62). That's exactly what the County of Pueblo, a little over one hundred miles south of Denver, pursued after Amendment 64 passed. Although the city of Pueblo banned marijuana sales, the county sought to entice growers to move to Pueblo County—and they did. Pueblo County in short order garnered fifty entities licensed to grow cannabis, in part because of "use by right" regulations that allow marijuana growers to avoid time-consuming special reviews and approvals by the local government, and in part because County officials applied those same "use by right" regulations to agricultural land. With abundant sunshine and near-perfect growing conditions, a large number of growers are foregoing indoor cultivation and building greenhouses on agricultural land.

One such person taking advantage of Pueblo's regulations and abundant sunshine is Mark Morely, a Colorado Springs real estate developer who had a marijuana dispensary as a tenant and thought, "Why am I not doing this myself?" Morely bought 30 acres of agricultural land in Pueblo County and is growing 14,400 cannabis plants. If he were growing corn he could expect revenues of $768 dollars on those 30 acres, but with cannabis his revenues are likely to be $6 million. And Morely is not the only one to benefit: Pueblo County has generated $1.8 million in fees and taxes, commercial real estate has doubled in price to $50 per square foot, the price of agricultural land has doubled to $10,000 an acre, and the 1,300 new jobs have had a $120 million impact on the local economy.

Most significantly, Pueblo County established a scholarship fund based largely on the cannabis tax, for students who are residents of Pueblo County to attend either Pueblo Community College or the University of Colorado-Pueblo. With over $475,000 in scholarship money and a guideline to provide $1,000 scholarships, Pueblo County will help 400 local students attend college. A Pueblo County Board of Commissioner's press release stated that "The full roll-out of our cannabis-funded scholarship program is groundbreaking. We are the first community in the world to provide a cannabis-funded scholarship to every graduating high school senior. It is so critically important to make college affordable for our youth if we want to provide long-term economic opportunity to our community. Too many kids can't afford to go to college. With this program we are taking cannabis-tax revenue and using it to provide for a brighter future in Pueblo." Prior to a county-wide ballot initiative in 2015 to earmark cannabis taxes to scholarships, Pueblo County provided scholarships to only 23 students for $50,000.[4]

Pueblo County's marijuana excise tax is a tax on all marijuana grown in Pueblo County. The tax is charged to the marijuana cultivator only once, when the marijuana is first sold or transferred to a retail store or manufacturer. Pueblo County has been collecting excise tax, by voter approval, since January 1, 2016. The excise tax rate is currently at two percent and will increase by one percent annually until a five percent excise tax rate is achieved. No less than half of the excise tax collected by the County is required to go into the Pueblo County Scholarship Fund and the remainder of the excise tax revenue must go towards a specific list of capital improvement projects.

HOME GROWERS

The most significant aspect of Colorado's Amendment 64 is the right of individuals over age 21 to possess, grow, process, and transport no more than six plants, three of which are mature. Specifically, Amendment 64 states the following:

Notwithstanding any other provision of law, the following acts are not unlawful and shall not be an offense under Colorado law or the law of any locality within Colorado or be a basis for seizure or forfeiture of assets under Colorado law for persons twenty-one years of age or older: possessing, growing, processing, or transporting no more than six marijuana plants, with three or fewer being mature, flowering plants, and possession of the marijuana produced by the plants on the premises where the plants were grown, provided that the growing takes place in an enclosed, locked space, is not conducted openly or publicly, and is not made available for sale (Amendment 64 Ballot Initiative, 2012:4).

Colorado's Constitutional amendment on cannabis legalization differs dramatically from Washington's in this one significant regard: by allowing home growing Colorado provides individual freedoms to its constituents; Washington restricts those individual liberties and instead forces all consumers to purchase marijuana through the regulated market. Whether the State of Washington did this for monetary reasons (since marijuana grown at home is not taxed) or whether the cannabis industry provided leverage to retain total control of the marijuana market by taking potential competitors out of the market, is unknown. In Colorado, however, home growing is not viewed as a threat by cannabis industry participants, nor by the regulators. Home growing never came up as an issue in any of my interviews with State regulators and in fact there was broad agreement that home growing is a key element of Amendment 64. State of Colorado Senator Pat Steadman said, "The smoke is out of the bottle," and Christian Sederberg, author of Amendment 64 and a marijuana policy reform activist, said the exact same words: "The smoke is out of the bottle."

There is no turning back to any other system once home growing is allowed, short of a military-like police state that secures warrants to search every private residence and private land holding in the State. The constitutionality of a tactic like that would certainly be challenged and whether Americans would appropriate the billions of dollars to undertake a military operation on

American citizens raises serious questions about a drug war that has already cost billions and impacted the lives of millions of people.

One motivation to grow cannabis yourself is certainly economic, especially if a person is a heavy user. A market and demand study conducted by the Marijuana Policy Group for the Colorado Department of Revenue provides estimates of cannabis use in Colorado in 2014, quantity of cannabis consumed, and frequency (2014). The researchers estimate that a "heavy user"—a person who consumes cannabis daily—uses on average 1.6 grams of cannabis per day, or a total of 584 grams annually. Since there are 28 grams in an ounce, the heavy user would consume 20 ounces in a year. A low-end price for an ounce of cannabis is $185, while premium strains retail for $300 or more. So a heavy user would spend anywhere from $3,700 to $6,000 per year for cannabis—plus another 20 percent for sales tax. Cannabis consumers who use less frequently, what the researchers term "regular users," average 0.67 grams per use. A person who used cannabis ten times a month would consume 80 grams in a year, or about 3 ounces, for a total expenditure of $555 to $900 per year. [5]

Colorado has a climate well-suited to growing outdoors and doing so would be very cost-efficient but there is only one growing season which makes the supply of cannabis year-round difficult. It's feast or famine for the outdoor grower. Instead, most home growers grow indoors and the total expense can be as little as $500 dollars, according to the website, "Denver Party Ride," which has a pamphlet describing materials needed and the steps a grower needs to take during the entire growing process. For starters, a home grower will need a room, like a closet, attic, or basement and if those aren't available, there are "grow tents" which as the term implies, is an enclosure specifically designed for indoor cultivation of cannabis. A grow tent is small—about 5 feet high, 3 feet deep, and 5 feet wide—and can be purchased used on the internet for under $300, or new at one of the many businesses catering to the surging home growing market for about the same price. The home grower will need plastic buckets, soil, nutrients, an electric heater, a humidifier, which are all relatively inexpensive. The biggest expense are the lights—1,000-watt high pressure sodium lights that run $120-$140 per light. And the home grower will need the cannabis plant which can be started from seed or the recommended route, by clone, for $10-15 per clone.

The people I met who are home growers weren't growing necessarily for cost savings, but for the personal freedom the Constitutional Amendment afforded, and because they actually liked the plant and enjoyed the process of growing it, much like any gardener. For example, I met with Michelle Wright, who is the founder of the Boulder Cannabis Meetup, a monthly meeting focused on cannabis business issues and challenges, and networking within the industry. I was curious about home growing and so Michelle invited me to her house to view her grow.

"I really don't know anything about growing marijuana," I said to Michelle as I entered her house.

"That's not surprising," she responded, "if you're not a user you would never really think about the plant at all."

"Well, how did you get interested in the plant?"

"In college someone gave some seeds to me and a friend and I thought, 'Well, we should try to grow this,' and we tried to grow it in his dorm room and it didn't work out at all. But I was a biology major and took a botany class and I researched the plant, learned the genetics of it, and when it became legal I got some seeds and started growing."

"Where do you get the seeds, at a dispensary?"

"I don't know if you can get them from a dispensary. I got mine off the internet."

"Really? Is that easy to do?"

"Yeah," she responded, "They're about the size of a mustard seed so they just get mailed in a regular envelope. For cannabis you don't want any males because they will pollinate the females and lower the THC levels. So that can be a problem when you start from seed, because you don't know what you have until it starts to flower. But you can buy feminized seeds, seeds that are guaranteed to be female, which is what I did. I got five feminized seeds for $80 dollars."

Michelle opened a door to a side bedroom and as we stepped in I saw that she had a grow tent with two cannabis plants, each about a foot high. "So this is my setup," she said as she waved her arm across the setup.

"I got the tent from a friend for $100, and the light was $200, and that's basically all you need to get going. That, and some good soil and nutrients. You just stick them in the dirt and they grow. When they get to one inch high, you turn the lights on for 20 hours and 4 hours of dark."

"That's all you have?" I asked. "Just two plants?"

"I'll get three ounces from each and that's way more than I can use. I make lotions and moisturizers, for your skin and to relax muscles, with coconut oil, and I give it away. I don't sell it. Most the time I give it to people I know, but sometimes I just give it away. The other day I was in the parking lot at the mall and my car wouldn't start and I got a jumpstart from a guy there and I gave him some pot as a thank you, and he was like, 'cool. Thanks!'"

"I guess I don't know how much six ounces really is."

"It's a lot, at least for me. But I'm not totally out of the pot market. If I want an *Indica* I'll go to Terrapin Station and buy some there. But there are other people growing around here and I can trade with my neighbors who have different strains, but I mostly use and give away what I have."

"So is it difficult to grow cannabis?"

"Not really. I have a thermometer and a hydrometer to make sure everything stays at the right temperature and humidity, and I check the PH levels to make sure everything's ok and if not, I just use baking soda and vinegar to get the PH levels right."

"It seems like you're excited about it."

"Yes. When it was illegal I didn't show anyone, didn't tell anyone, I kept it completely under wraps. But now that it's legal it's like my own little art project and I like to show people, share the information about the plant and educate them. I give people a biology lesson about cannabis and I want to share what I'm passionate about."

"Have you seen a big change in your life since cannabis became legal?"

"It's huge," she responded. "The attitude is changing, the culture is changing. Two years ago I didn't go to my family reunion because I didn't want to answer the question, 'so, what are you doing these days?' I was putting together a business plan for a cultivation facility—ultimately, I ended up not doing that and started the Boulder Cannabis Meetup instead—but our extended family has a lot of law enforcement people, FBI, and that kind of thing and I just couldn't go to the reunion and tell them that I was doing a business plan to grow marijuana. This year? This year I'll go and I'll tell them what I do and I don't care what they think."

"You know," I stated, "there are a lot of people that think Big Tobacco is coming in here and that all the people in the cannabis business now will get pushed out because they won't be able to compete. Obviously, that won't impact you, but what are your thoughts on that?"

"Oh, I think they're coming but I don't think they'll create a very good product. There are growers out there now without ethics, they spray the plants with pesticides—why spray the plants with pesticides? So they can grow a lot and sell to pot heads. That's very Philip Morris-like. But we don't know what happens when you combust cannabis and inhale, like a cigarette. You heard Andy LaFrate speak at the Cannabis Meetup. He said that there are over 10,000 pesticides we could test for, plus heavy metals. I like the fact that I know what soil I'm using, I know the nutrients, and I know how the plant is grown."

"Have you ever experimented with hydroponics?" I asked. "I know some growers who are using only hydroponics and I was wondering if there's a difference in the final result."

"No. I grow in soil because that's what the plant is designed to do. I make sure my plants are happy. I think if you treat something that's alive you should err on the side of caution."

PESTICIDES AND POT

Michelle's approach to growing cannabis—natural, no pesticides, and keeping the plants happy—is at odds with large-scale growers in Colorado who are increasingly coming under scrutiny from a number of state and local agencies for misuse of pesticides. In March and April 2015 the Denver Department of Environmental Health quarantined 100,000 marijuana plants from ten grows, including 60,000 plants from Colorado's largest grower, for pesticide misuse. In a *Denver Post* investigation city spokesperson Dan Rowland stated, "There is clear language on the labels to guide their usage, saying it's not for indoor use, or that the product isn't intended to be used on items grown for human consumption, like marijuana."

In July 2015, an edibles company was cited for "lack of temperature control" during manufacturing and the tincture they manufactured could develop a bacteria, clostridium botulinum, that forms botulism, which is fatal. Another edibles company was cited for unsanitary equipment in producing their hashish in a washing machine. In September 2015, two more growing operations and several extracts companies were cited for using dangerous pesticides. And LivWell, the largest cultivator in Colorado, was sued in October 2015 by two individuals who contend that the company knowingly used Eagle 20, a fungicide that contains myclobutanil. When heated, myclobutanil breaks down to "poisonous hydrogen cyanide." States the attorney for the Plaintiffs, Steven Woodrow, "Myclobutanil is not on any product you will consume through inhalation. On a grape it doesn't break down into cyanide."[6]

The primary enforcement agency for pesticide use on cannabis, the Colorado Department of Agriculture, received very little guidance from the Environmental Protection Agency on which pesticides were safe for cannabis. Because cannabis is illegal federally, the EPA did not respond to Colorado Department of Agriculture inquiries about pesticides, and because the science of cannabis pesticides is sorely lacking, the Colorado Department of Agriculture was left to create a regulatory framework on its own. Initially, the agency waited for consumer complaints before investigating cannabis companies, but it has taken a more proactive approach recently. A draft of proposed allowable pesticides was provided to cannabis industry participants, which was met with resistance. States former Colorado Agriculture Commissioner John Salazar, "We were caught between a rock and a hard spot. Anything we wanted to allow simply was not enough for that industry." The pesticide issue is ongoing and it remains to be seen how Colorado and other states regulate cultivation and manufacturing of cannabis products.

Cannabis consumers would be far better off growing their own cannabis and controlling all the inputs, the growing environment, and the quality. The cannabis industry is now big business and the profit motive means that commercial cannabis producers are focused on doing everything in their power to maximize yields, including using pesticides with unknown consequences and, of course, using large amounts of energy. There is a third group of cannabis producers that grow neither for themselves nor for commercial sale, the caregivers, who grow for the medical benefit of others.

JEFF ULLMAN, THE CAREGIVER

I met Jeff Ullman multiple times during my research because we were both interested in cannabis and would attend the Boulder Cannabis Meetup as well as other seminars and conferences. He introduced himself as a "caregiver," and within the medical marijuana context a caregiver is someone who grows marijuana for a medical marijuana patient…and then gives them the marijuana. A caregiver can't charge money for the marijuana because technically, the cannabis plants belong to the patient and the caregiver grows the cannabis for the patient. In reality, patients pay for the cannabis they receive, but it's not required.

The requirements to be a caregiver in Colorado are few: you must be 18 or older, be a Colorado resident, not be the patient's physician, not have a primary caregiver of your own, and you must submit a "caregiver acknowledgment form" with the patient's application. Of the 3,083 caregivers in Colorado 76.8 percent of them (2,369) have just one patient; only 15 caregivers have more than five patients. The caregiver role, based on these numbers, appears to be nearly a one-to-one relationship but even so, the State of Colorado is convinced that the caregiver market is fueling the black market.

Jeff Ullman is certainly not in the black market, however, and I met with him at a restaurant in Superior, Colorado, a relatively upscale suburb north of Denver. Jeff is 60 years old, has five kids, and is loquacious—especially when it comes to cannabis.

"Has anyone told you this yet?" he asked me as soon as we sat down. "I'm curious who, if anyone, has suggested that policy makers, legal, law enforcement, religious and judicial professionals who deliberately and vehemently oppose all forms of medical cannabis, should be denied any access or usage of medical cannabis whenever they might get around to requesting and acquiescing to its usage. These people continue to ruin the lives of millions and should be denied its proven medicinal benefits when they finally come around to asking for it. Has anyone suggested that to you?"

"No," I stated, "you're the first person to come up with that."

"At some point marijuana, at least medical marijuana, is going to be legal at the Federal level and I think all these people who have spent a lifetime harassing us should be denied marijuana. They shouldn't be allowed to use it."

"Yeah," I responded, "that's probably not going to happen."

"Well, I know it's not *going* to happen," he said emphatically, "but at the very least I think these people who have spent their life prosecuting marijuana should *choose* not to use it. They should stick with pharmaceutical medicines."

I decided to change the subject. "So as a caregiver, what do you do?"

"Well right now I'm mostly a consultant to a growing facility in Denver. They've got 15,000 square feet and the owner is a younger guy that was put in there by his father. He doesn't know that much about growing and frankly, doesn't have any interest in business. So I help him out. I also have a fabulous idea for a new delivery mechanism for cannabis and I'm in clinical trials now with that and talking to investors. That business will revolutionize how we consume marijuana."

He told me about his delivery mechanism and if it works the way he says it works it will revolutionize how people consume marijuana, but he also asked that I not share the innovation.

"What are some of the challenges in growing medical marijuana?" I asked. "Is it different from growing for the recreational market?"

"It's faster to grow marijuana with high levels of THC, so a lot of people do that. But it's more difficult to grow with high CBD, more challenging, so it's only the people like me, who are interested in the health benefits of CBD that are pursuing that."

"Are you growing marijuana then?"

"Oh, yes, of course. I have twelve plants at home."

Jeff looked across the table at me as if he's seen something interesting, "Hey, what's wrong with your hand?"

"Oh, this?" I responded as I look at my hand, "I have super dry skin and we were in Santa Fe last weekend and it was both incredibly hot and dry…so, it's not a big deal," I laughed. "It seems like I've always had dry hands and feet and I'm always putting on a lotion or moisturizer. I really don't even think about it; that's just the way it is."

"Well," Jeff said, "you shouldn't have to live with dry skin. Why don't you come over to my house and I'll give you a salve, an ointment for that. I live just five minutes away from here."

So I followed Jeff in my car to his house. He lives in an upscale neighborhood—quiet, manicured lawns, 4- to 5-bedroom homes that were built within the last fifteen years. It seems out of character to me that he's growing marijuana but who knows? Maybe there are a lot of people that are growing marijuana in upscale neighborhoods, just like Jeff.

After going inside and meeting his wife and kids Jeff pulled out a little plastic container with what looks like green petroleum jelly. "So," he said as he opened it up, "take just a little bit like this on your index finger and rub it on your dry skin. Just a little bit, see?" And he put a dab on his finger and rubbed it on my hand. "You just want a thin veneer, a thin layer wherever you need it. You don't need a lot." He handed me the plastic container. "The only thing I require is I want you to use this and report back to me how it worked. That's the only thing I need."

"Ok," I stated, "that's not a problem. I have a little wart here on my other hand. Do you think this will work for that?"

"Absolutely. Same thing. Take a small dab and rub it into your wart. Here," he stated, "let me show you my home grow," and he headed out a patio door to his back yard. Jeff's got twelve cannabis plants in his back yard. Each is in its own container sitting on top of his lawn, spaced three feet from each other. They are all about two feet in height and bushy.

"I didn't know you could grow marijuana outside," I stated.

"Yes, of course," he responded. "I had the City officials from Superior come out and look at this and they said, 'As long as your neighbors don't complain, and as long as it's locked we're fine with it.' And it's locked—I have a padlock on that gate right there and the only other way in is through the house. Don't mind this," he says, as he taook a blue tarp and threw it to the side. "I ran over this with the lawnmower and it's all torn up."

"What is the tarp for, for low temperatures?"

"No, it's for hail. Hail will ruin all the plants, so I keep this handy to protect them."

"When will these be ready, and how much do you expect to get from them in terms of yield?"

"We'll harvest them in October. I'm not sure about the amount of cannabis we'll get. It can vary anywhere from a half a pound to a pound and a half." Later that year, in October, Jeff sent me the following email:

"This is partly about: botany, chemistry, horticulture, family activities, living in Colorado and medical cannabis.... The day we've been awaiting since May 2nd when Head Grower, Elijah, gingerly opened legal cannabis seeds given to us by (strain) breeder friends who are multi-Cup winners (translation: **spectacular** *strains you just don't find in commercial stores) has arrived. We started with 27 seeds (no clones this year) and seven strains. After six weeks, our plants were about 3' feet tall and just entering the post-vegetative, flowering stage. Upon close inspection, we could now identify their gender. When we find males, we kill 'em, because they're no good for growing cannabis, and in fact, injurious to their growth. Ergo, we ended up with just eight females. The results: some were almost TREE sized—nearly 7-feet tall, 4-feet across, and finely topped to propagate massive quantities of our quality plant. We do not sell anything (but you should know how to get on our good side). If interested in anything, contact me about: flower, trim (excellent for smoking, concentrates and baking), tea leaves (8-inchers, just for bragging rights and art projects, and slapping Republicans across the face), and concentrates (shatter @ THC 80+%)."*

Using the Colorado Demand Survey as a baseline, the average joint or bowl of cannabis is about a half a gram and if Jeff were to average a pound per plant, just one plant would provide 900 joints, enough for over two joints a day for one person. He's got eight plants and presumably much higher yields, so significantly more, which he will share.

"One other thing you should write in your book," Jeff continued, "is you should say something about these 'budtenders,'" (people who work in marijuana dispensaries as the retail sales clerk). "The budtender has way too much power to sway the customer and the information they have is anecdotal. You've been in the dispensaries, you've seen them, right?"

"Sure. They're all young people in their twenties, from what I've seen."

"Yeah," he responded, "and they mostly don't know what they're talking about, especially when it comes to edibles. And that's where we've been having problems in Colorado, with the edibles."

I reported back to Jeff several days later that my dry skin had completely cleared up. Several weeks later, my wart was gone. I have a little of the salve left over and I've found it helpful for other ailments. For example, after riding my bike my knee was sore and I searched the house for Ibuprofen, which I couldn't find and then I thought to myself, "I should just rub Jeff's ointment on this sore knee." So I did, and it worked. When I mentioned that to my mom she said, "You should bring some with you next time you come to visit. It could be really helpful to your father."

"Well," I responded, "it's a Federal offense to transport marijuana out of the state of Colorado and I'm not going to do that." But it would be incredibly helpful to my dad who has a lot of skin problems, sore muscles, and all the things that go along with old age. Besides that, the salve Jeff gave me is a 1:1 ratio of THC to CBD so there's no chance of having a psychoactive effect, just a therapeutic effect.

The provision of home growing in the Colorado Constitution changes the dynamics of cannabis production, and consumption in significant ways, and it is the key to Amendment 64. Cannabis has been available worldwide for thousands of years, not just since Colorado legalized it. With over 180 million monthly users globally and 20-24 million users in the United States, it is hardly surprising that there are a number of people growing marijuana. The ability of a person with internet access to order cannabis seeds and have them delivered to their residence—undetected—certainly contributes to the prevalence of home grown cannabis, as does the multitude of educational materials that teach people the process to cultivate. But by denying home growing state regulators are essentially forcing consumers to put their trust in growers who use dangerous pesticides. As Mowgli Holmes, a board member of the Cannabis Safety Institute in Oregon told the *Denver Post,* "I think everyone thought marijuana growers were a bunch of organic growers who would never use pesticides on pot, but that's definitely not the case. A lot of this pesticide use is new and driven by commercial pressures."[7]

Pesticide use on cannabis is an unsettled question. Without guidelines from the EPA, and with the competitive pressures facing industry producers and manufacturers to maximize yields, regulatory agencies like the Colorado Department of Agriculture face a daunting task to ensure the health and safety of the cannabis consuming public. Fortunately, Colorado residents can opt out of the recreational for-profit market completely and grow their own marijuana, in a tent in their house, or in their backyard. And they can control all the critical variables: light, soil, nutrients, pesticides. That's true in Oregon and Alaska, but not Washington.

Notes to Chapter Two

[1] The United Nations Drug Report estimates worldwide drug use for all illicit drugs. The relevant chapter for cannabis can be found here: http://www.unodc.org/documents/data-and-analysis/WDR2011/The_cannabis_market.pdf

[2] I draw heavily on the work of Hazekamp (2007) in this chapter on the biology and pharmacological properties of cannabis. His work can be accessed here: http://www.oregon.gov/pharmacy/imports/marijuana/staffinfo/cannabisreview.pdf

[3] The full report on potency can be accessed here: http://home.olemiss.edu/~suman/potancy%20paper%202010.pdf

[4] Information on Pueblo County scholarships can be found here: http://county.pueblo.org/nearly-475000-available-pueblo-county-mj-scholarship

[5] The full report, "Market Size and Demand for Marijuana in Colorado" can be found here:
https://www.colorado.gov/pacific/sites/default/files/Market%20Size%20and%20Demand%20Study%2C%20July%209%2C%202

[6]   See   http://www.denverpost.com/news/ci_28924681/col-orados-largest-pot-grower-sued-by-two-con-sumers?source=infinite-up for more details on pesticides used in cannabis cultivation.

[7]   https://www.denverpost.com/2015/10/03/colorado-yields-to-marijuana-industry-pressure-on-pesticides/

CHAPTER 3.

THE START-UP CANNABIS ENTREPRENEUR

Eric, the established cannabis operator featured in Chapter 2, bemoaned the fact that he received hundreds of emails and phone calls a day, from people he didn't know, and who "wanted his money." His situation is not unique in the cannabis industry and he's not paranoid: there's a perception that Colorado is on the cusp of the next BIG thing, and that the cannabis industry will make lots of people lots of money. In fact, the cannabis industry in Colorado has been dubbed the "green rush," and not only are people from around the country moving to Colorado, but investors from around the world are seeking business and financial opportunities in the cannabis industry, too.

When I attended a "Boulder Cannabis Meetup" in the fall of 2014 it was one of the first networking events for the cannabis industry. The organizer, Michelle Wright, promoted the event as a place where people inside and outside of the industry could "focus on issues surrounding owning a cannabis business, discuss challenges, and network within our community." But at that first meeting, and all subsequent meetings, the only people who showed up to "network" were people trying to sell their services to the true power-holders in the cannabis industry: the cultivators, manufacturers, and dispensary owners. There were people selling legal services, bookkeeping, accounting, financial services, retirement plans, marketing, software development, and a host of other ancillary services, but absent at the cannabis meetup were the people in the industry who owned the means of production, who actually touched the plant, grew it, transformed it into an edible, or sold it at retail.

An established cannabis entrepreneur, like Eric, already outsources most of the ancillary services offered by the members of the cannabis meetup. He has a lawyer, an accountant, a marketing firm, a web designer, a real estate broker, a security firm, and he and his partners have been growing cannabis at a large scale for the better part of six years and selling at retail in a highly regulated market for five years. Prior to legal cannabis sales, Eric and his partners were carrying out all those activities in the black market, and they did just fine on their own. Any hope of selling ancillary services to established cannabis operators, of joining in the "Green Rush," would be dashed if someone like Eric were to show up to the Cannabis Meetup because he doesn't need any of the services these vendors are providing.

But the would-be vendor might have a chance to sell to a start-up cannabis entrepreneur, who would presumably need all those services, especially if the entrepreneur wanted to enter the cannabis industry in a big way as a cultivator, manufacturer, or retailer. But again, the start-up cannabis entrepreneurs were also absent from the Boulder Cannabis Meetup. The reason for the start-up entrepreneur's absence differs from the established cannabis entrepreneur and is actually quite simple: there are almost no opportunities to start a cannabis business in Colorado, for a number of reasons. First, there's a residency requirement and anyone wanting a cannabis license must be a resident of Colorado for two years, a fact that was lost on a number of people. For instance, at the cannabis meetup people would show up and excitedly announce that they just moved to Colorado from Ohio, for example, and were going to start a grow operation. But that residency requirement stops everyone in their tracks.

Second, the Colorado constitution allows local jurisdictions (county and city) to determine whether or not recreational or medical marijuana sales, cultivation, or manufacturing can take place within their boundaries. Counties and cities are not bound by the same rules regarding marijuana and it's possible for a county like Weld to ban any and all forms of marijuana within the county (which it did), but a city within Weld county, like Garden City, to allow medical and recreational sales and cultivation (which it did). And there are various other arrangements. Some counties allow existing marijuana establishments to remain, but no new ones can enter; others allow cultivation but no marijuana sales, or they allow medical but not recreational marijuana. And some jurisdictions put a cap on the total number of establishments and then close the gates.

According to the Colorado Municipal League, nearly 72 percent of all jurisdictions in Colorado prohibit recreational marijuana sales, cultivation, or manufacturing, 5 percent have moratoria and have tabled a decision to be determined at some future date, and 23 percent allow some form of marijuana production or sales. Of the jurisdictions that do allow marijuana production or sales, about 40 percent of all dispensaries are located in Denver. The other operations are concentrated along the Front Range or in a few isolated tourist destinations such as Telluride, Durango, Aspen, and Breckenridge. In the eastern third of the state, and in the vast expanses of the western part of the state, there are a scattering of recreational and medical dispensaries, but the vast area is mostly devoid of any dispensaries.

A third reason it's so difficult to open a marijuana cultivation, manufacturing, or dispensary business is that, for the first few months of legal sales, only current medical marijuana cultivators, manufacturers, and dispensary owners could obtain a license for recreational marijuana. That moratorium allowing only medical marijuana dispensary owners to operate a recreational license was set to expire January 1, 2016 and would have allowed others to enter the industry. But in November of 2015 Denver's marijuana policy office recommended extending the moratorium on new marijuana businesses for another two years, from January 1, 2016 to January 1, 2018.

This rule obviously provides significant first-mover advantages to the medical marijuana industry, and effectively blocks all entrants to the industry in Denver, the most populated part of the state. Between the jurisdictions that ban all forms of cannabis production and sales, to those jurisdictions that have imposed a moratorium, to those that have reached maximum capacity and are not expanding further, getting a license to operate a marijuana facility is the key hurdle to overcome, no matter how highly motivated someone might be to join the cannabis industry. It's also expensive to get a marijuana license. At a minimum, the application from the state of Colorado is $5000 and the license fee is $3000. One would also have to apply for a license, pay an annual license fee, and an additional operating fee at the county level and also at the city level. All told, the fees just to get a single license are close to $20,000.

The alternative is to purchase an existing license and an existing business, assuming one has the two years of state residency. But going this route is cost-prohibitive for the average person: several hundred thousand dollars to purchase a license, and several million dollars to purchase an existing cultivation facility or dispensary. But either way, buying a license or buying a business, entering the cannabis industry is expensive and since banks are not making loans to the cannabis industry, a cannabis start-up entrepreneur would need to have capital in the millions, or the ability to raise millions, to get into the industry. And, if you need to get investors, you'll need a business plan. That requirement led "Johnny," a start-up cannabis entrepreneur, to me.

JOHNNY, THE START-UP CANNABIS ENTREPRENEUR

I received a call from Johnny within a week of meeting with

Eric, the established cannabis operator. Like Eric, Johnny used the same website to find someone to help him write a business plan. He stated quite briefly in his query on the website: *"Business Plans. Company structure, scale of the economy, human resource, and funding."*

I sent a proposal and Johnny called me within minutes.

"I'm putting together a business plan for a recreational dispensary and want to know what you bring to the table," he asked in our initial phone conversation. "What do you know about the cannabis industry?"

"Ha," I responded. "That's funny you should ask because actually, I have another client in the cannabis industry and I'm writing a business plan for him. It's early in the process but I have been through his cultivation facility and understand something of the business, but not a lot."

"Cool," Johnny replied. "What I'm trying to do is create a high-end, vertically integrated recreational chain and it's going to be different than anyone else out there," his voice rises with excitement.

Nearly everybody who has the wherewithal to enter the cannabis industry has designs to be vertically integrated and Johnny told me that he is in the process of leasing 30,000 square feet of growing capacity, leasing a $3.2 million-dollar retail space for his dispensary, and putting together equipment to manufacture edibles at his growing operation.

"We're going to have the best cannabis, we're going to feature artists with original art, and we're teaming up with some super cool skateboard and clothing companies to offer apparel and things that will appeal to the cannabis community. Eventually I'd like to franchise and have five to ten stores and I saw where you wrote a book about that."

"Yeah, I wrote a book on franchising, but I don't know if you can franchise in the cannabis industry."

"Anyway," he continued, "I have some investors in New York, Florida, and Mexico that are interested, and I need to get them something that lets them see the full picture."

"What's the picture? Why can't the investors understand what you're doing?"

"I can tell you more about it," Johnny said, "but let's talk about that when we get together. What's your Thursday like?"

"I'm open."

"Let's meet at the coffee shop over on Iris at 10:00."

We met several days later. Johnny is in his early thirties, thin, tall, with dark hair that he pulls back into a bun. He is the definition of "cool," with an air of self-confidence, deep knowledge about cannabis, and a direct and engaging manner of speaking. He is the type of person that has a refined look and appears well-dressed and stylish even when wearing blue jeans and a t-shirt. But while his appearance and clothes scream "marijuana culture,"—the laid-back, slacker, free-spirit persona—he is just the opposite: a relentless worker with a voracious intellectual curiosity, a decisive decision-maker, and quick to take action. Johnny has a vision to dominate the cannabis market, the confidence to make it work, and the skills, too, based on a world-wide reputation for developing high-quality and sought-after cannabis strains. Although only thirty years old, Johnny has several years of high finishes in international cannabis cup events that pit the best cultivators in the world against each other in judged competitions.

"It's not a big project," Johnny stated as we got settled in the coffee shop. "I already have a business plan. You just need to go over the document and edit and revise it. It's mostly done. I'll email you the plan we put together and then we can talk about how to tweak it," he told me during our initial meeting.

"Ok, that should be no problem. But one quick question. Are there any financial models in the plan, or any financial modeling that I would have to do? I'm asking because that's a ton more work if I have to create or modify the financials."

"We have some financials that you can look over. I have a partner, Josh, who's helping me and he and I wrote the business plan and he did most of the financials. If you want to look over them that would be great, but I don't think you'll have to do any work on them."

"Ok. How soon do you want this done?"

"As soon as possible. There's intense interest in cannabis right now and I'm getting interest from people all over the country. There's a group of guys from New York City, a group from Florida, Houston, North Carolina. I even got some Mexicans that are interested."

"That's a lot of people, but why Mexicans?"

"They said they were in the agriculture business, that they grew fruit, and wanted to get into the cannabis business."

"They're fruit growers? Don't you think they're really in the cannabis business?"

"Probably," he responded, "but we'll see. They have to come here to Colorado for some reason and I'll set up a meeting."

"Ok. Well, I'm going to write the business plan in English, anyway."

"Oh, yeah," Johnny stated. "Don't even bother writing it in Spanish."

Several days later I reconnected with Johnny and he gave me more details on who some of these investors were. "The Florida guys own a chain of dry cleaners," he told me, "and the guy in North Carolina is super interested but he only has $250,000. I need a million, maybe more, so that's probably not going to work."

"Wait a minute," I broke in. "The Florida guys own some dry-cleaning businesses?"

"Yeah, that's what they said."

"Johnny! That's how people launder drug money. That's not the only way, but dry cleaning is a cash business with a lot of transactions and it's notorious for being a prime way to get illegal money into the banking system. You need to steer clear of those guys."

"Ok. Well, I like the New York group and the Houston group, so we'll see where that leads. How are you coming on the business plan?"

The truthful answer was, not so good. The business plan that Johnny and Josh put together was totally useless to me and I could see why Johnny wasn't generating much interest from investors. It looked like they found a template on the internet on business model generation, and they wrote a series of questions and stated their responses.

Question: What are our target markets?

Answer: We have a segmented and diversified market. The 21+ section of the dispensary will target all socio-economic classes of the cannabis market. The retail side (18-20) of the dispensary will target the same market as the 21+ side, but will also target the markets of 18-20 year-olds involved with the cannabis culture, long board skaters, and the art community.

Question: How will we be new and unique?

Answer: Our dispensary will be the first art gallery style dispensary in Colorado. We will have a larger variety of retail products for sale than any dispensary in Colorado. This will allow us to target every angle of the cannabis culture. We will have a user friendly website that will allow anyone in the United States to purchase our products. Blogs and forums on our website will allow us to gain a stronger social media following than any of our competitors.

Johnny and Josh went on and on with this boilerplate business plan, tediously, for twenty-five pages. The document made Johnny look less sophisticated than he really was, it lacked credibility, raised questions, and didn't convey at all his true expertise as a cannabis cultivator. Johnny grew up on the east coast and his mother was well-known as a gardener and he learned the nuances of growing plants from her. He has been growing cannabis since he was fourteen years old and is well-known within the cannabis industry, but he neglected to mention this skill, and the awards he won, in his business plan. The business plan made him seem like a person with big dreams but no skills to pull anything off, and consequently, no investor would take him seriously. When I got to the financials I ran into the same problems—not easy to read or understand and the document lacked credibility. Over the next several weeks I spent time with Johnny and Josh going over the plan and financials and one day I received an unexpected call from Johnny.

"Pete, Josh and I want you to come over and we'll help you finish up the business plan."

"Ok," I responded, "but I have the information I need. It's just a matter of putting everything together, and that takes time."

"Well, we'd like you to come over anyway. And another thing, all these investors keep asking what my internal rate of return is. I don't know what to say to them."

"It's pretty easy to calculate, and the numbers are right there for the investor to figure out. I can calculate that for you, but I don't know why the investors you've sent the financials to can't do the same analysis."

When I got over to Josh's house, Johnny was late, and I pulled out a package from my backpack to show Josh. "I went to one of your competitors to see what the buying experience was like in a dispensary," I said. "Look," and I pulled out a ziplocked bag, opened it up, and produced a small, prescription container with three "buds" in there. "I bought one gram of marijuana and this is what I got. What do you think?" I asked Josh. The buds were about the size of a thumbnail.

"Wow!" he roared with laughter. "How much did you pay for that?"

"$17," I replied, "plus $2 for the childproof container."

"Look at our buds," he said as he stood up from the table, walked to the kitchen and returned with a Mason jar of marijuana. Inside were several buds ranging in size from pineconesized to softball-sized.

Johnny walked in just then, talking on the phone. When he finished Josh said, "Look what Pete bought," and showed him my three little buds, "for $17 dollars," Josh continued, laughing.

"Brotha," Johnny replied, "if you wanted some herb you should have just asked me, man."

"No, it wasn't that," I replied, "I was just going in to the dispensary to figure out the experience, to see who was there as a customer, to compare it to what you're trying to do, and to just understand the buying experience."

"You got ripped off. That's what these guys do at the dispensary. Did the budtender ask you how long it's been since you last smoked?"

"Yeah," I replied.

"And what did you say, like, thirty years ago?"

"Yes."

"So then the guy knows you're not a savvy cannabis consumer and he gives you the bad shit because he knows you won't know the difference. We will never do that in our dispensary."

"Well, anyway, I'm not going to use it, so it really doesn't matter. I just wanted to experience the whole thing."

"So, that was an investor from New York," Johnny said, changing the subject. "He asked what our internal rate of return is. Everybody's asking for that. We got to give them that number."

"Ok," I said as I opened a spreadsheet on my computer. Josh leaned over and looked carefully at the data.

"I can do that," he said with some trepidation.

"Here," Johnny said as he stood up and moved next to the computer. "Let me do it. I was pretty good at math when I was in high school."

And he's good at math now. I've seen Johnny work all sorts of calculations on pounds of cannabis, yields of extract, prices, costs, and margins in his head and confirm with his cell phone calculator. And he's always right.

Johnny stared intently at the formula for the internal rate of return for several minutes:

$$NPV = \sum_{n=0}^{N} \frac{C_n}{(1+r)^n} = 0$$

Finally, he asked, "What's r?"

"That's what we're solving for," said Josh. "I can do that."

"Hold on a second," I stated, "you guys don't understand. That's just the formula, the computer will solve for r. We just have to provide a series of numbers and apply the formula. I already did that based on your monthly results and for you guys your year one internal rate of return is 73 percent."

"Is that good?" asked Johnny.

"That's unbelievably good," I stated. "I did the internal rate of return for Eric's new dispensary and it was negative in year one. So, yeah, 73 percent is great. But the thing is, any serious investor ought to be able to do this analysis, or find someone in their company to do it. If they can't figure this out on their own then that says something about them, and it's not good."

"Cool," said Johnny, ignoring my caution. "Anyway, we got the number."

"It's all based on the numbers we put in, though. We said that a pound of cannabis costs $500 to produce and sells for $2000 wholesale and $7000 retail, right? So your year one sales are $6.8 million. And you break even within a couple of months of opening. That's why the internal rate of return is so good. But if it costs more to produce and if the wholesale price drops, your internal rate of return will be a lot lower than 73 percent."

"The price is not going to drop right away," Johnny responded thoughtfully. "Prices will stay where they are for a couple of years at least, maybe five years."

"If it's ok with you, I'd like to have my finance guy look over the plan and numbers, just to make sure everything is correct."

"Yeah, sure. I'm cool with that," said Johnny.

So I did that. I gave the business plan Johnny wrote to Jeff Rosenfeld, a friend of mine who has a finance degree from the Wharton School and who has also helped to raise millions of dollars in investment money for companies. Jeff's a feisty critical thinker and I figured he would have some good ideas on how to improve the presentation of the business plan.

"Peter!" Jeff exclaimed when I spoke with him on the phone. "There's absolutely no VC who would do this the way it's set up. Yes, the numbers are attractive — what other investment pays 35 percent per year? But does this guy know what he's doing?"

"He doesn't know a lot about business, but he knows a lot about cannabis."

"Does he understand the difference between debt and equity? Why is he giving up so much and paying it all back in two years? Where does the two years come from?"

"I don't know where the two years come from," I responded, "but I'm guessing that he wants to get his money, scale quickly, and get rid of the investor."

"But if the investor gets the money back, why give up equity?" Jeff asked. "Is this just a dream by the guy or is there a real market?" He reflected for a moment then continued, "I'm assuming there's a real market, but he's got to convince the investors that he has the ability to pull this off. You need to get him to understand the business part, you need to find an analog for this." Jeff continued, "Like coffee, the roasting guy we worked with in Minneapolis. Who was that guy?"

"Greg," I responded.

"Yes! Like Greg. I mean that guy had a nice roasting business and then decided to go into retail sales like Starbuck's and he didn't have any skills for that. Maybe this guy would understand that. Vertical integration might be an advantage, but maybe just keep the warehouse and sell the product to others. Why does he want to do the retail? And why does he want to sell all these knickknacks? I mean skateboards, art, pins, tags, and clothing, in addition to all the marijuana paraphernalia. He's got to know going in that if the knickknacks don't work, close it down and go with the marijuana."

"I agree," I stated, "but it will be hard for him to change anything. He's fanatical about this vertically integrated business and about the art and all that cool stuff. Did you see the line in the business plan where he stated that his company will be the first art gallery style cannabis company in Colorado?"

"Yes," Jeff laughed, "but does anybody really want that? That's the thing that he needs to figure out, otherwise it's just expensive stuff he has sitting in inventory."

"Also," I stated, "he wants to be a C-Corp and everyone else in the industry is an LLC, but I couldn't get him to understand the implications."

"A C-Corp! Why would anyone start out that way? Is he crazy? Doesn't he realize that he'll need audited financials, reports to the SEC, and a board of directors? Plus, the taxes are so high."

"Yeah, I told him all that, but he thinks he'll grow really quickly and will want shareholders. He doesn't listen to me all that much."

Jeff was silent for a moment.

"I'm surprised people are seeing him. He hasn't sent this to anybody, has he?"

"I think he's sent it to a couple of potential investors."

"Who are they, do you know?"

"I've never met any of them, but he's told me he has a group from Mexico, New York, Florida, Houston, North Carolina, and just the other day he told me he had a pornographer here in Colorado lined up."

"Peter! A pornographer? How do these people find him? You can't let him do that, that's a terrible idea. I mean, you can't expect those guys to follow the same standards as a regular business person."

"No, I won't let him do that."

"What about the other investors?" Jeff asked. "What about the group from Mexico?"

"Yeah, they told him they were farmers, that they were growing fruit."

"What is this?" Jeff asked, "Is everyone investing in this business a drug cartel or running sketchy businesses?"

"Maybe," I responded, "the Florida guys own a bunch of dry cleaning businesses."

Jeff burst out in laughter. "That's the very definition of money laundering!"

"I know. I told Johnny that."

"Well, now I see why people are seeing him. But you can't let him do a deal with any of these investors. Does he have a confidentiality agreement?"

"Not that I know of."

"If he doesn't have a confidentiality agreement he's just advertising his ideas to them. Does he have a trademark?"

"No," I answered reluctantly. I know where this is going, and Jeff's frustration level was rising. He deals with people all the time who know a lot about their product or service, but little about some of the things that can derail a good idea, like confidentiality agreements and trademark registrations.

I did a search of Johnny's company name when I first started working with him and found that it was registered to a poetry publication in New York City, and I talked to him about that.

"Hey, Johnny, I did a Google search of your company name and found that somebody has already trademarked your name."

"Who are they?" he asked.

"A poetry magazine in New York City," I responded.

"A poetry magazine!" he exclaimed, "We're in a totally different business."

"It doesn't matter, what matters is that they own the trademark and they could sue you and get damages."

"But I love our name, it's cool."

"Yeah, but what they could do is wait for you to get big and then come after you for millions of dollars."

"Ha! I don't think that's going to happen. How would they know, if they're in New York City?"

"Well, they can do a Google search like I did, or they can hire a lawyer to do a search. Either way, if they find you they'll first send a threatening cease and desist letter so they have documentation that they tried to work something out with you in good faith, and then they'll wait for you to grow big and then they'll send their lawyers in to take a lot of money from you. You should contact them and see if you can use the name, or find a different name that you can trademark and own."

Johnny thought about those two options for a moment and then responded, "Nah. We'll just deal with that later if it comes up."

I relayed this story about the trademark to Jeff. "Is he crazy? They're just going to steal his money. Didn't you tell him that?"

"Yeah, sure I did, but he doesn't listen to me on everything."

"I don't know, Peter," he said with some resignation. "This is basic business 101. Does he really have the expertise and skill set to do this? What is it?" And then Jeff answered his own question, "He probably doesn't."

"Well he's a master gardener for a top tier medical dispensary and he has placed high in cannabis Cup competitions —"

"But has he thought about Day 1?" Jeff interrupted. "What does Day 1 look like? Does he have a mock-up of what the retail site looks like? How does he get customers in the door? He can't be serious," Jeff laughed, "about having college girls wear sweatpants with his company name on their butt. I mean, this is something high school or junior high school kids would think up!"

"Yeah, I couldn't believe it when I read that either."

"But to get any serious investor," Jeff continued, "he's going to have to create a good business model and he's going to have to answer the question that each investor will have which is, 'How can he pull this off?'"

In the end I had to rewrite everything Josh and Johnny came up with, and had to change things substantially in the business plan. Based on Josh's research Johnny figured out that it was illegal to combine a retail store within a dispensary and to let 18 to 20-year-olds into the store. And they dropped the idea of having college girls wear sweatpants with the company logo. But I struggled to figure out a role for Josh and mentioned that to Johnny.

"Johnny, I can't figure out a role for Josh in the business."

"What do you mean?" he asked.

"I'm looking at his bio and he's basically done nothing of substance. He can't be the CFO since he's not good with numbers, and he can't really be in charge of operations since he doesn't know how to grow and—"

Johnny interrupted me, "Yeah, I got guys in my current grow operation that will do all the cultivation so there's nothing there for him." He was silent for a moment. "Let me talk to him and see what he says."

A few days later Johnny got back to me on Josh's role. "He says he wants the title CEO."

"What?" I asked. "The CEO? That's your job!"

"I know," said Johnny. "He said that titles are really important to him."

"Well, I'm not going to do that," I responded. "I'll think of something but for now, for the business plan, I'll just put him in there as a manager."

And a few days after that conversation Johnny called me and said, "I let Josh go."

"You got rid of him?"

"Yeah. He was angry about it, but ever since you said you couldn't figure out a role for him, couldn't come up with a title for him, I started thinking that he's not the right person. And then when he said he wanted to be CEO I knew he wasn't the right person."

"Well, good for you. That's tough to fire a friend, but better now than later."

"You know," Johnny said in a reflective moment, "the worst thing you can do is start a business with your friends. A lot of people do it, but if it doesn't work out you could lose your business and your friend."

With Josh gone Johnny lost a potential $300,000 investment from Josh's father, but even with that money Johnny would still need another million dollars, and figuring out how to get that million dollars became his sole focus over the next eight months.

THE INVESTORS

Since Johnny already had a license for cultivation, a license for infused products, and a license for a retail dispensary, he went ahead and leased a building for the cultivation and manufacturing of edibles in Boulder. And although he couldn't afford to start up any operations, that was probably a good thing to do at the time because commercial real estate in Denver, Boulder, and the Front Range is increasingly difficult to come by and vacancy rates are some of the lowest in the country. Between 2009 and 2014 marijuana cultivation operations accounted for 35.8 percent of all leased industrial space in Denver, and by 2015 one in eleven industrial buildings in Denver was a marijuana grow operation. In total, marijuana accounts for over 3.7 million square feet of industrial space, most of it C properties—buildings that are the poorest quality, obsolete, and should be scrapped or redeveloped.

Despite the poor quality of marijuana grow buildings, cultivators often pay two to three times higher rents than other tenants. In Johnny's case he leased 30,000 square feet and his monthly payment was close to $35,000 a month. But he showed me one of his weekly checks from his medical marijuana growing operations and it was $23,000, enough to cover the monthly rent for his new growing facility. Even so, he was desperate to find an investor.

And, surprisingly, it was difficult to find an investor. The numbers for Johnny's cultivation facility alone are staggering, but adding in the infused products and retail store of a fully vertically integrated business makes it one of the most attractive investment opportunities available. His business would generate revenues of $6.8 million in year one, nearly double to $12.5 million in year three, and would generate cumulative profits of $7.3 million over that three-year timespan. There's risk involved for the investor who wants to be in the cannabis industry, but the risk stems from the federal government shutting down the industry, not from the marijuana growing operations or from market demand. In fact, compared to growing corn the marijuana growing cycle is far superior.

Johnny said to me, "A farmer has to buy the seeds, plant the corn, fertilize, and then he's at the whims of Mother Nature in terms of water, humidity, sunshine—"

"Plus," I broke in, "don't forget that the farmer has to spend hundreds of thousands of dollars on equipment."

"Right," said Johnny. "And at the end, he gets one result, an ear of corn, and the rest is waste. For me, I control every variable—the soil, the nutrients, the amount of light, the water, the temperature and humidity. I don't need seeds, and I use every part of the plant—the trim, the fan leaves, the flower, and even the stalk. There's no waste. And," he continued, "I can get four crops a year and the farmer can only get one crop."

From an investment standpoint, cannabis (legal cannabis) has to be one of the best investments out there, but one reason Johnny was not finding investors was that he was listed on an obscure venture capital website in Denver and he's constrained about how much he can say about his opportunity. What he did say was generic: *"Seeking $1 million investment for an equity position* *in my company, share of profits, and the ability to grow with the company."* Since I knew the financials in Eric's business, and I knew Eric was interested in making as much money as possible in the shortest amount of time, I told him that Johnny was looking for money. "How much does he need?" Eric asked.

"A million" I responded.

"I'll give him the million bucks," said Eric, without needing a pro forma, or meeting Johnny, and without thinking about it for more than a few seconds.

I went back to Johnny with this information. "Johnny, I mentioned to Eric that you were looking for a million dollars and he said, 'I'll give him the million.' Do you want to go to Denver and meet with Eric?"

"Pete! No! I don't want to work with Eric." Normally reserved and thoughtful, Johnny had an outburst of emotion. "I'll sell him some flower, but he might try to take over my business."

"I don't think he's going to do that, and I don't think he could take over your business unless you give him a controlling interest. I think he's looking at it as an investment opportunity, which is the way I presented it."

"No," Johnny continued, more calmly, "we have a lot of opportunities with the other investors. I don't want to do it."

Several months later, after Johnny had hit dead end after dead end with investors, he came back to me and said, "Why don't you go back to Eric and see if he would like to invest?"

When I approached Eric a second time, I got a totally different response. "Why would I want to help put a competitor in business?" he asked.

"Well, it's a good investment opportunity for one, and two, I don't think Boulder and Denver are in the same market."

Eric thought for a moment and said, "Well, I guess we could help run his dispensary if he wants that, but otherwise I don't see a play for us."

"One thing," I note, "he's a C-Corp, not an LLC."

"A C-Corp! Why isn't he an LLC? That's just stupid."

"I tried to get him to be an LLC and he wouldn't listen to me."

"Yah," Eric said in a long, drawn-out voice, "I don't want to do a deal with someone who won't listen to you, and I don't want to do a deal with a guy as a C-Corp. Nah, I don't think so. We're going to Nevada anyway. We think medical will get started soon there."

When I circled back to Johnny I said, "Eric's not interested anymore," expecting him to be disappointed.

"Doesn't matter!" he stated with excitement, "I found a new guy. Saul, from New York. I think this might be the guy."

"Why do you think that?"

"He's got a ton of experience in marketing, has been an executive in marketing, and wants to work in the business as head of marketing. He's been successful as a marketer. And he's got a son that lives here and wants to work in the growing operations and learn that."

"Well, what's the deal you're talking about?"

"40 percent for $2 million, plus working in the business for Saul and his son. Here," he said as he wrote Saul's name on a piece of paper, "take a look around the internet and see what you can find out about him."

A few days later I returned to Johnny with my assessment of Saul. "Johnny, this guy hasn't done anything since 1983. That's the last time he worked. What does he know about marketing in 2014?"

"I like the guy," said Johnny, "we've had several conversations and we've hit it off."

"Ok. Let me run one scenario past you. Saul brings his $2 million dollars and you give him an office and a salary of $400,000. At the end of the year you have a profit of a million and you have to give Saul another $400,000. Meanwhile, he doesn't do anything for your marketing, he just makes phone calls to marketing companies to do the work. Do you actually think a guy like Saul, who is pushing seventy years old, is going to set up your website? Do the programming? Create and execute your blog? No.

He's going to come here to Colorado and delegate everything, and buy a vacation home in Vail and spend his weekends there. Oh, and he's going to put his son in the business to learn all of your knowledge and then the two of them are going to start their own business and compete with you."

In the end my opinion of Saul didn't matter because Johnny figured out that Saul was a fraud. When we finally came up with a contract for Saul to sign he told Johnny that he actually didn't have the money and needed to get a friend of his to sign off on the deal. And worse for Johnny, that he wouldn't be able to get the money until February or March at the earliest. After months of discussions, working through financial models, and thinking through the options, Saul finally revealed his true self, which was a person posing as a serious investor. After that Johnny was much more skeptical and wary of investors and I came up with a list of three questions for him to ask to vet people, so that he wouldn't waste his time and get his hopes up.

1. Are you an accredited investor?
2. Do you have 3X of funds available? Show us your bank statement to prove it.
3. Why do you want to invest with us?

Those questions provided a reality check for Johnny, and for the potential investors, too, and it ended up taking a lot of them out of the equation. After instituting our three-question rule, we were only left with one serious investor, Derek, who I met at a Boulder Cannabis Meetup.

DEREK, THE CANNABIS INVESTOR

I walked in to my first Boulder Cannabis Meetup with Derek—we were both there for the first time, and the speaker was Andy LaFrate of Charas Scientific, talking about cannabis testing labs.

"Have you been here before?" I asked him, as we walked down stairs to the basement of the Riverside, in Boulder.

"No," he responded. "This is my first time. How about you?"

"Same," I stated. "First time."

"What are you here for?" he asked.

"Well, I have a couple of cannabis clients that I'm working with. I'm writing business plans for them, and I need to help them get some money. But I'm mostly a writer and I'm writing a book on the cannabis industry. What about you?"

"I'm an investor. I'm looking to do something in the cannabis industry."

I immediately turned to Derek and said, "I got a guy for you."

"Great," he replied, "what does he do?"

"He's a startup here in Boulder with plans to be vertically integrated. He's leasing 30,000 square feet of commercial space for his growing operations and is looking for retail space in Boulder."

"That sounds interesting," Derek replied.

"Yeah, I tell you what, let me text him and see if he's around this week. Are you near here?"

"Yeah, I grew up in Boulder and just moved back, so I'm flexible and can meet when your guy can. Send me a half-page with what he wants and why and I'll run it by my investors and see if there's any interest."

I did that, and Johnny and I met with Derek the following week. We learned a lot about how investors are thinking about the cannabis industry in Colorado, and a lot about Derek, as it turned out. Derek is in his early thirties and has a weightlifter frame—big arms, thick thighs, and overall, very muscular. He told us he played football both in Boulder and at a Division 1 school in California and without checking, that seemed plausible. After college Derek joined the Army Special Forces Operations unit, doing several tours in Afghanistan. For the past several years he has been working with venture capitalists to vet projects for funding, but now he was working with his father and some of his father's friends in a consortium to invest in opportunities. Derek mentioned that they prefer deals in the $1-$5 million dollar range; any smaller and the payoff isn't worth it. Any larger and the risk is too high. Derek had the green light from the investors to seek out opportunities in the cannabis industry, preferably deals that involved real estate, so the consortium would have a hard asset for collateral.

"There are a lot of guys approaching people in the cannabis industry with a 40/40 deal," said Derek at our first meeting, at the same coffee shop where I first met Johnny.

We must have had blank stares on our faces because Derek continued explaining, "That's 40 percent for 40 months."

"Ok," I clairified, "so if you loan us $1.5 million you'll want both the $1.5 and 40 percent of that, say $600,000, within 40 months?"

"Yeah," said Derek, "that's with no collateral. That's a hard loan. But," he said as he turned to Johnny, "you need to figure out what you want to do. We could come in and buy the property that you have, the 30,000 square feet, and then we'd give you a really good, long-term lease. But we'd have to make improvements to the building in order to have an asset. Or we could look for a building for your retail site. If you have some collateral I could probably talk the investors down to 20-25 percent."

"I'm working on the retail site," Johnny stated, "but there are other investors involved. I'll get half the building and the current owner will downsize his restaurant and stay in the other half, and I'll have the whole top floor."

"What's your cost?" asked Derek.

"$3.5 million" replied Johnny.

Derek quickly responded, "So you really need $5 million."

"I can fund the $3.5 million" stated Johnny, "once I get the growing operations up and running. That's the key because now with no vertical integration I can sell to anyone. So my phase 1 is to get the growing up and running, in phase 2 I start the edibles, and in phase 3, the retail."

"But if you got the $5 million you could do it all at once, right?" asked Derek. "No one is going to give you $5 million with a 40/40 deal. It needs to be collateralized. You'll need to give up some equity. You'll have to give up a stake in your company to move this."

"Ok," said Johnny. "Tell me, how do you work with someone like me."

"We're hands off, as long as you're making your payments. If you miss a payment, it's not a big deal, but if you miss a couple then the investors start to get nervous and then they start to turn up the heat. We like to be the first ones in on a deal, but if we're last then we will back you into a corner because we know you're desperate."

"But," Derek continued, "for this deal, we'd be first, right?"

"Yes," I responded.

"Then this deal is totally different. There's a lot of interest in the cannabis industry right now. I have a guy in Washington who has growing operations and he's got money to play with, and what I'm really thinking is that I'd like to get a guy I grew up with here in Boulder involved, Jay. His dad gave him a lot of money and Jay's been afraid to do deals because he's afraid of losing money. His dad doesn't care if he loses money, but Jay has been sitting on the sidelines. He knows a lot about cannabis, especially around Portland, where he lives, and I think this would be something he could get really interested in."

After meeting with Derek, Johnny and I walked outside, and Johnny turned to me and said, "Did you hear Derek say that they like to push a guy into the corner?"

"Yeah, that's investors for you."

"I'm not sure I want to do anything with somebody who treats me like that. That doesn't sound right to me. I'm thinking more of a partnership, not a guy telling me what to do and backing me into a corner."

"I agree. But let's just wait for them to come up with something and if they want to come to Boulder to see your operations, that's a sign of interest. Otherwise, it's just talking."

A few days later, Derek called me. "There's a lot of interest in what Johnny is doing. I'm working with Jay to get him out here. He's interested, and I think this would be a good opportunity for him. One thing you should know about Jay, he has a very skeptical approach to things. He will ask a lot of questions, he will challenge Johnny on things, but you need to ignore that."

"Ok, I know the type."

"I'm thinking that Jay will come out here in the next several weeks. Do you know Johnny's schedule?"

"No, I don't know his schedule, but you know that the cannabis business is seven days a week, and nearly all day long. So, whenever Jay gets here we'll be able to show him around."

Several weeks later, Jay arrived and we all met up at Johnny's future retail location: Jay, Derek, me, Johnny, and his wife, Kate. The property is owned by a family that has been in the restaurant business for decades and they're ready to sell out and retire. It's an old, tired piece of property, but the location is supreme.

"Hey, Brotha," Johnny said as he shook Jay's hand.

"Hey," Jay responded. "So this property is off the table? This is not part of the deal that we're looking at?"

"Right," said Johnny. "It's a great location" as he pointed to the south, "there's a bank right there with an ATM, the mall is just beyond it and we're right between the two biggest dispensaries in town. This is actually a better location than either one of those."

"Yeah," responded Jay, "I'm familiar with Boulder, and when Derek told me about this property I was super interested because it is a nice piece of property and will be for years to come."

Clearly, Jay and Derek are very interested in the retail space but Johnny understands commercial real estate and knows that his business model will work: build out the cultivation in year one, monetize that, and then by year three build out the retail space. He doesn't need or want investors for his retail space, but he sure needs money to get off the ground.

"We can talk about that," said Johnny. "Let's go over to the medical marijuana grow."

Johnny is the master gardener at this medical dispensary and a one-third owner, which is why he makes $20,000 a week, and why he can afford to build out the retail space on his own and, if he has to, the cultivation facility itself. The grow is located on the east side of town in an old industrial park. Most of the buildings in this part of town are also growing operations. We all follow Johnny there and I have followed Johnny before and know that he is a slow, cautious driver. Unlike Eric, with his $100,000 Mercedes, Johnny drives an old Lexus he bought from his aunt who needed the money. In fact, Johnny funds nearly everybody in his family—his brother, his mom and dad, and others. Although he makes $20,000 a week, he also gives most of that money away. But he's a slow driver for good reason since he's had run-ins with cops before. While over at Johnny's house for a meeting he was worried about driving to his niece's high school graduation in Idaho.

"We don't want to fly, with the baby and all her stuff, it would be a lot, plus we want to bring the dogs. We have to go through either Wyoming or Utah to get to Idaho and in all three states the cops target Colorado plates. Pete," he said as he looked at me with concern, "I'm going to wear a nice suit and tie, drive under the speed limit, and tuck my hair up underneath a baseball cap. What do you think?"

"Well, I've driven all those places since Colorado legalized marijuana and I've never been pulled over, and I usually drive faster than the speed limit. I've heard that the State Patrol in all the states surrounding us are targeting Colorado drivers, but I don't know if that's anecdotal or true."

"I can't risk it. I have herb in my car every day and no matter how thorough I am in cleaning it—and I'm meticulous—if there's even one little leaf or seed or bud and I get pulled over and searched, the cops will find it. Seriously, Pete, it's impossible to have a totally clean car if you're hauling marijuana around."

I thought for a moment. "You know what you should do, is just rent a minivan for the trip. There would be virtually no chance of marijuana being in the car and you might get lucky and get a car with Utah or Idaho plates."

So, the fact that Johnny is driving very slowly to his growing operations is something I expected. When we got there Johnny and Jay had a conversation in the parking lot.

"So, Brotha, what's your story?" asked Johnny.

"I grew up here with Derek and he called me after meeting with you guys, and I'm interested in the space. I invested in a grow operation in Oregon and this looks like a good opportunity." Jay continued with questions to Johnny about plant count, how many plants per light, and the wattage of the lights. Jay tried to give Johnny advice based on what he had seen in Portland, but Johnny would have none of it and I could see him tense up a bit and become irritated at the suggestions.

"Let's just go inside," said Johnny, "and I'll show you what we've got."

Johnny's grow house is a lot smaller than Eric's but essentially the same—high ceilings, multiple lights hanging from the ceiling, and a ventilation system that runs throughout the facility. He's got several rooms completely filled with cannabis plants at various stages of growth, and a drying room for the harvested product. It was a very quick tour, and because we were getting in the way of Johnny's workers, we went back to the entrance within five minutes of getting inside. At the entrance, Johnny has one room that serves as an office, a meeting room, a datacenter (with charts, graphs, and logs of the operations), a secure vault for cash and cannabis, and cafeteria. Johnny walked over to a safe, opened it, and pulled out a tray with cannabis—a large tray, probably two feet by four feet. The buds in the tray are the softball-sized ones Johnny showed me earlier, and Jay is astounded at their size and quality. He picked up one bud, smelled it, and told Johnny, "This is really good stuff you have."

"Yes," Johnny replied, "I've won Cannabis Cup competitions and have been doing this for over fifteen years. So, this is pretty much what you should expect in terms of quality. So, I want to show you my new grow house, up in Gunbarrel. That's where everything comes together."

We arrived at the industrial park in Gunbarrel, and Johnny's building is a relic from the 1970's. It is definitely a "C" space and the property owner must have considered Johnny a gift from heaven when he came looking for space. Already Johnny has paid the owner six figures in rent. Once inside Johnny took us up to the third floor which is 9,800 square feet. "This is where we'll start phase 1," Johnny said. "And phase 2 we'll build out the second floor with some growing but also with a MIPS production lab."

"These ceilings aren't very high," stated Jay.

"Oh, they're high enough," said Johnny, "it depends on how many plants you're putting under the lights and we'll probably have three or four, so the height of the ceiling won't matter. Let me show you the roof."

Jay and Johnny headed up to the roof while Kate, Derek, and I waited below on the third floor. When they returned Johnny turned to Jay and said, "So, Brotha, what do you think? Is this something you'd be interested in?"

"Yes, definitely. We'll have to work the numbers. You're sure about the retail space?"

"For now I am, but that could change."

Derek spoke up. "We can have the money to you by the end of the month. How long will the build-out take?"

"I told the contractor we were on a tight schedule, so it ought to be completed within three months."

"And another three months to get your first crop?" Derek asked.

"Yep," replied Johnny.

"So we would be cash flowing by May or June of next year," Derek confirmed.

And on that note we ended the tour of Johnny's growing facility and parted ways. Several hours later I got a call from Johnny, which was rare because he mostly sends me texts. "Pete, I don't like Jay. I don't want to work with him."

"Derek told me he was annoying—"

"I can't stand the guy. I can't work with him. I think he would be constantly meddling in my business, telling me what to do. He's a trustafarian. He's a wealthy guy who never earned a nickel in his life, never had to work. He only went to school because his parents paid for it."

"Ok, I hear you. Let me talk to Derek and get back to you."

I immediately called Derek. "Hey, what did you guys think of Johnny's opportunity?"

"Jay's real excited about it. He likes Johnny. The only questions was, why are your electricity costs so high?"

"Oh, right. That's because in Boulder you have to have 100 percent of your power from renewable energy, like wind or solar. You can't use fossil fuels like coal or natural gas, at least, not for marijuana growing operations, I don't know about other businesses."

"Wow. I didn't know that. That makes a huge difference."

"Sure does. Say, what does Jay bring to the table in this deal?"

"Well, he brings some money and he knows a lot about the industry, so some expertise."

"Johnny didn't like Jay. Doesn't want to work with him."

"Really?"

"Yeah, that's what he told me on the phone just now."

"Well, I know Jay's a tough person to be around and that he rubs people the wrong way. I really wanted him to do this deal and get off the sidelines. Ok, that's not a problem. I'll take him out."

I was surprised that Derek took his buddy out of the deal so quickly, so maybe they really are interested in funding Johnny. "So what are the next steps?"

"Well, I'll talk to Jay and make sure he understands where we're at, but there are five other guys that have opinions and it will take a while to get them organized."

Over the course of the next month or so we had numerous conversations with Derek and worked through various models. Derek and his investors were willing to provide the $1.5 million loan for a 25 percent equity stake in Johnny's business for five years. That seemed like a good deal but there were two hitches. First, there was a substantial penalty for paying off the loan early and it's easy to see why: by year five Johnny's sales will be above $15 million and why give up the equity position early with a payout of nearly $4 million looming? Second, the investors weren't willing to budge without some collateral, and they really wanted an equity position in Johnny's medical marijuana cultivation facility, for "a certain amount of time."

The problem was, Johnny didn't tell the owner of the medical marijuana cultivation and dispensary that he was breaking out on his own to pursue the recreational market. Johnny floated the idea by the owner when Colorado first legalized cannabis, but the owner was hesitant and decided to stick with medical marijuana. Johnny, however, pursued the recreational market and purchased the three licenses—growing, MIPS, and dispensary—that would allow him to be vertically integrated. He also rented the growing space at $35,000 per month, and put together a business plan for securing capital. So, anything that involved the medical marijuana part of Johnny's business was off the table.

Next the investors suggested that Johnny put his retail space into play, and that the investors and Johnny partner and develop that together and be 50-50 owners. Johnny rejected that plan because firstly, the retail site is a class A location and will be worth a substantial amount of money if Johnny's business gets derailed, if the federal government decides to enforce marijuana laws, or any of a myriad of reasons that prevent him from developing the site as a marijuana dispensary. Also, there's no need for Johnny to bring the investors into the retail space since he can fund it himself and why should he give the investors 50 percent of that value? After concluding that the retail space wouldn't work, the investors then suggested that they purchase the 30,000 square foot building in Gunbarrel where Johnny will start his cultivation facility. Their plan was to provide Johnny a 20-year lease at a preferred rent rate and then the $1.5 million could be paid back over time. They reasoned that it would allow Johnny to get in to business and they would roll the money into the building for the improvements that Johnny needs. But Johnny already negotiated a good lease with the landlords, under $8 per square foot, which is very good in Boulder County and very good for a marijuana growing facility. So, the cultivation facility was off the table.

Johnny and I were getting frustrated with the delays in getting a deal put together with Derek and his investors, especially since they had already been to Boulder to tour the facilities, had face-to-face meetings with Johnny, and had indicated that they had a lot of interest. Then, two days before Christmas Derek called me and suggested a meeting with Johnny.

"Ok," stated Derek at the meeting, "here's the deal. If it's not an asset-based deal then it's risky. The hard loan is risky and if you were to go to a venture capitalist they would want to earn at least 25-30 percent on their money. Investors want 5x to 20x on their money—that's if you do a hard loan, like the 40/40 deal we talked about before.

"If you take the risk out by throwing an asset in there, like the Gunbarrel property or the retail property or the medical marijuana property, then we could come down to 15 percent for 60 months, and no payments for the first twelve months."

"That sounds good!" said Johnny, with excitement.

"Ideally what we could do is pay off the $1.5 million in year two, and then have a 15 percent equity position for 60 months," stated Derek. "Basically, if we give you the money we want you to be successful, we don't want to make it difficult for you to make payments to us, if it hurts your business. We're interested in getting our money back and you need to stay in business to do that.

"Now, I'll bring this back to the investors. We need a pitch deck for them and once they make their decision it takes about ten days to complete. I know you can't put your properties up as collateral, so I want you to put your current cash flow from the medical marijuana company into a spreadsheet. And any personal and business debt needs to be listed, too. I'll need the operating agreement between you and the owner at the medical dispensary, and any other loans or debts that you have. We'll want to be a part of the next deal. We'll write that into the contract and don't worry about legal fees. I'll have my lawyer draw up the contracts and all you'll have to do is sign them."

After Derek left, Johnny and I stood outside talking about the deal Derek had proposed: $1.5 million loan, paid back within two years, and a 15 percent equity position for another five years. Johnny was ecstatic, exuberant, as happy as I'd seen him in months.

"This gives us everything we want," Johnny said excitedly. "If we can get the money by February 1st then I can call my contractor and have him start pulling permits—that will take some time with the City of Boulder. But we could have a crop in the ground by April or May. I have to call Kate. Let me know when Derek gets back to you and have a great Christmas!"

Derek did get back to me several days later and had several questions about Johnny's ownership interest in the medical marijuana retail dispensary, and the legal structure of the growing operations. Derek strongly suggested that Johnny organize as an LLC versus a C-Corp or any other structure, and after being hounded by every business person for the past six months about the issue, Johnny finally agreed that "LLC is the way to go." But what Derek sent back to me, Johnny, and Kate was confusing and wasn't anything close to what we had talked about just before Christmas. Derek said that the current deal he is working on with investors is a sliding scale of 15-30 percent with personal recourse, 22-37 percent with recourse. In addition, the investors wanted a quick payoff where the investor would get 90 percent of the profit until the money is paid back, and then has a 20-25 percent equity position.

Johnny and Kate were stunned. "Pete," Johnny said to me, "Kate and I just read through the email from Derek and we are super confused as to what he is proposing versus what we spoke about last week."

"I know. I'm totally surprised myself."

Johnny continued, "We have our notes from the meeting and what he's saying we never talked about. We can handle the 15 percent of profits and I understand that if we default that they need to step in, but the numbers he mentioned are huge."

"The numbers are way more than what he talked about," I responded.

"That whole concept of 90 percent of profits going to the investor until they're paid off is a tough way to grow the business. It seems like the investor is positioning themselves to be the source for all future money, and when we go to them we'll have to give away equity every time we want to expand."

"Yeah, I don't know where this is coming from. I've never met any of Derek's investors other than Jay, so I don't know what's going on."

"Really," Johnny stated, "the deal breaker here is the huge amount of equity being asked beyond that 15 percent. For a $1.5 million loan which is being paid back, to receive equity higher than 15 percent is a lot. To give away upwards of 25-30 percent is taking us back to an investor who would ideally be buying into the company and not be a loan. Does that make sense?" he asked.

"Absolutely. It makes total sense. It's kind of like the Saul deal. He wanted a lot of equity and also a job that we knew he would never do. These guys just want the equity and no job. But they are both freeloading off of you."

"Circle back with Derek. We need to get this figured out."

The three of us, Johnny, Kate, and me met with Derek the next day, December 31.

"I'm working with a couple of investor groups that are interested," Derek began. "The guy in Washington, Brad, can fund by February 1st, and he's the main money guy. The other group, the Japanese, can't fund by February 1st but they also want to structure the deal with the retail."

"Nah," Johnny broke in. "I don't want to mix the retail and the growing. I want to keep those separate."

"Ok. Then the investor from Washington wants a twelve month lead-in and you can pay off the $1.5 when you're able, within forty months. If you don't pay by then there will be penalties. One other thing. Your management fee is light. Investors don't like to see somebody not paying themselves, it makes them uncomfortable. You should put in at least $200,000 for yourself."

"Yeah," I agreed, "that was an oversight on my part. Is there any equity involved in this deal?"

"Yeah, with this deal it's 20 percent for five years. And if you return the capital within two years we'll roll it forward to start phase 2 and phase 3."

"Sounds great!" Johnny exclaimed.

"Yes," said Kate. "We were confused about that 90 percent of profits."

"Don't worry about it," said Derek. "This guy is already a grower, has the money, and wants to diversify to Colorado, so it's no big deal."

"One thing," Johnny interjected, "Kate and Pete and I have talked about having you work with us as a CFO. That way you can keep track of the money for your investors, and you can help us out too."

"It's something to think about," responded Derek, "but I'm not looking for a full-time job."

"No, it wouldn't be that, it would be a part-time deal. We're just thinking that since you live here in Boulder and know us and our business, you could help out and make a little money. Probably $150,000 a year just to keep our books straight."

"Well, let's get this first deal done," said Derek, "and then we can think about ways to work together."

After the meeting Johnny, Kate, and I talked outside about our take on things. Both Johnny and Kate were ecstatic about the possibilities with the investor. The great thing about the offer was that Johnny wouldn't have to bring in other investors to realize his vision, which is a huge time-waster. Over the past several months he has tried to figure out who was a legitimate investor and who was just kicking his tires, like Saul, for example, a person just pretending to be somebody serious. The investor groups from Houston, Florida, New York, and Mexico, and the individuals from North Carolina and Colorado were a huge drain emotionally for Johnny and Kate, and a huge drain in their time. Those investors either didn't have the money or didn't have enough money to move the needle. But with this latest offer from Derek, it appeared that all of those troubles were behind them.

It was premature to believe that. About a week later Derek sent me a text: "I just heard from an investor. Johnny will need to sacrifice a payment in perpetuity to sell this deal. i.e. equity is inevitable without a termination date. We can also call it a fee (like the first $500K) that is always adjusted for inflation. That way the percentage slides depending on revenue. Semantics."

I forwarded that text to Johnny. He called me a few days later, distraught.

"Pete, don't take this the wrong way. I know Derek is your guy, but Kate and I checked him out and he's never done a deal. We checked all over the place and couldn't find any record that he's done anything."

"Well, I didn't know that. I only met him about a week before he met you, so we basically understand him the same way."

"But here's the thing," Johnny continued. "I don't want to work with the guy. I think he's dishonest and he goes back on his word. Every time we meet with him we come to a conclusion that we like, an agreement that works, and every time he comes back a week later with something completely different that we didn't talk about. And every time it's something that's way worse for us.

"This $500,000 payment that goes on forever?? No way! Kate and I are not interested in that. We're not interested in doing this even if there is a buyout date. It doesn't work. We have no desire to take more time to meet this guy. After all Derek has been telling us during the last two meetings, and this is what he came back with?"

"Ok, I'll tell him. I agree with you. I don't know if Derek is dishonest or if he really doesn't know what the investors want, but all these deals are lousy for you."

"Thanks, Pete. We'll be Ok once I get the growing facility up and running at my medical grow, and that should be February."

"What about the retail space? He'll ask about that and who knows? Maybe that's what they wanted all along."

"Yeah, that's done. We got an SBA loan, so we won't need any investors at all."

When I contacted Derek and told him that Johnny was not interested in any investment, he responded, "You mean for the cultivation facility?"

"Yes, that and the retail site."

"How's he going to fund that $3.5 million then?"

"He got an SBA loan."

"Are you kidding me?" Derek responded in an angry tone. "That sucks. That's totally dishonest. It takes a long time to get an SBA loan. He didn't just start that process last month. So he's been playing us all along. That's not right, that's not being honest with us."

"I agree, but the SBA loan took me totally by surprise. Johnny doesn't share everything with me."

SIX MONTHS LATER

Several months after trying to get financing for Johnny I circled back to Derek to get his insight on the investor perspective for the cannabis industry, who is investing, and what changes he's seen since Colorado legalized marijuana. We met at a coffee shop, where Derek provided details that highlight the differing world perspectives of the cannabis culture, and the investment culture.

"At first, when it first became legal there was a lot of interest from people," Derek started out. "The investors could see the dollar signs with the industry, but it's restricted to invest directly, so that makes it a little more difficult. That's why there are so many real estate deals. But those first guys that got in, I'd say three out of five went tits up.

"People are so willing to trust guys like Johnny, but it's hard to get the cannabis guys to really be forthright. Like Johnny with that SBA loan, you know? But I've seen a lot of deals go down to the wire and then at the last minute the cannabis guys pull out. No one in the cannabis industry has a clue on their fiduciary responsibility. There's an utter disconnect between the business guys and the cannabis guys."

"What is the reason for that, do you know?" I asked.

"I'm not sure. The operators are very close to each other, and they have more growing sense than business sense. But I think it might just be a different moral perspective, or maybe I should say a different ideology with the growers. I don't know. It feels like an inside game to me. There's risk in the industry, not only from the Federal government, but from the cannabis guys themselves.

"We've done some deals but we only want to do something if we can control a hard asset, like land. That's what Jay did on his first deal. He funded an irrigation system for a grower. So we stay on the periphery. At first, we thought, 'This is going to change a lot of things,' but now it seems like it's moved the needle a little bit, not a lot. If you had asked me about hemp, that I could get excited about. Hemp could change everything. But cannabis…it's not logarithmic."

"What isn't logarithmic?"

"The growth. The banking issue hasn't been solved and now more investors are passing. Cannabis for our guys is off the table for at least another 24 months. At first we were like 'Yeah!' but now we're more sensitive. Now you really better be clever with your concept or don't waste my time."

"When we were trying to get Johnny some money you mentioned some groups from Japan…is there interest internationally in cannabis?"

"Yeah, there's a lot of interest. Mostly Japan, Russia, and Israel. Some from Germany, too. I wouldn't do anything with the Russians. Would never trust them. For the Japanese group it wasn't so much that they wanted to be in the cannabis industry, but they wanted to get their money out of Asia and they mostly wanted real estate."

"Is the cannabis industry the same as all the other industries or is it different in some way?"

"I don't have a lot of confidence in comparing cannabis to other industries, not at this point. And I don't think you can compare it to prohibition of alcohol. That's too hard. It's so hard as an investor to calculate your winnings. And it's tough to figure out what a good investment is. My guy in Washington who is a grower loaned another grower $2 million and expected payback in two years. Now he's getting a 15 percent return and he's happy. It's tough, and like I said, we're sitting on the sidelines for the next couple of years."

Johnny was not sitting on the sidelines, he was all in, and moving forward with his plans for vertical integration. I spoke with him several months after everything fell apart with Derek. His addition to the existing medical marijuana grow was done and that will provide him with an extra eighty pounds of cannabis monthly, which he will sell wholesale. At $2,000 a pound that's another $160,000 per month, which he will uss for the build-out of the 30,000 square foot cultivation building.

"We're actually on track to finish early, probably by November," Johnny told me.

"Wow. Good job!"

"Yeah, I found a contractor that has worked with other growers before and I told the guy the situation and he's like, 'Don't worry about paying us. We'll do the work and you can pay us once you get a couple of crops.' So that's what we're doing.

"You know," Johnny continued in a reflective moment, "I never liked a person who had money. Never liked an investor that I met. The best thing you can do is find a company who makes you stronger, like with this contractor. He does what he does best and I do what I do best. And then you grow together and you each make a lot of money. I bought property up in the mountains and I'm going to cultivate there, but use greenhouses instead of buildings. You know that traditional LED's only have red and blue spectrum, right? Plants respond best to the full spectrum, so I'm going with the sun next."

"With the same contractor?"

"Yep."

I was impressed with the near total transformation of Johnny from a person who was naïve about business, to savvy about business and investors. His thoughts on the win-win partnership with the contractor, where they both do what each does best and grow together and make a lot of money, is the definition of a "strategic partnership." Most people figure out the benefits of a strategic partnership in business school, but Johnny figured it out by pursuing his vision of vertical integration and never giving up on that vision.

CHAPTER 4.

THE REGULATORS

A critical factor in legalizing marijuana stems from the inter-action between the industry—including trade associations, lob-byists, and operators—and the regulators and legislators who create the framework for industry regulations. When I attended the Mile High Young Professionals panel discussion and all three groups were represented, but I was particularly interested in speaking with the regulators and lawmakers, including Frank McNulty, former Speaker of the House, Andrew Freedman, Director of Marijuana Coordination, and Representative Jonathan Singer. Eventually, I interviewed all three of them, and also Senator Pat Steadman, an expert in the finances and tax implications of the cannabis industry. I also interviewed Gover-nor John Hickenlooper, who has overall strategic and regulatory oversight of the industry. Together they provided key insights of the inner dynamics of the industry transitioning from illegal to legal markets, including the challenges they faced and the solu-tions they put forward.

FRANK McNULTY
FORMER SPEAKER OF THE HOUSE

I met Frank McNulty shortly after the panel discussion in Sep-tember 2014. I was impressed with Frank's candor during the panel discussion because he is opposed to marijuana legalization and the audience was decidedly pro-marijuana and were intently interested in hearing from the activists and industry insiders. One question moderator Brandon Rittiman asked was, "How has the image of Colorado changed, both positive and negative, since implementation of Amendment 64?"

One panelist responded, "Well, our tourism numbers are very high," and that comment received immediate applause, clapping, and cheering from the audience.

Frank McNulty leaned forward into the microphone and responded, "There's more homeless people here now. And there's statistical evidence for that. I don't think anyone saw that coming. It gives us a black eye. Yes, we're trend setters on legalizing marijuana but we're also the test case for America's homeless population. If you were to ask me, 'Would you do this again?' I would absolutely not legalize marijuana. I am opposed to legalizing it."

There were no cheers from the audience after that comment.

Frank McNulty is no longer serving in the Colorado House, because of State constitutional term limits, but he is a force to be reckoned with and I was grateful to get the opportunity to speak with him about his experience in legalizing marijuana. We met at a coffee shop and as he entered, I could see him look to the side and walk to greet a patron, speak with that person for a while, and shake his hand as he walked away. The life of a politician never ends, even after serving in office, I guess. Frank has an easygoing, affable demeanor that belies a tougher, no-nonsense and practical approach to politics. Once we get settled, I asked, "What is the current reality in the cannabis industry?"

Frank looks at me for a moment, somewhat perplexed, and then states, "It's here! It was very confusing from my perspective because it happened very fast, and because of the Federal rules. We had to think about every part of the economy and society in putting this together."

It **was** fast, as Frank stated. The election and vote on the Constitutional Amendment in 2012 was in November, and Amendment 64 had a drop-dead date of complete rules and regulations by July 1, 2013, in anticipation of a January 1, 2014 opening for recreational marijuana sales.

"I was—and am—opposed to Amendment 64," he continued. "I don't think it's a good idea. And when someone communicates something to you and starts their sentence with 'This is not as bad as…' then I think we have a problem," he stated with some forcefulness. "Look, research shows that marijuana has a negative impact on a developing person's brain. A teenager, or even someone in their early twenties can be harmed by marijuana. But," he contemplates for a moment, shakes his head and says, "it's here."

"What was the biggest surprise to you after it became legal?" I ask.

"Whew!" He shakes his head and quickly answers, "The edibles! That took us completely by surprise. Nobody knew how dangerous edibles were. We weren't familiar with them at all. Basically, a company takes a known piece of candy, like a gummy bear, and they lace it with marijuana. It's a very powerful mix and, if you look at a marijuana-laced gummy bear and a regular gummy bear, you can't see a difference based on looks. Also," he continues, "the sheer number of products that are edibles is enormous. Those guys knew what they were doing, the edibles manufacturers, and they had no plan to educate consumers on the product. They had an obligation to tell consumers, but they didn't."

The popularity of edibles is astounding. By the end of 2014 nearly five million edible products had been sold in Colorado, in both the medical and recreational markets, surprising regulators and industry insiders alike. Many of the consumers of edibles were first-time users and they didn't understand the differences between smoking marijuana and ingesting it through an edible, leading to several well-documented exposés of the industry. But there were also two high-profile deaths involving edibles that spurred state regulators to re-think how edibles are packaged and labeled. In the first instance, in March of 2014, Wyoming college student Levy Thamba, 19, ate a marijuana-infused cookie, became agitated and leapt to his death from a Denver hotel balcony. Several weeks later, Richard Kirk allegedly shot and killed his wife after eating a marijuana-infused caramel candy.

Understandably, the public outcry was national in scope and the Marijuana Enforcement Division proactively created a working task force, the Retail Marijuana Product, Potency, and Serving Size Work Group, to determine a reasonable serving size of an edible in proportion to THC levels. The issue was that a brownie or cookie, for example, could be one serving but could also contain 100 mg of THC—ten times more potent than the recommended single serving amount. Naturally, a consumer could easily be confused into thinking that one brownie was one serving, not ten servings.

Frank McNulty was a member of that task force. "I served on the edible sizing task force," he stated. "I was interested first," he raised his finger, "that there should be no black eye for the state and second," he raised his other finger, "that there should be no marketing of edibles to kids." He put his hand down and asked, "How do you keep edibles out of the schools? I mean, seriously, how can you do that? A kid can carry it in their pocket and eat it at lunch, and no one would know."

"Is that your biggest fear, then, with legalization?" I asked.

"Yes. I worry about an increase in marijuana products getting into the schools, and I'm not just talking about high schools," he states as his voice rises, "but about middle schools and grade schools. The problem is that state regulators couldn't establish a baseline to track an increase in edibles, since they really weren't on the market before 2014."

"What about the black-market, do you have any fears there?"

"None at all," he states as he waves his hand. "There's a black market in every market now, in alcohol, in tobacco...electronics...black markets are here and marijuana is no different. I do think that Colorado is becoming, or already is, the marijuana cultivation center for the rest of the United States. For example, U.S. Postal seizures of marijuana have increased. Same is true at FedEx and at small airports." He looks at me intently, "there's no way that taxes from marijuana can compensate for the social costs." The tax revenues were a key, prominent, point made by advocates for marijuana legalization, and Frank wants me to know that he doesn't buy that argument.

"Was the edibles issue the only big unknown when you started," I asked, "or were there other things that surprised you, or that you just didn't know?"

"Everything was an unknown!" He exclaimed. "It was like building an airplane while you're flying it," he said with a laugh. "We didn't have enough time to come up with a regulatory regime that would be tight and thorough. The policymakers were thoughtful, but we were playing catch-up the whole time. Amendment 64 passed in November of 2012 and we had to have a complete set of regulations by July 1, 2013. It happened very quickly. More time would have been helpful. It would have helped to eliminate some problems."

"Let's shift focus a bit," I state. "A couple of weeks ago I attended a Colorado Public Health hearing where they tried to limit the number of patients that a caregiver could have. What are your thoughts on the medical marijuana market in general, and in caregivers in particular?"

"The medical and recreational markets are different," he responded. "Medical is cheaper, for one, but if they're different, if marijuana really is a medicine, then the State needs to regulate it like prescriptions for other drugs. Otherwise, people should use the recreational market. That's how the industry gets started, through medical marijuana first. It's how they get a foothold."

"What about the caregivers?"

"If properly implemented, caregivers could be a positive," he states.

This surprises me. As someone who is adamantly opposed to marijuana, I thought that he would be opposed to the caregiver market, which has all the elements of a black market. But I was wrong on that.

"Some people take it seriously," he says, "They are actually caregivers," he states, bringing both hands up to make the 'quote' mark, "and they grow plants for people and help them with medical issues. The State regulators have the authority to determine who is actually a helper and who is just making money by selling in the grey market or the black market. We can just enforce what we have, and we can change the structure so that regulators can encourage more of the helpers rather than the black market operators."

"I don't understand why that hasn't been done yet. The hearing on caregivers was emotionally charged and the proposed rule change only effected, literally, fewer than five people."

"The caregivers are politically powerful and the regulators are afraid of them."

"Oh," I stated, "Ok. I get it. That makes sense. Well, let me ask you this. If you had advice for other states contemplating legalizing marijuana, what advice would you give them?"

"If you **have** to do this," he responded with an emphasis on 'have,' "take your time. Don't let the industry write the rules, and don't be bullied by them. The amount of money that is involved in this makes it easy to care about the industry, but no other industry gets that benefit. I also wouldn't cut and paste from Colorado and Washington. I would start with a blank slate knowing what Colorado and Washington have done, but I wouldn't cut and paste in a hodgepodge way. I think every regulator will do it this way, but make sure that you track each plant, and make sure that you have adequate enforcement. Having all the rules and regulations but lacking resources for enforcement will cause problems. Do it the right way. Follow the rules."

"Marijuana has been legal in Colorado now for nine months," I continued, "but if a Republican governor is elected, could things change? What do you expect in the future?"

"Well," Frank stated as he contemplated the questions. "Because it's in the Constitution there is no easy way to derail it, but a governor could put up all sorts of sideboards and make things difficult. A single act by the Federal government could bring the whole thing down. What happens if Federal enforcement agencies enforce Federal law in Colorado? For the future I don't see any drastic changes at the Federal level. It's not a motivating issue for Congress. But in five years, when we have better data and better insight, then I think you'll see some changes, one way or the other. Either more states will legalize, or those that have will make it illegal again."

That conversation with Frank McNulty took place in September of 2014, but I circled back to him in June of 2015 to understand his perspective given eighteen months of legalization, not just nine months. The circumstances for Frank were different in 2015 and he was now in the private sector, working as a lawyer for a top firm in Denver. We met in a conference room at his law firm, thirty floors up and with a half-mile view to the golden dome of the state capitol.

"So," I state, "it's been nine months since we last spoke, and now eighteen months since Colorado legalized marijuana. I assume you're still opposed?"

"Ha!" He roared with laughter. "Yes. Still opposed."

"I figured as much. But I wanted to get your thinking now that we've had more runway on this."

"We're starting to see the societal impact," he stated. "The homelessness is still a big and growing problem. Kids are getting into their parents' stash and we're starting to prosecute parents for that. And the edibles! The edibles are still a major problem.

"The regulatory regime should have had more time. That lack of time is an issue for the industry and for the regulators. The industry says, 'You keep changing the rules and it costs us at every point.' And they're right about that. We've changed all sorts of rules and regulations and the industry pays for that. But we should do better, be more robust in regulating edibles. Edibles are still marketed to kids because they make the marijuana-laced candy look like kid candy. The edibles are not regulated correctly."

"Do you have any idea of the sales figures for the edibles?" I asked.

He shook his head. "No. It's hard to get. They don't want to share the numbers."

"So, it seems like your thoughts and perspective are pretty much the same as they were in September of last year, but with a little more data and experience. Is that right?"

"Yes. My overriding concerns are: how do you keep people safe? And, how do you keep marijuana out of the hands of kids?"

JONATHAN SINGER
STATE REPRESENTATIVE

I met Jonathan Singer, a Democratic State Representative, at a coffee shop in Longmont, a city equidistant from Fort Collins and Denver, and a jurisdiction that Jonathan represents in the State House. I heard him speak at the Mile High Professional panel six months earlier but he was busy with his re-election campaign and with Session, so it took a while to connect. Jonathan is in his mid-thirties, I'm guessing, and is an affable person, relaxed and open.

"Do you care if this conversation is on the record or not?"

"Naw, I don't care," he said with a wave of his hand. "There's nothing I wouldn't say and besides, I don't know that anything I say will be all that earth shattering," he laughed.

"Well," I responded, "you're one of the most prolific bill-writers in the House of Representatives, having authored a number of bills to regulate marijuana. Have you always been supportive of marijuana legalization, or did your thinking evolve over time?"

Jonathan laughed, "Yeah, me and Shawn Mitchel were the only two lawmakers to publicly support Amendment 64. But I understood marijuana as a treatment provider, as someone coming from the social services sector, and to stick people in jail for smoking marijuana is a waste of money."

Jonathan has a college degree in social work, and his career prior to becoming an elected official has been working in Boulder County Social Services.

"Is that view widespread, do you think, within the House and Senate?"

"No, but people are coming around, and it's truly a bipartisan effort. There are staunch Republicans who are in favor, and liberal Democrats who are not. I'm not sure what draws people to one side or the other. But something had to change in Colorado. The caregiver market before 2009 was one that required licenses and registrations but we had no real oversight, we had no idea what was going on."

In January of 2009 there were 5,051 registered medical marijuana patients in Colorado, people who had a prescription from their doctor for one of the eight qualifying conditions (Cachexia, Cancer, Glaucoma, HIV/AIDS, muscle spasms, seizures, severe pain, severe nausea). Two years later, in January of 2011, there were 118,895 medical marijuana patients, an increase over 24 months of 2,200 percent.[1] The Colorado Department of Public Health collects data on the number of patient registrations, the number of people who have died or are otherwise no longer on the registry, and also reports age, gender, and medical condition. The Department also sets the registration fee and from 2009-2011 the fee was the same at $90 dollars. Yet over 90 percent of the people on the Colorado medical marijuana registry list "severe pain" as the condition necessitating marijuana use. The explosion in number of patient registrations, along with the significant number of patients reporting "severe pain" was a source of concern for regulators.

Jonathan continued, "Initially, I was on the side of decriminalization versus legalization, but I was frustrated with the medical model. People were forced to lie for the substance and it was bad for everybody, for the doctors and the people. Also, I think it's a dumb idea to jail people for marijuana use. It's costly. It ruins lives.

"One of the things that changed my mind, going back to the caregiver market in 2009, was that people with a Red Card felt that they had a license to use marijuana anytime, anywhere. That led my thinking to recreational and legalizing marijuana. Medical marijuana had consequences for kids. People would smoke and drive while taking their kids to school. And if you confronted them with that they said, 'I have a Red Card. I'm entitled to use this marijuana for my medical condition.' They really weren't responsible about their use at all and it put law enforcement in a bad position."

"Ok," I said, "if you had a blank slate, if you could do it all over again knowing what you know now, would you change anything?"

"I would start with legalizing the recreational market...or legalize the recreational and medical markets together. I would get rid of the notion that medical is different. The way we did it with medical first helped and it hurt."

"How so?"

"Well, it helped to bring greater awareness, it helped in establishing cultivation on a large scale and dispensaries for retail sales. It changed the black market a bit, but it was largely unregulated. Law enforcement didn't have clear guidelines on what to do if someone was using marijuana and they had a Red Card. They didn't have clear direction on what to do if someone had 200 plants in their house."

"So, take me back to the passage of Amendment 64. It passed in November of 2012, and you show up in January of 2013 as a first-time representative. What were the other Representatives and Senators thinking, and how did the regulatory framework come about?"

"One of the things I've learned about the State of Colorado is that if you want a seat at the table you need to just show up. You can't wait to be asked. The Governor put together a Task Force with all the players — District Attorneys, defense lawyers, opponents of marijuana, supporters of marijuana. It was a brilliant move, but I wasn't invited to be on the Task Force..."

"Hold on a second," I interrupted, "what was the make-up of that Task Force?"

"You mean besides what I just said?"

"Yeah. Women, men, age, race. That kind of thing," I responded.

"Oh, ok. It was a fairly even mix of men and women, and the ages ranged from the 20's to the 60's. I didn't notice this at the time, but I feel terrible that there were no Blacks on the Task Force. In fact, I met a woman named Wanda James after we had our findings and she asked, 'Why weren't any Blacks involved on the Task Force?' She's Black, and owns a dispensary, but she is the only Black dispensary owner, out of over 300 dispensaries. The Black community has been most harmed by the War on Drugs and I see that as a big oversight on our part in creating the Task Force."

Jonathan is right about the impact of the War on Drugs for Blacks in the United States. An American Civil Liberties Union report in 2013 stated that between 2001 and 2010 over eight million marijuana possession arrests were made, and that the United States spent $3.6 billion on marijuana enforcement in 2010 alone. Despite nearly equal usage of marijuana, the report states that "a Black person is 3.73 times more likely to be arrested for marijuana possession than a white person (P. 6)." This significantly higher arrest rate for Blacks is true throughout the United

States — in all regions of the country, in all counties, in both urban and rural communities, in wealthy and poor communities, and regardless of the size of the Black population. [2]

Jonathan continued, "But then I was approached to be on the Task Force—I know I'm going against what I just told you—but I was invited because I was one of only two legislators to publicly support marijuana legalization and I was trusted by supporters of marijuana, by Brian, Christian, and Mason (the authors of Amendment 64) and they wanted me on the Task Force.

"The Task Force was exhaustive in its process. We looked at every angle. We looked at how legalization would impact crime, we looked at social components, we looked at it from addiction, we looked to see the impact on kids. I mean, no stone was left unturned. And then once the Task Force was done it gave recommendations to the Legislature, and the legislative process involved a joint committee with members from half of the house and half of the senate. Out of that came three bills."

"And what was that like, the joint committee. Were people open to moving forward or was it politically divisive?

"It was really collegial. The political lines were not drawn like it is with abortion, for example, with decades of hardline approaches. It was a blank tablet, and we didn't have the same level of lobbying activity. You didn't have people talking with you and speaking in your ear. We were focused on doing the right thing."

"It almost didn't happen," he said with some excitement.

"What didn't happen?" I asked

"The whole thing, the legalization!" he exclaimed. "There were three bills that were coming out of the joint committee and I was creating the one on taxes, and at the eleventh hour two Senators came in to my office and asked, 'What are you going to do if your bill doesn't pass?' I didn't really have an answer for that and they came back and said, 'Well, if it doesn't pass then marijuana won't be taxed and if it's not taxed then it can't be sold.' So they could kill my bill and pass their own bill to prevent marijuana sales."

"Luckily a Democratic House Leader who heard what they were doing intervened and walked into their office and said to them, 'Hey, you know this isn't right. This isn't what the people of Colorado asked for when they voted for Amendment 64,' and so they backed off and we passed the Bill. But it almost didn't happen," he stated as he shook his head and laughed.

"There are some interesting aspects to how Colorado went about regulating recreational marijuana," I stated. "For example, the Vertical Integration rule is unique, where a grower has to sell 30 percent of what he or she grows on the wholesale market."

"Yeah," responded Jonathan, shaking his head. "That wasn't us. That was the medical marijuana guys. They came to us and said, 'We want the first bite out of the apple. We already have growing operations and dispensaries and the easiest way to do this is to start with us.' So that's what we did, but we put the Vertical Integration rule in there to stop those first recreational dispensaries from creating a monopoly."

"Hmm, smart," I said. "I'd like to shift focus a bit, and think about the present and future. Colorado has now had legal recreational marijuana for 18 months and how have things gone from your perspective? Do you have any concerns or any surprises?"

"My concerns have changed over time, actually. Initially we were concerned about the Federal Government coming in and shutting the whole thing down, so we were very socially responsible. We put tight regulations in place in terms of "seed to sale" (the practice of tracking a marijuana plant from seedling to final sale to a consumer), we put in restrictions on hours of operation for a dispensary, setbacks from schools and other public places. It is heavily regulated because we didn't want any Federal involvement. Now there are more big money players coming in. Is Big Tobacco coming in? I expect them to. The industry has matured, and they have a lot of money and power.

"But, I would actually like to see more Federal regulations for the industry," he stated.

"Hold on a second," I interrupted. "Really? More regulation? There's already more regulation in marijuana than almost any other industry."

"Yeah, but I would like to see the FDA get involved, to do the studies on the effectiveness of marijuana for particular conditions. The question is, what is marijuana?" he asked with a shrug of his shoulders. "If you have Oxycontin on one end of the spectrum," he said while holding his arm to the side, "and Aspirin on the other," spreading his other arm to the side, "where does marijuana fall in? It's not a drug, but IF it's an herb," and he emphasized the word 'IF,' "then it probably falls somewhere in there closer to aspirin. I would like to see marijuana sold at a Rite-Aid or a Walgreens. It should be in the supplement section, or the nutritional section."

"That's probably going to anger a lot of people," I said.

Jonathan shrugged his shoulders, "So what? These guys came in and said, 'We want the first bite out of the apple' and they have gotten that. But I'm a Democrat and I believe in regulating things for the public good. Earlier this week I submitted a bill to further regulate the caregiver industry, I mean, there are so many gaps in the medical marijuana industry and we've known for a long time that the caregivers are diverting marijuana to the black market. Not all of them, there are a lot of good caregivers out there, a lot of people who put in the time and effort and follow the rules, but there is an element that are just growing for the black market. There were no limits on the number of plants a caregiver could grow, so we capped it at 99. Opponents to marijuana wanted to cap it at 36 plants and after some intense discussions we finally passed the bill as written, with a 99-plant cap. [3]

"Someone asked me," he continued, "how many more bills I'm going to introduce to regulate the industry. And I don't know if I'm going to introduce bills, but I can see us passing ten bills a year for the next five years."

"Wow," I say, "that's a lot of regulation."

"Yeah, well it's a patchwork of things when you start with medical marijuana and like I said before, I'm a Democrat and I think we should regulate the industry, keep marijuana out of kids' hands, and reduce the black market."

PAT STEADMAN
FORMER STATE SENATOR

Every person I spoke with from the government in Colorado told me to speak with Senator Pat Steadman, telling me that he was deeply involved in cannabis legislation and particularly, that he was the expert on the taxes and financing of regulations. After the legislative session ended in 2015 I was finally able to meet up with him in his office. Like everyone else I spoke with on the regulatory side of cannabis legalization, Pat Steadman wanted to make sure that I understood the evolution of the legal recreational cannabis market.

Pat started speaking before I asked a question.

"So, in the summer of 2009, there was a rule change and medical dispensaries were allowed to open, and they did. People in the city started to panic, like, 'Oh My God! There are going to be dispensaries on every street corner!' And by 2010 the horse was out of the barn. There was an explosion of Red Cards, from 5,000 to over 120,000 in a period of six months," he looked at me and continued. "If you need it I can get you the data on that."

"Oh, thanks," I responded, "I think I've seen that."

"Ok. So in 2010 we had two bills, House Bill 1284 and Senate Bill 109 and they both passed. Senate Bill 109 regulated the patient – physician relationship and basically stipulated that the physician had to actually see the patient before issuing a Red Card. And House Bill 1284 was the bill that set forth regulations for medical marijuana, including seed-to-sale tracking and a lot of other areas. The feeling at the State Capitol in 2010 was that we couldn't put the smoke back in the bottle.

"Having said that, though, I can say that this process has been fascinating. The regulation of marijuana has been so interesting."

"Is it interesting from a financial perspective?" I asked.

"I'm more motivated by the individual and personal freedom to choose to use marijuana, and I see it as a social justice issue. I was involved in the Drug War—trying to get it stopped," he stated as he sat back in his chair. "Over the last several years I worked on re-writing the sentencing laws and the criminal code to allow persons over twenty-one to possess an ounce of marijuana. Because of my involvement with a lot of marijuana legislation people assume that I endorsed Amendment 64. But I did not endorse Amendment 64, and that surprises people."

"Yes, that is surprising because I thought for sure that you were totally in favor of Amendment 64."

"I was" he responded, "and I am, but I am a purist for the Constitution and now it's getting filled with all sorts of amendments and details. It is so easy to get a constitutional amendment on the ballot in Colorado that we've essentially watered down our constitution. I prefer to keep it simple."

"Well, everyone has mentioned that you played a big role in the taxes and financing of Amendment 64. Can you speak to that a bit?"

"Sure. I worked on the ballot language with Jonathan Singer. He was new to the House and he asked me to look over his bill and when I saw it I knew that because of the wording of his bill, that it would not get passed. So I helped to shape that and it did get passed.

"But, to answer your questions on the taxes, the taxes from Amendment 64 are all new revenue streams for us. There's a 2.9 percent sales tax that both medical and recreational marijuana consumers pay, and a 10 percent sales tax that only recreational consumers pay. And then there is a 15 percent excise tax that is imposed on sales of wholesale marijuana, between a grower and retailer. The retailer pays it but passes that cost on to the consumer.

"One of the clever approaches of Amendment 64 was to state that the 15 percent excise tax would be devoted solely to school infrastructure, school construction, up to $40 million dollars. From a voter's perspective that makes a lot of sense, it's like 'Why not?' Colorado has historically not funded capital construction for schools, leaving that to school districts to figure out through local property taxes…and they haven't been good at that. So there is a need statewide for capital outlays for school districts and this new revenue stream meets that. But, they were optimistic in stating the $40 million because all of last year the excise tax generated a little over $13 million."

"That's it?" I asked, surprised.

"Yeah. I mean, it's better than nothing but we did an assessment of capital outlay needs for infrastructure, and the state of Colorado needs at least a billion dollars, probably two billion. So, in perspective, $40 million is not going to change much.

"We also have licensing fees that we impose on everyone in the marijuana industry—the cultivator, the manufacturer, the retailer, the testing lab—but the licensing fees can't support the regulators and enforcement of the industry, so we have to subsidize that with the sales tax. But the same is true with the alcohol industry.

"This year," he continued as he pulled out a spreadsheet and showed it to me. "This year we're poised to generate $79.6 million dollars in revenues from the entire industry—the sales tax, the special marijuana sales tax, the excise tax, and licensing fees."

"Wow," I stated, "new-found money."

"Yes," he replied, "but it got me to thinking. Looking at the marijuana tax revenues changed my mindset on alcohol. Statewide we netted $40 million from alcohol sales. That's wine, beer, and spirits, but we got nearly $80 million from marijuana? Alcohol has all these societal consequences, but they don't pay. Marijuana is taxed, and it pays. Do you know what it costs to run felony DUI's for a year?"

"I have no idea."

"It costs us $9.5 million to pay for all of those. So, why the free pass for alcohol? Why not legalize and tax cocaine and heroin? We could regulate those markets and set up treatment centers with the tax revenues."

"I'm guessing you're standing alone on that, with respect to the other senators and representatives."

"Oh yeah, it will never happen, but thinking about marijuana and these other illicit drugs...it makes you wonder if legalizing and taxing and regulating...it makes you wonder if that's a better approach. For example, there's a treatment center in Grand Junction called Summit View. They had a problem several years ago with meth addiction and one of the problems associated with that is that there's a big step for the addict to take going from detox to productive member of society, and the recidivism rate is like 95 percent."

"Wait a second," I interjected, "the recidivism rate refers to the percentage of people that have a relapse, right?"

"Yes."

"So, only 5 percent of the people are actually successful in getting their life back? Am I understanding that right?"

"Yeah," he stated, "that's right. So the county created a treatment center that involves parents, child welfare, mental health, the criminal justice system, all focused on helping the meth addict make the transition to productive society member. Their recidivism rate is 41 percent so," he looked at me to make sure that I understood the terminology, "that means that 59 percent of the people are successful, are living a life without drugs."

"That's amazing," I stated.

"Yes. I have a desire to replicate that. We should be doing what they've done in Grand Junction and replicate it in other Colorado communities. Grand Junction is not the only community with drug problems. Well, why not take the tax money we create from legalizing these drugs and put that into programs that actually take people off drugs and help them lead better lives?"

I nodded my head in agreement. "Looking over the past year and a half, are there any surprises that have emerged, any challenges that you didn't think about before?"

"Yes, there are a lot of challenges. We've already done a lot of tinkering through the legislature, by passing a dozen laws. That's an indication that we didn't foresee some things. For example, the pesticides issues were unanticipated. The Department of Agriculture is involved in that and they go by the mantra, 'The label is the law.' The use of a pesticide has to be approved by the FDA but once it's approved you can use it on corn, hay, tobacco…you can use it on anything that's approved for human consumption. There is no available product for marijuana since it's illegal under Federal law. We're looking for something that can be consumed by people, like lettuce, something that can be used on marijuana.

"The other challenge and we knew this last year, is the banking issue. We introduced a bill in 2011 but it failed, and the administration was against it. The bill wouldn't solve the banking problem anyway. Then in 2014 we authorized financial co-ops, but that's not working because everyone is using the old credit union laws to prevent the industry from access to banking. I've come to the conclusion that states can't solve a Federal problem, like the banking issue. It has to be solved by the Federal government."

"Well," I stated, "speaking of the Federal government, what are your thoughts for the future?"

"I'm cautious past 2016. Will the next president and attorney general be tolerant of what we're doing, or will they shut it down? I don't think we'll ever stop it because we're making some money from the industry. But the Federal government, that's an unknown."

"Finally," I asked, "what advice would you give to other states, if they decide to legalize marijuana?"

"I would do it differently than what we did. I would do it all at once, not do an Amendment 20 (medical marijuana) and then an Amendment 64 (recreational marijuana). We have a bifurcated system with different sets of rules, and it's confusing and complex. I would be proactive on the regulations and taxes before it's done to you. But I would just legalize marijuana and make special provisions for medical, I wouldn't separate them."

ANDREW FREEDMAN
DIRECTOR OF MARIJUANA COORDINATION

Andrew Freedman was a speaker at the Mile High Young Professional panel and introduced himself by saying that his mom proudly mentioned to her friends that he worked with Governor Hickenlooper, but now that he is Director of Marijuana Coordination, she says that he "works for the State government." That introduction by Andrew highlights one fact about marijuana legalization: the people that are opposed to marijuana have strong opinions on that. But during our interview Andrew mentioned that one of the things that was a highlight of his first year on the job was the sense of collaboration, despite the divisive topic of marijuana legalization.

"This is a really divisive issue for the State of Colorado and the people that are against it are very against it. But when it came time to sit down together and work out the regulations, everyone did that. It wasn't partisan, and there were no backroom deals or coalitions that tried to block things or have things done their way. It was truly collaborative."

We met in Andrew's office at the Department of Revenue building. It is as plain and Spartan as an office can be and consists of a desk, chair, and some filing cabinets. Andrew's youthful looks belie a long career in government, first as an intern on Governor Hickenlooper's first campaign, then as Chief of Staff to the Lieutenant Governor, and now as Director of Marijuana Coordination. He has responsibility and oversight for Colorado's marijuana industry, and has worked with both the industry, other regulators, and legislators in crafting the rules that shape the legal marijuana markets.

"What do you attribute that collaboration to?" I asked.

"I'm not sure. Maybe the fact that we were first, that this was a chance for the industry to establish itself. We were really breaking ground and we had to work really fast since we had a firm deadline within six months to have all the regulations put together."

"Did the fact that medical marijuana was already highly regulated help?" I asked.

"Absolutely. There were fewer unknowns and we had to do a lot less catch-up. Medical and recreational look similar at the retail level but the element of caregivers changes medical a lot."

"I went to the Colorado Department of Health meeting earlier in the month on caregiver limits...."

"There are a lot of good caregivers out there," Andrew broke in. "For some people it's a belief system, a spiritual, religious belief system that both the patient and the caregiver subscribe to. For those people, the caregiver system works well, but there are others who are just growing for the black market. We created a nebulous system when we legalized medical marijuana. Local law enforcement didn't know how to proceed. If someone has a Red Card, can they possess marijuana? And how much can they possess? And if they're a caregiver, can they grow it in their own home? The local district attorneys also didn't know how to go about enforcing marijuana laws. We could change all that by changing the structure of what we have, by tightening up the medical marijuana registry. That would solve a lot of problems."

"Were there any surprises for you after legalizing marijuana?" I asked.

"The element of the edibles," he stated. "With medical marijuana we had no problems or issues with edibles, but in the recreational market there were all sorts of issues with sizing, dosing, packaging. It will get worked out, but the problems with edibles were unexpected."

"If you had advice for other states contemplating legalizing marijuana, what would that be?"

"First, if you're doing this for the taxes, you're way off base. You can never fix education or transportation with the money generated from marijuana sales. Our demand is flat and most people who wanted to use marijuana legally were already using it when it was illegal. We haven't seen a big jump in usage and I think the maximum tax revenues we'll see is somewhere between $100 to $130 million. But if you are going to legalize marijuana, I would roll it out narrow and with strict regulations and then relax those strict regulations once you have a better idea of how things are going. I would also treat medical and recreational the same in terms of vertical integration, and I would keep the plant counts low for both industries. I think if you did it that way there would be fewer exceptions and it would be easier to provide oversight and enforcement."

"Are there any outstanding issues that you feel need to be addressed?"

"There are some murky areas, like banking and pesticides that need to be cleared up. One of the things that we struggle with is what data to collect and how to benchmark the data. What should we be measuring? Even base demographics are hard to come by. How many women and minorities are using? What's going on in the middle schools and the high schools? We don't know. So, it will take a couple of years before we really know what's going on. My hope is that over the next five years we can still approach this as experimental...not go into camps. Not have partisan politics with the industry on one side and the regulators on the other," he stated wistfully. "That's my hope."

GOVERNOR JOHN HICKENLOOPER

On August 3, 2015 I had the opportunity to interview Governor John Hickenlooper about his thoughts on cannabis legalization. By the time I had this interview I had already spoken with the leading lawmakers involved in creating a regulatory framework for cannabis, so I understood some of the early challenges in making legalization a reality. And I knew something about Gov. Hickenlooper's personal ideas on cannabis based on articles and interviews in the popular press — he was adamantly opposed to cannabis legalization. But I was mostly interested in his perspective of the new legal cannabis industry and the people in it, I was interested in knowing what sorts of discussions he had with the Federal Government on Colorado's legalization efforts, and I was interested in his ideas on Colorado and what led the people to vote "yes" on Amendment 64.

I was shadowed by a young woman, Amanda Ford, who had been working in her role of Assistant Communications Director for only three weeks and who's job, at the moment, was to keep track of me. "How is your book coming along?" she asked.

"It's coming along. It will be important to have this interview, with Governor Hickenlooper."

"Yes," she replied. "He will have some interesting ideas."

My allotted time was being eaten up by a prior staff meeting that involved a conference call, and Amanda is incredibly apologetic, as if I am an important guest. "I'm sorry about the delay," she said, "but your meeting should happen pretty soon." She's right, and we proceeded through a door with a key lock, walked around the corner, stepped over the Governor's dog lying lazily in the middle of the entryway, and entered the Governor's private office.

It is a large office, probably eighty feet long and forty feet wide, with forty-foot high ceilings and royal blue carpeting. There is a photograph of a Colorado landscape covering nearly the entire north side of the room, measuring twenty feet high by forty feet wide. The Governor was standing at a rectangular conference table that could comfortably seat twelve people, shuffling papers from the previous meeting. He turned around as we entered and with a broad smile, walked the thirty feet from the conference table to where Amanda and I were standing. Amanda introduced us and as he shook my hand he said, "let's sit over here," and gestured to the oval table. Before we could get situated he stated, "So, you work with Norton?" I must have looked puzzled because he continued, "in Crested Butte."

"Oh, yes," I responded.

"Me and a friend hiked the trail from Maroon Bells to Crested Butte last weekend," he offers, "and it was spectacular."

Frankly, I was impressed that Governor Hickenlooper, or his staff, did an internet search of my bio, and that he used that as an icebreaker. As I sat down to get organized Amanda broke in, "Because of the earlier meeting you only have fifteen minutes." As with my other interviews, I have several questions written out on 5×7 note cards which I placed on the table in front of me, most of which are high-level policy questions. I was interested in the Governor's initial reaction to the passage of Amendment 64, interested with his early interactions with the cannabis industry, and with the challenges moving forward. Now that the meeting was truncated I knew I would have to be judicious with my questions. The Governor sat back in his chair, relaxed, smiled and said, "fire away." I wasn't going to ask Governor Hickenlooper about his personal viewpoint on marijuana because it's well-known that he is opposed to cannabis legalization, but he offered it anyway.

He leaned forward in his chair and before I could ask my first question, said with a smile and shake of his head, "If I had a magic wand after the 2012 vote I would have reversed the vote. But now I think this is *thee* great social experiment of the 21st century." He emphasized the word "thee" and continued, "U.S. Supreme Court Justice Louis Brandeis said that the States ought to be the social laboratories for new ideas, to be the place where experiments take place, and that's what we're doing here in Colorado."

"Well, I agree with that. What was the biggest surprise to you about the cannabis industry?"

"It was that the cannabis industry was like any other industry, that they were a responsible industry. They had a communal self-interest and were willing to have very strict regulations applied to them to assure their long-term viability. The other big surprise was the edibles. Nobody anticipated that edibles would be so problematic. If you go back to those first days the edibles people didn't have labels on their packaging, they didn't show the dosages. And we have had a lot of problems associated with the edibles. Kids that we're seeing in the ER are kids who have ingested an edible. It's not a kid who's smoked pot, but someone who ingested a brownie or a piece of candy."

"Who are the edibles people, do you know?"

He shook his head, "No, I assume they're black market people."

Amanda broke in again, "There's time for one more question."

Governor Hickenlooper turned around in his chair to Amanda and with a dismissive wave of his hand said, "Oh, I think we can keep going a little longer."

I scrambled for the last questions to ask. "The idea of ending prohibition, of legalizing a previously illegal good has been theorized by economists for decades," I said. "The argument is that if a society legalizes a drug the price will go down, the crime rate will go down, the quality will go up, and the black market will disappear. The opponents of legalization don't have a theory other than to say, 'Well, not that.' They argue that crime will go up, teen use will go up, DUI's will go up, that violence will go up, and that the black market will thrive. Based on the experience in Colorado, where do you see things going? I know prices have dropped and that the quality of the marijuana has gone up, and I know that the black market has shrunk — I'm not sure if it has disappeared. But what are your thoughts?"

"The crime rate has gone down, and teen use is not up. We've always had a higher marijuana use in Colorado compared to the rest of the nation, but there wasn't an upward trend in use and it even came down a bit for teen use."

"I spoke with a district attorney in San Diego recently," I responded, "and she believes that if you make marijuana legal everybody will do it and I responded to her, 'Well, it's legal here in Colorado and I haven't started using marijuana and neither has my wife, and neither have our neighbors or our friends.'"

Governor Hickenlooper leaned forward in his chair and stated emphatically, "Everybody who was using before is still using, and everybody who was not using before is still not using."

He leaned back in his chair and continued, "I had a young man interview me awhile back, he was seventeen years old and he told me that marijuana has always been easy to get. And legalization hasn't changed that. But what he did say was that our efforts to curtail marijuana use among young people, because it impacts the development of their brain, *that* message might have an impact.

"I guess Willie Nelson is the spokesperson for marijuana now. He's eighty years old and still performs, and when he performs, sings fifty songs, never forgets the words, and never misses a note. And he smokes pot every day. But he didn't start smoking until he was an adult, is what I understand. So, who knows?" he asked with a shrug of his shoulders.

As I stood to leave I had one final question to ask. "Governor, what has been your relationship with the Federal Government during the legalization process? Have you had discussions with them, or have there been threats by them?"

"Well, they are in a tough, tough spot. They have been hand's off and believe, I think, that the States are the laboratories of democracy. This is the great social experiment of the twenty-first century. It's early in the process but as we gather more information we'll learn a lot."

"That's interesting," I stated. As he walked me to the door he said, "I'm looking forward to reading your article on 'Why is there a Nebraska?' My sister lives in Nebraska, and I am interested to see what you have to say."

"Ha!" I responded. "Thanks. I thought that might get people's interest. I will send you a copy when it's done. Thanks again for your time and insights."

"You're welcome."

REGULATING EDIBLES

The regulator's perspective on cannabis legalization is similar across all the people I interviewed. They all said that a lack of time was a contributing factor to the process of regulating marijuana, that they were "building an airplane while flying it," and that the "smoke was out of the bottle." Every single person also identified the edibles manufacturers as the bad actors in the industry, as the people who were deceptive in labeling, who did not educate the customer on differences between smoking pot and ingesting it, and who marketed their products to children. In fact, during my conversations I asked each person the following question: "If you had to fill out a report card for the following groups involved in the legalization process, what grade would you give to lawmakers, regulators, enforcement, growers, retailers, infused manufacturers, testers, and communities?" The infused manufacturers, the part of the marijuana industry responsible for edibles, got grades of "D" and "F" from everyone I interviewed. Even Brian Vicente, who plays a big part in the marijuana industry, gave infused manufacturers the lowest grade on his report card.

There were numerous loopholes in the original regulations concerning edibles. Prior to 2014, the regulations required manufacturers to individually package each edible in a sealed container, with labels, to be shipped to the retail dispensary. However, manufacturers were not required to provide child-resistant packaging. More importantly, they were not required to list the total number of servings in an edible product, nor did the regulations require each serving to be readily apparent. Child-resistant packaging and the labels were the responsibility of the retail dispensaries, not the manufacturer. To close the loopholes regarding edibles the marijuana enforcement division created two work groups. The first, "Retail Marijuana Product Potency and

Serving Size Work Group," had the relatively easy task to determine the maximum THC allowed in any edible, and to determine what constituted a "serving size." Additionally, the work group developed rules that led to child-resistant packaging for all edibles. But the second work group, "House Bill 14-1366 Work Group," was directed to recommend rules for edibles products that "can be clearly identifiable, when practicable, to indicate that they A) contain marijuana, B) are not for consumption by children, and C) are safe for consumers" (p.8). Ideally, the legislators of House Bill 14-1366 were also seeking a universal symbol that could be used to warn people that the product contained THC. But coming up with a universal symbol that worked with all marijuana edibles proved difficult. [4]

One challenge with edibles is working with the sheer variety of products that contain THC. The work group listed nine types of edibles, into the following categories. **Baked goods** (brownies, cookies, cakes, granola bars, breads), **bulk foods** (loose granola, crackers, popcorn, baking mixes, trail mix, nuts, potato chips), **chocolate** (bars, truffles, candy-coated, drop chocolate), **hard candy** (mints, suckers, throat lozenges), **liquids** (soft drinks, coffee, tea, cooking oils, dressings, sauces, honey, agave nectar), **mixes and effervesents** (oral dissolvables, powdered beverages, powdered candy, powdered food), **pills** (pressed pills, capsules), **soft candy** (gummies, chewing gum, taffy, chocolate chews, fruit chews, licorice), and **tinctures**. Even though there are several ways to label edibles, such as marking, shape, color, smell, or packaging, there was no universal symbol that worked for all of the edibles. Moreover, the work group didn't have clear legislative intent on whether edibles needed to be identifiable outside of their packaging, and also no direction on how to proceed if a product (like liquids) cannot be identified outside of packaging.

Three presentations were made to the working group: the Children's Hospital of Colorado, the Colorado Department of Public Health and Environment, and the Colorado Cannabis Chamber Association. The only point of agreement among these three organizations was the fact that the most common age for unintentional ingestion of marijuana is a two-year-old child. But there was no agreement on preventative measures, nor whether the frequency of accidental ingestion is alarmingly high, or actually "average" given the nearly five million edibles sold annually. The Children's Hospital presented data on unintentional ingestions, noting that the number of calls to regional poison centers saw nearly a fourfold increase from 7 callsof unintentional marijuana ingenstion, in 2001, to 26 calls in 2013 for unintentional marijuana ingestion. These numbers are low, but higher than other states. The Colorado Department of Public Health and Environment presented evidence that storing products safely at home is the most effective strategy to prevent unintentional poisonings. Nearly 75 percent of poisonings occur when products are not stored safely at home. Further, they stated that child-resistant packaging is more effective than labels, colors, or other approaches to identify marijuana, since young children don't recognize products as dangerous based on colors or symbols.

Finally, the Colorado Cannabis Chamber Association presented data indicating that most accidental ingestions happen when children find common household items—not marijuana infused edibles—that are not protected with child-resistant packaging. (Marijuana edibles are protected with child-resistant packaging). Moreover, the Cannabis Chamber argued that any restrictions on what edible products can or cannot be manufactured and sold in Colorado are unconstitutional since Amendment 64 explicitly defines marijuana to include edibles.

Specifically, Amendment 64 states: *"MARIHUANA or MARIJUANA' means all parts of the plant whether growing or not, the seeds thereof, the resin extracted from any part of the plant, and every compound, manufacture, salt, derivative, mixture, or preparation of the plant, its seeds, or its resin, including marihuana concentrates" (p.3).* Clearly, banning edibles would violate the Colorado constitution and that was the crux of the problem faced by the House Bill 14-1366 Work Group. Sixteen recommendations were put forth for the work group to consider and all of them divided the group into two camps, those in favor of stronger regulations, and those opposed to any interference or increased regulation. For instance, the CDPHE proposed banning all edibles except for tinctures and lozenges and similarly, law enforcement suggested a universal symbol on the actual edible visible outside of the package. In addition, law enforcement called for banning products that could not be marked with a universal symbol. But the people who dissented from those recommendations had a litany of arguments against the proposal:

- "Even if a system could be devised to readily identify products when outside their packaging, the markings could be readily removed or disguised by someone wanting to hide the identity of the product."

- "Banning products is likely to lead to an increase in black market production, where identification of products is even more difficult, tracking of production is impossible, there are no quality control standards to protect consumers, products are not tested, have unknown potency, and are not easily separated into 10mg or less servings."

- "No data has been collected to prove that imprinting edible marijuana products would help prevent accidental ingestion."

- "The only practical way to imprint all edible marijuana products with a universal symbol is to print the symbol on the product labels."

- "Limiting edible marijuana products falls outside the scope of HB 14-1366."

- "The recommendation to prohibit edibles is unconstitutional."

Similarly, several marijuana licensees proposed to increase consumer education campaigns, or to create a universal symbol on packaging that would identify a product as containing marijuana. These proposals, and any proposals that advocated for packaging, labels, and education were met with the same two arguments:

- "This recommendation ignores the intent, language, and directives of the Colorado General Assembly when enacting HB 14-1366. The intent is that edible retail marijuana products, not their packaging or labeling, are readily identifiable by the general public."
- "This recommendation does not address identification of edible marijuana products outside their packaging."

There was no common ground for the work group, and in the end the group provided four strategic options to the General Assembly that would need to be pursued through further legislation. The options were:

1) Take no action at this time.
2) Strengthen packaging and labeling requirements.
3) Identify edible marijuana products outside their packaging.
4) Limit or ban edible marijuana products that cannot be identified outside of their packaging.

The Colorado General Assembly took up the issue again in 2015 and this time passed a new bill that supported item number three above. Now, manufacturers of marijuana edibles are required to display a universal symbol—a diamond shape with the letters THC and an exclamation point (THC!)—stamped or etched on all products for which that's feasible, like chocolate, hard candy, and lozenges. For other products, like liquids and loose granola, the serving sizes are limited to 10mg. Why was it so difficult to regulate the edibles manufacturers in the marijuana industry? And why are the manufacturers of edibles so resistant to regulating their products? Are the manufacturers of edibles so insensitive to public safety that they're unwilling to provide any identification of marijuana infused products for consumers? It's true that virtually no two-year-old accidentally smokes pot and must go to the emergency room. It is the enticing candy, the gummy bears, the knock-off, look-alike products laced with marijuana that manufacturers are selling, that children are unintentionally ingesting, and adults, too. The manufacturers of edible marijuana products clearly do not want to be regulated.

This was not the first time that marijuana infused producers operated with wanton disregard for public safety, having a history of doing so from inception of the industry. Make that, since the inception of the *recreational industry*. In the medical marijuana industry, no problems with edibles emerged and Ron Kammerzell, enforcement director for the Department of Revenue, which regulates marijuana businesses, noted that there were no reports of overdosing during the rollout of medical marijuana. A leading medical marijuana edibles manufacturer concurred, but like the regulators, legislators, and governor, was surprised at the demand for edibles, and mentioned that his company had a five-fold increase in sales once marijuana was legalized.

But in the newly created recreational marijuana industry the majority of manufacturers provided no product information on the labels, no dosage levels, no serving sizes, no child-resistant packaging. And the consumers of edibles differed significantly from consumers of marijuana flower. Consumers of edibles were more naïve, new to using marijuana, or were people returning to marijuana usage after a long time of not using. And they didn't understand that the time for an edible to take effect can be several hours after ingesting, not minutes, as with smoking.

I spoke with Jack, a client of mine who was creating a business focused on extractions and concentrates, about the edibles companies, and he told me the following.

"People who were growing before it was legal, are growing now, after it's legal, and people who were operating dispensaries in the medical market are operating dispensaries in the recreational market. But the edibles people, they are all new, they're corporate guys with MBA's and finance degrees. They came into the industry from other industries. They weren't the traditional marijuana growers and sellers."

"Wait," I responded. "Are you telling me that the people who are unethical, who are resisting regulations, who are marketing their harmful product to children...are you telling me that those are corporate people from legal businesses coming into the marijuana industry?"

"Yeah. Look," he continued, "brownies and cookies? That's just not what most people in the marijuana culture want. I mean, if you go to a concert and guy comes up to you with a saran-wrapped cookie you're just going to look at the guy and say, 'no thanks, man'" he stated with a look of disdain.

"I mean, it was rare to have a cookie or brownie with pot in it. Maybe you'd do it three times a year, for like your birthday or special occasions. But no, man, you couldn't make money selling edibles. You'd just do it for yourself for those special occasions. Besides, they taste extremely weedy, not like what they are now with concentrates."

I found what Jack said to be one of the most ironic things I've ever heard. The people who have been working in the black market, who have been villainized by law enforcement, by the DEA, by public media, are actually the honest and ethical people in the marijuana industry. They are the ones who embraced regulations, who worked with regulators and legislators to create a regulatory framework, who pay exorbitant taxes and take enormous risks. The people who have been working in Corporate America, or in legal businesses in the United States, the people who have been celebrated by the public press, have been speakers at college graduations and have been asked to serve on boards of directors for non-profits and other worthy causes—those people are the unethical people in the marijuana industry. Those are the people who don't want to be regulated, who feel no compunction about misleading labeling, who neglect to tell consumers about the dosage or potency of their product, who merely take existing candies, lace them with marijuana, and market them to children—those are the people from Corporate America.

Jack's belief on edibles manufacturers was confirmed several months later when I met Patrick and Dave, two people who wanted to invest in the edibles business. They actually wanted to do more than invest and they were clear about it: they wanted to create their own line of edibles and they just needed somebody with a license so that they could get started. Patrick was in his 50's and had made his fortune as a trader; Dave was in his 60's and made his money in commercial real estate. They were part of a consortium of high-powered investors that included a former governor and a best-selling business author. But they were outsiders to the marijuana industry, successful people who made their money elsewhere, and they were looking to cash in on the "green revolution." In dealing with Patrick over several months I heard him say repeatedly that they wanted to build a brand in the edibles space, to be the McDonald's of the industry.

The regulators had a tough task in creating a regulatory and enforcement framework for the newly legal cannabis industry, and it was compounded by the very short time frame to get everything done. But there was no alternative, the smoke was out of the bottle, and they covered a lot of ground. Even so, there are gaps in the regulations which the legislators will work to close over the next several years. The issues surrounding making edibles identifiable highlight the complexity of the problem and the entrenched stances taken by the work group participants. After a little more than a year of legal cannabis, the lines are drawn between people who want to make products safer, and those that want an unfettered ability to innovate, promote and monetize products.

Eventually, the Colorado Legislature passed a series of laws that forced edibles manufacturers to operate ethically. There is now a 100-milligram THC limit on edibles, split into 10-milligram servings, a THC! Symbol must be stamped on all edibles for which it's feasible, and since October 1, 2017, all edibles products must be gemoterically shaped—squares, triangles, or diamonds. No more edibles shaped like humans, animals, or fruit. It too three years after legalization to implement these changes, because the edibles manufacturers, the Corporate America stalwarts, were (and are) more interested in making as much money as possible, rather than in correcting the societal harm that their products produced.

Notes To Chapter Four

[1] Statistics on medical marijuana patients and caregivers dating from 2009 to the present can be found here:

https://www.colorado.gov/pacific/cdphe/medical-marijuana-statistics-and-data

[2] Access the full ACLU report here: https://www.aclu.org/feature/war-marijuana-black-and-white?redirect=billions-dollars-wasted-racially-biased-arrests

[3] The revised caregiver bill can be read in its entirety here:

http://www.leg.state.co.us/clics/clics2015a/csl.nsf/fsbillcont3/088E74361A7DCFB887257D900078263B?Open&file=014_enr.pdf

[4] The full report on edibles can be found here:
https://www.colorado.gov/pacific/sites/default/files/
HB%201366%20Work%20Group%20Report_FINAL.pdf

CHAPTER 5.

WHY COLORADO, WHY 2012?

I heard an expert on the cannabis industry speak in March of 2015 and they were asked the question, "Why did Colorado and Washington legalize marijuana in 2012?" and the response was not very convincing. "The internet, and the research," they stated. No social scientist would accept the notion that a revolutionary social idea would become a reality without people bringing resources, skills, and tactics to bear on the issue. In Colorado, the impetus to legalize marijuana did not somehow magically emerge from the internet, but it was the result of a concerted effort by the people who drafted Amendment 64, the people who created the regulatory framework, and the people of Colorado who voted for Amendment 64 and set into motion the recreational sale of cannabis. I explored the nexus between activism for marijuana policy reform on the one hand, and cultural attitudes and peculiarities of Colorado voters on the other in bringing about the legalization of marijuana in 2012 and I asked a number of people who have been involved with marijuana legalization for years, how legalization came about.

BRIAN VICENTE AND CHRISTIAN SEDERBERG, AUTHORS OF AMENDMENT 64

I first became familiar with the key players in marijuana policy reform and regulation when I attended a panel discussion in September 2014, hosted by the Mile High Young Professionals. There were eight panelists included in the program, and they represented a broad spectrum of perspectives, from advocates, opponents, regulators, and legislators, to owners of cannabis businesses. I would run into most of the panelists at various other symposiums and conferences throughout the year because they were the key people who had worked on challenging issues prior to implementing Amendment 64 and were sought after for their insight and experience. Of the eight panelists, I interviewed five of them and they provided me with an extensive history of the marijuana reform movement in Colorado, as well as the time line, trajectory, key points and evolution of the early stages of legalized recreational marijuana. Two of the earliest marijuana reformers were Brian Vicente and Christian Sedeberg, founders of what *Rolling Stone Magazine* calls "the country's first power-house marijuana law firm," Vicente Sederberg. I spoke with each of them to understand the insider's account of how marijuana legalization emerged and became a reality.

Unlike other powerhouse law firms, the offices of Vicente Sederberg are in an unassuming, brownstone house several blocks from the Colorado State Capitol and from the Marijuana Enforcement Division offices. This location affords no spectacular views of the city nor of the mountains, and it is not near restaurants or entertainment venues; it is merely a house in an urban neighborhood. I entered the office and stepped into a large foyer with a fireplace and mantle, a staircase, and nothing else. There was no receptionist, and the first floor only consisted of a small parlor, small conference room, a kitchen and a small office. I met with Brian and Christian on separate occasions, but interviewed Brian first, in September of 2014. He came down the stairs to meet me and escorted me to his office on the second floor. Brian is probably in his late thirties, tall, thin, and was wearing a button-down shirt with blue jeans. After introductions and explaining my project to him, I handed him a dozen or so questions written on 5×7 notecards. He looked through all of the questions and said, "Yeah, that's fine."

"Do you need me to keep anything confidential?" I asked.

"No," he waved his hand, "I'm ok with everything."

"Ok," I responded. "Well, you and Christian are some of the key people instrumental in marijuana policy reform in Colorado, and probably in the world, right?"

"Yes. Colorado was the first jurisdiction in the world to fully legalize marijuana for recreational use, and we were instrumental in that. We are the authors of Amendment 64, along with Steve Fox."

"So, is there anything that surprises you about the early stages of legalization? Marijuana has been legal now, recreationally, for the past nine months and I'm wondering if anything surprises you."

"Well, after eighty years of prohibition I can tell you that the industry is thriving, and that we're setting the model for how other states will implement—"

"Oh," I interrupted, "I heard Christian say that forty lawmakers from Uruguay were here to see you guys, so it's more than just a few States that are thinking of legalizing marijuana."

"Right. Yes. We had forty lawmakers here and they didn't follow all of our model, but some of the Colorado model. Anyway, one surprise was that once legalization passed, it quickly became less novel and became mainstream. But really, everything was a surprise in a way since we were trailblazers in all of this. There were a fair amount of unknowns. We didn't know what the tax revenues would be, or even what tax rate would work best. We didn't know what the response of the federal government would be. We didn't know if there would be spikes in use, especially teenage use, or spikes in DUI's. It turns out that there has been a drop in both teen use and DUI's."

"Really? A drop in teen use?"

"Yes," stated Brian.

"That's funny because there's an organization totally devoted to keeping marijuana away from children, in the belief, I think, that just the opposite would happen."

"Yes, that's Smart Colorado. I agree with them that keeping marijuana out of the hands of children is important. I mean, I have kids of my own," he stated with a raised voice, "and I don't want them to use marijuana or accidentally consume an edible—who wants that? But a lot of the discussion around teenagers and marijuana use is hyperbole."

He may be correct in that assessment. The fear of marijuana being diverted to children is widespread among the opponents of marijuana legalization and to some extent, the advocates who, like Brian, fear that the Federal government will shut down the whole industry if marijuana is being diverted to children. Although the data so far do not support an increase of marijuana being diverted to minors, opponents of marijuana legalization have been outspoken about the issue nonetheless. In October 2014, the Denver police department posted a YouTube video warning parents of the potential for marijuana-laced candy to be handed out to children during Halloween. "With Halloween fast approaching, Colorado citizens are in a unique position in the country – watching our kids' candy for marijuana edibles," the video stated. The video was picked up by *Fox News*, which ran daily stories on the perils of marijuana edibles for children during Halloween, by the *Huffington Post*, and other national media outlets. Smart Colorado ran a billboard campaign in Denver with the title, "Can you spot the pot?" with pictures of common marijuana edibles like Swedish Fish and the tagline, "Marijuana candy. Trick or treat?"

But according to the Denver police and the Rocky Mountain Poison and Drug Center, there were zero cases of people giving marijuana candies to children during the 2014 Halloween holiday. The following year, in 2015, the Denver Police did not put up another YouTube video about marijuana edibles; instead, they posted on their Twitter page a message to "find a designated driver" if you plan to use adult beverages or products this year. Similarly, Smart Colorado changed their billboard from warnings of edibles going to children to warnings of high THC levels. "To be really honest," stated Smart Colorado co-founder Gina Carbone, "I doubt people are putting marijuana candy in little kids' baskets."

I turned back to Brian. "You had mentioned surprise that the cannabis industry quickly became mainstream after legalization. How would you compare the cannabis industry to other industries? In what ways is the cannabis industry similar or different from others?"

"It's similar in the way that things get played out at the State Capitol. There are trade associations, and lobbyists, and it's like any other industry trying to influence laws and regulations in their favor. But it's different in that the marijuana industry is interested in being taxed and regulated. The industry and the businesses want to go beyond self-regulation, and be regulated by the State."

"When you say that the industry wants to be regulated by the State, are you speaking about the medical marijuana industry, the recreational marijuana industry, or are they one and the same?"

"Oh, I should clarify," Brian stated. "I mean the recreational industry. The medical marijuana industry played an important role in the evolution of recreational marijuana. In the beginning there were no stores and there were people who knew how to grow marijuana for extremely sick people. But the medical industry grew radically in 2009 and there was abuse in the system. There were too many people with Red Cards, and too many people who were caregivers, and there was a temptation to abuse the system. I think the structure of the caregiver market will change and it will be regulated more."

"Following that line of thought," I stated, "of potential abuse in the system, or things not quite working the way they were anticipated, what are the pros and cons of legalizing marijuana? I know it's only been legal for nine months, but are there any definitive trends that are either positive or negative?"

"On the positive side, adults are no longer arrested for possession of small amounts of marijuana. I think there's less confusion on the part of law enforcement on how to deal with marijuana, and their attention is focused on more pressing concerns."

"What about the black market?" I asked. "That was one of the key points in the Ogden memo, preventing diversion."

"The cartels are less involved now, they're underground."

"And on the negative side? What are the social costs to legalizing?"

Brian considered for a moment, "I'm not convinced that there are social costs to legalizing marijuana. The revenues are coming in and the first $40 million is earmarked for schools and we haven't had a spike in crime or an influx of cartels. We need to study the effects further, we need to educate people, and we need to have consistent regulations. But I don't see social costs to legalizing marijuana."

"Washington also legalized marijuana in the 2012 election and I'm wondering what your thoughts are in comparing the two approaches?"

"Colorado's Amendment 64 is far superior to Washington's. And I'm not just saying that because I wrote it. Ours was a holistic process and we included a lot of stakeholders with strong laws, but only one or two people wrote it. Washington doesn't let communities opt out but we do. Washington has a much higher tax rate. Colorado's approach is superior to Washington's."

The differences between Washington and Colorado go beyond opting out by jurisdictions and tax rates, however. Colorado allows adults over age 21 to grow up to six plants while Washington does not allow home growing at all. Colorado provided a path for medical marijuana dispensaries to convert to the recreational market while Washington considers medical marijuana dispensaries to be illegal, and, in fact, by April of 2015 Washington shut down all medical marijuana dispensaries. Colorado created a new oversight department, the Medical Enforcement Division under the Department of Revenue, to regulate and enforce marijuana; Washington uses an existing department, the Liquor Control Board, to provide oversight to the industry. I do not know what all those differences mean, or what they amount to, but in the popular press when, for example, Presidential candidates are asked about marijuana, they most often respond, "Let's wait to see what happens in Colorado," not "Let's wait to see what happens in Washington." Brian is right: the Colorado approach to legalized marijuana seems to be more effective and it is the model that other states and jurisdictions are analyzing and following in their quest to legalize marijuana.

I have another question for Brian. "I heard someone speak at a conference recently and they believed that the driving forces for legalization were the internet and the vast amount of research that has accumulated on cannabis, also available on the internet. Is that your sense of how this all happened, or are they off the mark?"

"No," he shook his head, "that's not it at all. I started Sensible Colorado in 2004 and we had an eight-year strategy for legalization. I did have some benefactors who threw some money at it, George Soros and John Sperling, the founder of Phoenix University, but we were basically a penniless non-profit and we were trying to convince voters to legalize marijuana."

"But why 2012? Do you know? Did the internet play a role?"

"It was tactical on our part and I don't think the internet mattered at all. We knew, or we strongly suspected, that voter turnout would be high in 2012 and especially that the young person turnout would be high. And it's the young people that are in favor of legalizing marijuana. We also built support with older people because of our track record in medical marijuana. Colorado was the first state to seriously regulate medical marijuana growing, manufacturing, and dispensaries, with the seed-to-sale tracking software and other regulations. So, people in Colorado were already familiar with the medical marijuana model and recreational marijuana was not seen to be that different from medical marijuana. Also, people in Colorado tend to be more free-thinking than people in other states, more progressive, and that played in to it a bit."

When I met with Brian Vicente's law partner, Christian Sederberg, months after my initial meeting with Brian, I didn't even have to ask him the questions of "why Colorado, and why 2012?" because the first words he uttered to me were, "Do you know the timeline of how legalization came about?"

"I know some of it," I responded, "based on an earlier conversation with Brian. I do know that it didn't happen because of the internet or research, but because there were real people with real resources and real tactics behind it, but I don't know all the specifics."

"Yes, that's right. I don't think social media had much to do with it back then. Ok. I'll share that with you, the evolution of the marijuana policy movement. Basically, it was a seven-year campaign that we started in 2005. Mason Tvert did an incredible job of getting marijuana legalized in the City of Denver, through his SAFER organization. I give a lot of credit to Mason and SAFER. He had a lot of media attention, a lot of events, and billboards stating that marijuana is safer than alcohol. He even tried to have a smoke-off versus a drink-off with Governor Hickenlooper, who was the Mayor of Denver at the time. You know that Governor Hickenlooper owned microbreweries, so is tight with the alcohol industry, right?"

"Yeah," I stated, "I knew that."

"Well, Mason offered a competition where he would take a puff on a joint every time that Mayor Hickenlooper would have a drink, and they'd see what the results were. Hickenlooper never took him up on the offer. But it created a lot of media attention," he said with a laugh.

"There was a ballot initiative in 2005 to make it legal for anyone to possess an ounce of marijuana, Amendment 44. It failed, but we kept going, me and Brian through our Sensible Colorado organization, and Mason through SAFER. And then the Ogden memo of 2009 provided clarity for medical marijuana and dispensaries. You're familiar with that, right?"

"Yeah, that's the memo where Ogden said that as long as certain criteria were met, and that marijuana was really being used for medical purposes and not being diverted to the black market or to children, the Federal government would keep a hand's off approach."

"Right," said Christian. "After that, in 2010, the legislature passed bill 1284 and that led to the statewide regulation of medical marijuana, with growers, infused products manufacturers, and dispensaries all under oversight of the Marijuana Enforcement Division."

"But Christian, you make it seem as if the legalization movement was dependent on the Ogden memo. Certainly, you and Brian must have thought about how to make this a reality without the memo in place."

Christian was silent for a moment. "Well, if you think about it, marijuana is a plant, it's an herb. Really, it is a wellness product. I believe, fundamentally, that science will prove out the benefits of marijuana for all sorts of health-related issues, and it's a component of a lot of emerging drugs, but it is essentially an herb. The language that we used in Amendment 64 was 'medicine and patients' versus 'drugs and users,'" he said as he looked at me intently.

"Amendment 64 would never have passed if it was about drugs and users. Not in Colorado, not anywhere. But if it has medicinal benefits? That's a lot easier to sell and really, marijuana is a wellness product, an herb. It should be sold in a nutritional store, in a vitamin store, or in the supplement section of Target or Walmart."

From an insider's perspective, the answer to the questions of "why Colorado and why 2012?" have less to do with social media and the internet, and everything to do with tactical steps taken by Brian, Christian, and Mason, the authors of Amendment 64 and the activists who worked to generate traction around the Amendment eight years prior to the vote. They worded the Amendment in ways that would appeal to a broad group of voters by using the language of "medicine" and "patient" rather than "drug" and "user," and they campaigned for years before the actual vote to highlight the fact that marijuana is less harmful than alcohol. From their perspective the legalization of marijuana results directly from their individual and collective efforts, but from others' perspective, there is more to the passage of Amendment 64 than the activism of Brian Vicente, Christian Sederberg, and Mason Tvert.

REGULAOR'S PERSPECTIVE ON LEGALIZING MARIJUANA

During my interviews of the regulators (Chapter 4), I asked each person, "Why Colorado, and why 2012?"

Former Senator Frank McNulty: "It's ridiculously easy to get on the ballot in Colorado. But Colorado is more libertarian than other states, too. You know what a Libertarian is, right?"

"Yeah," I responded.

"A Libertarian is a Republican who likes to smoke pot," he stated with a laugh. "But we're more educated here, and we have more free-thinking people. Me personally? I didn't think it was going to pass. I was shocked that it passed."

Former Senator Pat Steadman: "It's the easiest state to get on the ballot. Also, we have higher per capita marijuana consumption here compared to other states."

State Representative Jonathan Singer: "Well, in November of 2012 I thought it was close (passage of Amendment 64) but I wasn't thinking it would actually pass," Jonathan stated. "I knocked on 10,000 doors in November of 2012 — I'm not making that up. I literally went door to door to introduce myself to voters and to understand what they were thinking. My district is only five percent Democrat heavy. Twenty-nine percent of voters are Republican and thirty-four percent are Democrat. Most people I spoke with didn't even bring up anything about any issues, they would just say, 'I'm voting yes on Amendment 64.' There were signs in people's yard that said 'Mitt Romney' and 'Vote YES on 64' so I knew it had legs. And I figured if Longmont had a chance then Colorado had a chance. There's a lot of blue collar, conservatives in Longmont. A lot of agriculture and industry. So, I thought it had a chance, but was I surprised that it passed? Absolutely."

Andrew Freedman, Director of the Marijuana Enforcement Division: "People in Colorado are open to experimentation. They're tired of the war on drugs and the dismal results we've gotten with that. I don't think it was because people smoke, I think it was more about ending the war on drugs and trying something different."

Frank McNulty and Pat Steadman are absolutely correct on the ease of getting an initiative on the ballot in Colorado. The requirements are straightforward and simple. A person merely submits their proposed constitutional amendment to the state legislative staff and legal services office for review and comment. At least one public hearing on the proposed amendment is required. The amendment is filed with the Colorado Secretary of State who convenes a "title board," to assign a title. The ballot title must describe completely the proposal and do so in yes or no format. Then, to be included on the election ballot, signatures of Colorado residents must be collected and there must be five percent of the total votes cast for the Colorado Secretary of State from the previous election. In 2012, 86,105 signatures were needed, but there is no distribution requirement and signatures can be collected from any county or congressional district. However, the signatures must be collected in person and no electronic signatures are allowed. That's the whole process. After the vote the Governor has thirty days to provide an official declaration and if approved, the amendment takes effect on the day of the proclamation.

When I interviewed Governor Hickenlooper I asked him for his thoughts on why Colorado. "Do you have ideas on why Colorado was the first state to legalize marijuana, and why it happened in 2012?"

He responded with a question of his own. "Are you familiar with my thoughts on the Millennials?"

"No" I stated.

"About ten years ago we started getting a lot of Millennials moving here. This is a place where young people with an active lifestyle want to live. We're close to the mountains and all they have to offer, and Colorado is the place to be now for Millennials. I like to draw the comparison to California in the 1970's. California had a laid-back culture, a leftover hippie culture, and everybody wanted to be there, and a lot of people did go there. And that influx of people fueled the economic growth of California for the next 30-40 years.

"If you look at our economic growth over the past several years you can see what's happening," Governor Hickenlooper said, as he sat back in his chair. He began to list off a number of milestones. "Boulder and Fort Collins are number one and two in high tech start-up density, our unemployment rate is lower than the national average, we've created more jobs than nearly every other state, our housing prices are up and demand is strong for both housing and rentals. We have more live music venues here than in Nashville—did you know that?" he asked me.

"I had no idea," I responded. "There are a lot of venues by us, but I thought it was a Boulder-Longmont thing."

"No, it's the whole State. Well, anyway, yeah, George Soros threw some money at it, but we have a lot of Millennials here and they are open and supportive of legal marijuana. They don't see it as an evil drug. So, if you ask me, 'Why Colorado?' I would say it's because we have a lot of young people, a lot of Millennials, and these people want to live here, and do live here."

He's right on both counts. Colorado does have a younger population than other states — ranked twelfth for median age based on 2010 Census data — and Millennials are much more supportive and open to marijuana legalization than other cohorts. In an April 2015 CBS News Poll that asked the question, "Do you think that the use of marijuana should be legal or not?" sixty percent of persons aged 18-29 responded "legal," followed by fifty-seven percent of those in the 30-44 age range, and forty-one percent in the 45-64 age bracket. Only thirty-seven percent of the 65+ respondents answered "legal." So, the belief in legalizing marijuana is nearly a linear progression based on age, with older people less likely to support legalization, and younger people more likely. [1]

Of course, age could be a contributing factor to Colorado's passage of Amendment 64, but it is most likely not the sole reason. Utah is the youngest state in the Union, with a median age of 29, yet has no strong movement to legalize marijuana. According to the Marijuana Policy Project, which follows marijuana legislation at both the State and Federal level, Utah's limited medical marijuana law only applies to people with intractable epilepsy and the extract used to treat the condition comes from hemp, not cannabis. On their website the Marijuana Policy Project states, "Because the law only applies to low-THC marijuana, MPP does not consider Utah a medical marijuana state. In addition, the law may well be unworkable" (www.mpp.org). Oregon, on the other hand, did legalize marijuana and it ranks 35th on median age. So, while age may be a contributing factor to marijuana legalization, it is not a causal factor.

Governor Hickenlooper continued with another thought. "Are you familiar with the theory on the risk-taking gene, RDR4?"

"No," I responded, "not really."

"They have isolated a gene that leads people to take bigger risks. Americans have the highest propensity of risk-taking in the world, entrepreneurs have higher than others. Maybe the people that move here also have the risk-taking gene."

"That's interesting," I stated, but I had nothing more than that to add to the conversation, and shortly after my time with Governor Hickenlooper was over.

A SHORT PRIMER ON COLORADO

Colorado is the eighth largest state in total land area at roughly 104,000 square miles, and can be divided into three major areas, the Eastern Plains, the Front Range, and the Western Slope. But the Rocky Mountains are the definitive feature of Colorado. Of the eighty-six peaks above 14,000 feet in North America, fifty-three are located in Colorado. Overall, Colorado has the highest average elevation in the nation, at 6,800 feet above sea level, and it contains three-quarters of the nation's land above 10,000 feet. Colorado is arguably the most significant 104,000 square miles on the face of the earth. Not only do the mountains alter the weather patterns across the world, four of the nation's major rivers, the Arkansas, Rio Grande, Platte, and Colorado, have their headwaters in Colorado and flow to other parts of the country. The Colorado river alone provides fresh water to over 30 million people, and power to roughly 780,000 households per year in the southwest and Mexico. The snowmelt from the Rockies east of the Continental Divide provides water to the High Plains Aquifer (also known as the Ogallala Aquifer) that supplies the nation's water to farms and people throughout the Midwest and allows crops to be grown for the United States and other countries throughout the world. Absent the aquifer, the Great Plains would be the Great Desert.

Over 80 percent of the 5.2 million Colorado residents live along the Front Range, which extends roughly 380 miles from Wyoming to New Mexico. Beyond the large population density, the Front Range is significant since it shares a boundary with the Eastern Plains, and when two habitats share a boundary the opportunity for greater biodiversity is likely. Ecologists refer to this boundary as an "edge effect," but in practical terms for Colorado it means that there are a lot of animals and people in close proximity to each other and encounters are common. In fact, it's estimated that there are between 3,000 and 7,000 mountain lions and 19,000 bears in Colorado, many of them along the Front Range, and rattlesnakes throughout the state below 8,000 feet, as well as coyotes and lynx. That doesn't stop many Coloradoans from enjoying the mountains and every day there are people hiking, skiing, kayaking, rock climbing, fishing, hunting, and dealing with extreme weather conditions—temperature changes, straight-line winds, lightning, snow on any given day, potential for fires and floods, and the risks associated with wildlife and extreme weather.

The risk in doing these activities is significant and every year people are killed by lightning, in floods, swept up in rivers or thrown overboard while whitewater rafting. They get killed in avalanches, they fall from mountains, they go hiking and are never heard from again. But despite these risks people are not deterred. There is no cry from Colorado residents to prevent people from rock climbing, or backcountry skiing, or whitewater rafting. The risks are accepted, embraced, and pursued.

The people I spoke with, the authors of Amendment 64, the regulators, the legislators, and the governor, all provided a different perspective on the questions of "Why Colorado, and why 2012?" Nobody even hinted that the internet had some sort of causal influence on the emergence and passage of Amendment 64, and no one suggested that the vast amount of research somehow persuaded people to vote in favor of legalization. Instead, Amendment 64 passed because of the strategic and tactical actions by Brian Vicente, Christian Sederberg, and Steve Fox, the authors of the amendment; because of the activism of Mason Tyvert; because of the "ridiculously easy" process to get constitutional amendments on the ballot in Colorado; because of demographic changes to Colorado and an increase in Millennials and others sympathetic to marijuana legalization who have moved to Colorado; and perhaps because of a risk-taking gene that may be prevalent in Colorado residents. It is all of those factors and perhaps something more about the culture, people, and attitudes of Colorado residents—a deep belief in individual rights, and being able to grow and consume cannabis is one such right the people of Colorado hold strongly.

Notes to Chapter Five

[1] For polling results on marijuana attitudes from CBS, Gallup, Pew Research, the Wall Street Journal, and others, see http://www.pollingreport.com/drugs.htm

CHAPTER 6

MEDICAL MARIJUANA

And the leaves shall be for the healing of the Nations
  Revelation 22:2

Nearly all the issues involving cannabis involve broad disagreements about the plant, perhaps none more divisive than the medicinal and therapeutic benefits of cannabis. On one hand, patients who use cannabis extol the benefits, but on the other hand, medical and science researchers argue that such evidence is "anecdotal," lacking standardized tests and studies. I spoke with leading experts on medical uses of cannabis to understand the current state of the industry and what we might expect in the future.

BRIGITTE MARS, THE HERBALIST

I first met Brigitte Mars during the University of Colorado Symposium on Cannabis, organized by Students for Sensible Drug Policy (SSDP). We both attended a morning session titled, "From Cannabinoids to Cannabidiol: Medicinal Value of Cannabis Flower," and there were four experts in medical marijuana who spoke about current developments in medical marijuana and trends to expect in the future. During the session two of the experts lost their train of thought mid-sentence and after the second person forgot what they were saying mid-sentence Brigitte, who was not a presenter, said, "One of the side effects of smoking too much marijuana is short-term memory loss." The forgetful presenter turned several shades of red and responded, "Well, I'm just nervous speaking in front of so many people, that's all."

I was surprised on two fronts. First, I had never heard anything negative about marijuana from the people who consume it, it's always presented as the miracle plant that has a plethora of positive benefits and no downsides ("No one has ever overdosed from smoking marijuana," is a comment I heard over and over). And second, I was impressed that Brigitte called these people out about their short-term memory loss and I thought, you must have a lot of confidence and expertise to mildly chastise several experts during a well-attended presentation. As it turned out, Brigitte had both of those qualities and that became clear when she presented her material later in an afternoon session.

In the presentation bio, Brigitte Mars was listed as an herbalist, author, raw food chef, and radio personality and she is known world-wide for her work with plants, especially herbs. She has written seventeen books on the subject, most notably on hemp. The Biblical quote at the beginning of this chapter, "And the leaves shall be for the healing of the Nations" was taken from her presentation and she provided an overview of the history and uses of cannabis *sativa*. She noted that both George Washington and Thomas Jefferson grew hemp and that George Washington wrote, "sow the hemp seed everywhere." Of course, the hemp that Washington and Jefferson grew had so little THC, as it does today, that it was impossible to have a psychoactive experience from smoking it. Most likely both farmers used the fiber for products like rope or clothes, and the seeds for oil.

She also mentioned that Henry Ford created a hemp-fueled car which produces one seventh of the pollution as a conventional car. Henry Ford also said, *"Why use up the forests which were cen-*

turies in the making and the mines which required ages to lay down, if we can get the equivalent of forest and mineral products in the annual growth of the hemp fields?"

Brigitte's main focus for her presentation was on hemp, which is a form of cannabis that has very low levels of the psychoactive component, THC. "It's a plant that needs very little water, can block out weeds if planted close together, and doesn't need pesticides or herbicides" she stated. "We have a bee problem in the United States and dandelions and thistle are good for the bees, but they often contain pesticides. Hemp is a food source for bees and birds. Plus, it roots quickly and if you grow it close together helps to prevent erosion." But, hemp is considered a Schedule I drug by the Federal government and the Controlled Substances Act defines cannabis sativa today exactly as it did in 1937, when the Marihuana Tax Act was passed.

Although people have argued that the mature stalks ought to be allowed given the definition of "marijuana," the DEA has refused that suggestion and hemp, with virtually no THC, still remains a Schedule I drug and is illegal. I asked relatives of mine who are farmers in Iowa if they knew anything about hemp and they responded, "No, we just ripped it out every year, it's called 'Ditch Weed.'" In fact, NORML, the cannabis activist group, claimed in 2004 that the Drug and Enforcement Agency destroyed 249 million marijuana plants, of which 243 million (98 percent) were 'ditch weed.' The DEA confirmed that those numbers were accurate.

But beyond being a source of food for bees and birds, and reducing soil erosion, hemp has unique health benefits. Like other healthy edible oils (flaxseed, linseed, fish-oil, and canola oil) hemp contains omega-6 and omega-3 fatty acids, but only hemp contains those fatty acids in a 3-to-1 ratio that matches human nutritional needs. Since these fatty acids cannot be made by human metabolism they have to be obtained through diet. While hemp can be purchased in the United States, all hemp is currently imported primarily from Canada, Europe, and China. And although it's possible to grow hemp, a person would need to get a permit to do so from the Drug Enforcement Agency.

To date, the DEA has denied every application, save for a quarter-acre research site in Hawaii from 1999-2003. Yet every major agriculture organization, including the National Farmer's Union, the National Association of State Departments of Agriculture, the American Farm Bureau Federation, and even the California State Sheriff's Association, have pleaded with the President, Attorney General, USDA, and the DEA to distinguish industrial hemp from marijuana and allow farmers to grow it without a DEA permit. So far, no action has been taken.

But the market for industrial hemp is potentially large, and the Controlled Substances Act, by defining industrial hemp—with no psychotropic properties—as a drug, precludes the United States from participating in a market with global demand. In fact, over thirty nations in Europe, Asia, North and South America allow the growing of hemp and the United States is one of the few industrialized nations that does not. The U.S. market is estimated to be $581 million, not yet large, but over 25,000 products in nine subsectors can be manufactured from hemp. These subsectors include agriculture, textiles, recycling, automobiles, furniture, food/nutrition/beverages, paper, construction materials, and personal products.

I asked Martha Montemayor, a leading patient's rights advocate for medical marijuana and an expert in the subject, her thoughts on hemp, since she has seen the medicinal benefits of the plant.

"What are your thoughts on a policy where the Federal Government spends billions of dollars to eradicate a plant that has no psychoactive properties and actually has significant medicinal value? And because of this social policy we as a society have to import it from other countries? Am I understanding this correctly, that we are essentially subsidizing Canada, Europe, and China to provide to us a helpful plant that grows naturally throughout the country?"

"Yes. You have that right. I think it is a completely boneheaded social policy. Several weeks ago, I met with State lawmakers and I had a bag of hemp meal, imported from Canada, that I bought at Whole Foods or Sam's Club, I can't remember which, and I laid it down on Representative Jonathan Singer's desk and I said, 'Why isn't this a Colorado product?' And he responded, 'It should be.' It's just crazy what the Federal Government has done to hemp."

Several weeks after her presentation I met up with Brigitte to learn more about hemp and marijuana.

"I wanted to follow up on your thoughts about marijuana and hemp," I began. "I didn't know anything about hemp before your presentation and I thought it was really interesting. But first I wanted to ask if you see a difference in how men and women view marijuana, because, in going to symposiums and conferences and talking to people in the industry, I've found that men and women see marijuana differently and I wondered if you see the same dynamic."

"Yes," she responded, "for women, I think we see the plant as something that can do so much good in the world. Hemp can inhibit noxious plants, it's food for birds, and decreases the number of insects. There are so many struggling small towns in America and people could create so many cottage industries with hemp, making paper, fuel, rope, clothing. I have a friend that makes hemp concrete. And hemp can be grown everywhere in the world—Iceland, Africa, Haiti. Just think how much that could change the lives of people, if they could take this plant and create something useful from it."

"Well," I responded, "I didn't realize that hemp was used for medicinal purposes, and most of the women I met at the symposium were involved in medical marijuana, not growing or dispensaries."

"Hemp is very high in CBD, and that's the element that does the healing, not just the THC. It calms anxiety, helps people sleep, helps in menopause, helps prevent organ transplant rejection. No other plant can do as much. But yes, I think women are much more interested in the healing properties of cannabis, more nurturing."

"And for the men? What's their view?"

"The masculine view is high tech, it's extracting as much from one part of the plant as possible, looking for ways to get as much THC as possible. The cannabis plant represents the feminine. They only want the female plant, they are controlling the genetics to prevent propagation, and they kill the males. You've seen the flowers on these plants, they look like a vulva and they're screaming 'pollinate me, pollinate me.' They're turning the plant into a drug. For me, I'm an herbalist and I believe in using the whole plant."

"Is it surprising to you that the industry is so focused on high THC and has become high tech?"

"Very much so. I expected peace and love, not this edgy, head-banging music. We should keep it special, bring some sacredness to it. It's not just tap water. We should take the opportunity to take this to the highest level, offering it to the highest good."

"Well, it's surprising to me that hemp was made illegal in the first place," I stated.

"Do you know how it all came about?"

"Not really," I responded.

"Dupont had just invented Nylon, in the 1930's, and hemp was a competitor, and I think that Henry Anslinger, the person responsible for the Marijuana Tax Act, was married to a Dupont. But Jack Daniels had something to do with it, and so did Hearst, because of the paper. And there were lots of media reports, which Hearst printed, suggesting that when your daughter goes to college she will smoke marijuana and have sex with black men. That was the plot of the movie, *Reefer Madness.* You should read the book, *The Emperor Wears no Clothes* by Jack Herer. That would give you a good idea of the history."

"I had heard about the Dupont and Hearst connection before," I replied, "but is there anything else that led to the Marihuana Tax Act?"

"Well, the other driving factor was the Flexnor report—are you familiar with that?"

"Yes, as a matter of fact, I am."

Written by Abraham Flexnor in the early 1900's, the report led to the closing of 124 medical schools, advocated stronger entrance requirements at the remaining 31 medical schools, increased medical education to four years, and prevented a number of medical specialties deemed unscientific from receiving research funding or legitimacy as a field of practice. Medical marijuana was a victim of that report.

"Oh, one other thing," Brigitte continued, "you should talk to my co-author, Richard Rose. He knows more about hemp than anyone and he would be happy to speak with you. And Michael Jacobs has the hempcrete business. And," as an afterthought, "you should talk with Rav Ivker. He's a doctor in Boulder and can help with the spiritual and health benefits of cannabis."

RAV IVKER, M.D.
"FROM HEALTH CARE TO SELF-CARE"

I took Brigitte's advice and contacted Rav Ivker, MD. He's a holistic, integrative general practitioner that focuses on the mind, body, and spirit. Dr. Ivker is also a writer, with a series of books written about health: *Backache Survival, Migraine Survival, Arthritis Survival, Sinus Survival,* and *Asthma Survival.* I explained my project to him.

"So, I'm writing a book about cannabis and Brigitte suggested I talk to you, that you use cannabis as part of your approach to health."

"Ah," he exclaimed, "Brigitte. Wonderful person, and very knowledgeable about herbs."

"Yeah," I responded. "Not only did I speak with her, but I went to a presentation that she had at Baumann College and I learned a lot about, I'm guessing, thirty herbs or so."

"Well," he replied, "I do use cannabis in my medical practice, although it's not a focus of mine. It's part of a total approach to health, and it's not for everybody, just for some of my patients. Right now there are over 3,000 Board Certified doctors in integrative medicine and they come from every specialty and like me, they treat the whole person, not just the symptom. The word 'doctor' means 'teacher' in Latin, and the word 'health' means 'healing, holy, to make whole.' So, it's not an absence of disease or illness that we're seeking, but an approach to health that involves mind, body, and spirit. Conventional medicine manages chronic conditions, but conventional medicine is not good at curing chronic conditions. And that's the number one reason why people go to see a doctor in the first place: chronic pain. It's anywhere from 90-95 percent of the people who go to visit a doctor do so because they have chronic pain."

"So how does cannabis fit in to all of this?" I asked.

"Medical marijuana is the most effective treatment for chronic pain. *The most effective treatment*" he emphasized. "Marijuana is a major, major complement to western medicine. I use high CBD strains of *indica*, and all of them are hybrids. There's an infinite variety of strains but we're just beginning to scratch the surface of the plant."

"Why is that? Cannabis has been known for thousands of years."

"We haven't been able to study it," he replied "because of Federal laws. In Israel they have been studying cannabis for 60 years, but we've been constrained. One of the major findings from the Israeli research is that marijuana is most effective as a treatment with both THC and CBD present. It's synergistic, for example, if treating someone for cancer with THC, to have CBD in there. There's a drug on the market now, Marinol, that is synthetic THC—it's pure THC, but it's not nearly as effective as the plant. When you use the plant you have the benefit of the blend, the synergy is greater, more beneficial than isolating one component. There are 60-100 known cannabinoids in cannabis and a hundred terrapins, and a number of them are highly therapeutic. There is an infinite variety of different combinations of CBD's and terrapins, and CDB is not psychoactive. Nor is CBN."

"From your experience, with your patients, what are some of the results that you're finding?"

"If I prescribe marijuana as part of a treatment for a patient I always schedule a follow-up appointment two weeks later. I ask each one 'How is the treatment helping you the most?' and the same two responses come up. They say, 'the pain is gone' and 'I'm sleeping much better.' CBD is terrific for seizures and pain, but it has many other benefits, like anti-inflammatory benefits. It is a real help to people with arthritis. It is a muscle relaxant, helps with sleep, reduces anxiety.

"From a recreational standpoint marijuana is so much less harmful than alcohol. The only real risk in adolescents who use it daily—" he emphasized each word, 'use-it-daily'— "is an increased potential for psychosis. That's the THC. But there is very little downside to marijuana. On the other hand, opiate addiction is a huge problem in this country. Addiction medicine is a big specialty now. But people hate taking those prescription medicines, they hate the effects. Most of the side-effects are undesirable. Do you know that there are a thousand people a year who die from Ibuprofen?"

"No, I didn't know that."

"Yes. They get intestinal bleeding, but nobody tries to stop anyone from buying it."

"I'm guessing that the pharmaceutical industry will be opposed to medical marijuana?"

"I think they're highly threatened," Dr. Ivker responded. "They're probably already feeling the effects of it. The pharmaceutical industry is number two in profitability after oil and gas, and they control the health care industry...."

Dr. Ivker is right about the opiate addiction problem in the United States. In fact, the Centers for Disease Control and Prevention has an entire section on its website devoted to "understanding the epidemic," and includes the statistic that 44 people a day overdose on prescription painkillers. That's over 16,000 people a year. However, researchers from the University of Pennsylvania found that, in states with medical marijuana laws, opioid deaths were 24.8 percent lower than in states without medical marijuana laws. Lead researcher Dr. Marcus Bachhuber, in an interview on Healthline, states, "I've seen people who would tell me that they had tried prescription painkillers like Vicodin, Percocet, or OxyContin but the only thing that worked for them was marijuana. We thought maybe, if people chose marijuana over prescription painkillers on a large scale, medical marijuana states might see relatively lower rates of painkiller overdoses — and even overdose deaths." But the challenge still remains with the medical professionals themselves: will current medical practitioners accept cannabis as a viable painkiller?[1]

I asked Dr. Ivker about that possibility. "And how about your colleagues? I mean, other doctors? How receptive are they to your approach?"

"Most doctors are not really supportive of an approach that integrates marijuana with conventional medicine. They think everybody's getting high."

"Well," I stated, "I think that's a common perception of medical marijuana. People don't know that medical marijuana is loaded with CBD and CBD is non-psychoactive. I think that's an especially true belief that people have about younger people who use medical marijuana—that there's really not a valid symptom and younger people are just using medical marijuana to get high."

"That's absolutely true," he responded. "The State of Colorado Board of Medical Examiners has just come out with a directive that 'No physician should be authorizing marijuana' and also, they are trying to limit the percentage of medical marijuana patients under age thirty. They are saying that the number of patients under age thirty should not exceed 33 percent. In Boulder, mine is 38 percent. We're in a college town and there are a lot of young people here. Boulder is the healthiest and happiest city in America. And these young people bang themselves up. They rock climb and mountain bike, and they get serious injuries that leave them with chronic pain. The regulations are arbitrary and don't take into account that we have a huge population of young people here."

"Yeah, I met a woman who is a CU student, probably twenty years old, and she's a medical marijuana patient because she has a twisted spine and marijuana is the only thing that lets her live a fairly normal life. Her dad is a physician and doesn't believe in marijuana as a treatment, but she told me he said, 'Well, if it works....'"

"We're at a major change in society right now," Dr. Ivker continued, "we're going from health care to what I call 'self-care.' 21st century medicine will become 'self-care.' People will not be dependent on the medical profession to cure them. The medical practitioners can't cure them because the system won't let them. There was a Journal of American Medicine Association report in 2000 that stated that medical treatment, *medical treatment,* is the number two cause of death after heart disease. It's the second most common cause of death!" he stated with excitement. "So self-care will have to be the foundation for people, and from a holistic approach we have to teach people how to be healthy, not how to call the doctor. Marijuana offers safe, effective, temporary relief of symptoms with very little downside. The market for medical marijuana will be huge in the future."

MEDICAL MARIJUANA TODAY

The first state to explicitly address and promote marijuana as a therapeutic benefit to patients was California, in 1996. Proposition 215, "The Compassionate Use Act" received 56 percent of the vote and became a state law. The law allowed for patients to cultivate and possess cannabis with a physician's recommendation for essentially any ailment. In addition to a half-dozen specific conditions, the law included the term, "any other illness for which marijuana provides relief." The progressive stance by California motivated the Clinton Administration, and the Institute for Medicine in particular, to re-think marijuana policy. The Institute for Medicine urged greater research into medical benefits of marijuana, but also cautioned that any research be as controlled as possible. The Clinton Administration, in response, required all marijuana research to be reviewed by the Department of Health and Human Services, which created the Public Health Services Review to independently review all applications for all marijuana research. In effect, the PHS hindered research for marijuana, making it more difficult for scientists and medical professionals to study marijuana than to study cocaine and heroin.

Despite the lack of scientific research on cannabis, states continued to create medical marijuana laws and regulatory frameworks. By 2006 (10 years after California created the nation's first medical marijuana laws) an additional 10 states legalized medical marijuana, providing a pathway for approximately 51 million Americans (20 percent of U.S. citizens) to alleviate pain and suffering. By 2016, an additional 18 states had legalized medical marijuana, providing cannabis to an additional 105 million people. By 2017, 29 states and Washington D.C. had legal medical marijuana, or 62.9 percent of the U.S. population.[2] But despite the widespread public support for medical marijuana, the

DEA, which has final say on any and all research of the plant, has done everything in its power to curb and thwart scientific research of *cannabis Sativa L.*

The draconian approach by the DEA to medical marijuana research is well-documented. [3] It might seem that a plausible strategy for scientists and medical researchers would be to petition the DEA—which has sole authority over drug classifications—to change the classification of marijuana from Schedule I (with "no currently accepted medical use") to Schedule II ("having currently accepted use, with severe restrictions"), but that path has been pursued and, in every instance, has been met with extreme resistance by the DEA. For instance, NORML (National Organization for the Reform of Marijuana Laws) followed precisely that path and in 1972 petitioned the DEA to reschedule marijuana. The DEA did not take up the issue until 1986 (and under duress, with three federal courts requiring the agency to address the issue), and finally, in 1994—22 years after the initial petition—rejected it. Other petitions have met the same fate. In fact, in its 45-year history, the DEA has only reclassified any drug 39 times, and only 5 times has a drug been reclassified from Schedule I to Schedule II. Both Vicodin and Ritalin—widely prescribed and used—were Schedule I drugs reclassified as Schedule II drugs, as are cocaine, methamphetamine and oxycondone. And the latter three are deemed risky, dangerous, and prone to abuse.

Surprisingly, in 2016 the DEA relaxed its chokehold on medical marijuana research and in particular, allowed organizations other than the University of Mississippi to legally cultivate cannabis for medical research. Part of the impetus to allow other organizations to cultivate cannabis stemmed from the 2015 landmark CARERS Act, bipartisan legislation introduced in both the house and senate that sought to amend the Controlled Substances Act. In particular, the CARERS Act ("Comprehensive Access, Research Expansion, and Respect States Act") sought to ensure that the CSA does not apply to "a person who produces, possesses, distributes, dispenses, administers, tests, recommends, or delivers *medical marijuana* in compliance with state law." [4] And, additionally, the Act sought to ensure patient access in states with medical marijuana laws, expand opportunities for medical and scientific research, and allow marijuana organizations access to traditional banking systems.

Prior to that 2016 decision by the DEA, the University of Mississippi had a 50-year monopoly on cannabis research in the United States, and on its 5-acre plot produced less than 45 pounds annually—hardly enough cannabis to provide researchers with adequate supplies to conduct double-blind studies. In fact, a home grower in Colorado can produce more cannabis with just 12 plants than the entire DEA-sponsored University of Mississippi program.

How far behind is the United States in medical marijuana research because of the DEA? World leader in medical marijuana research, Israel, currently has 110 clinical trials underway, according to the Ministry of Health medical cannabis unit,[5] and one organization (Breadth of Life Pharma) has over 1 million square feet of cultivation, producing over 175,000 pounds of medical-grade cannabis.[6] By contrast, between 1990 and 2011 the United States funded only 21 double-blind research studies on human subjects using plant material. [7] No wonder the DEA claimed on its website that, because there have been few controlled scientific studies, cannabis is particularly dangerous and has no accepted medical use. It is a convenient claim and one the DEA has been perpetuating for the past 45 years to justify the War on Drugs.

Medical researchers, however, have a different perspective on the benefits of cannabis. The American Medical Association, in a 2015 referendum, stated that, "Statistically significant evidence now exists supporting cannabis use in patients with neuropathic pain and chronic pain with additional data and professional opinion endorsing its use in multiple sclerosis associated spasticity."[8] And Dr. Tod Mikuriya, MD, a psychiatrist and addiction medicine specialist, provided a list of 259 conditions for which cannabis could be helpful.[9] The operative word is "could," since the federal government has largely prevented the scientific and medical study of cannabis. Nearly any person who has spent any time on this earth is likely to have experienced one (or more) of the conditions Dr. Mikuriya identified. As more states create medical marijuana laws and regulatory frameworks, the momentum ought to shift and researchers will be able to study cannabis and determine its efficacy for a multitude of conditions.

For millions of people, research and scientific studies cannot happen quick enough, and Americans are very much faced with Dr. Ivkar's prediction that health care in the 21st century is in fact, "self-care."

Notes to Chapter Six

[1] For research and results on opioid deaths and medical marijuana, see http://www.healthline.com/health-news/states-with-legal-marijuana-have-fewer-overdose-deaths-082614

[2] For a listing of states that have medical marijuana laws, along with the date, form of passage (amendment, house and senate bills) see the ProCon.org website at https://medicalmarijuana.procon.org/view.resource.php?resourceID=000881.

For a thorough and unbiased list of each medical marijuana and recreational marijuana bill introduced by state, results, and form of passage, see the National Council of State Legislatures at http://www.ncsl.org/research/health/state-medical-marijuana-laws.aspx

[3] A very good and unbiased review of the politics of medial marijuana research, along with the hurdles that must be overcome, is provided by the centrist Brookings institute, and can be found here: https://www.brookings.edu/blog/fixgov/2016/04/13/why-the-carers-act-is-so-significant-for-marijuana-policy-reform/

[4] Details of the CARERS ACT can be found at: https://www.congress.gov/bill/115th-congress/house-bill/2920

[5] For details on Israel's medical marijuana research program, see https://www.usnews.com/news/best-countries/articles/2017-04-11/israel-is-a-global-leader-in-marijuana-research

[6] Additional details of Israel's medical research program can be found here: https://www.rollingstone.com/culture/features/how-booming-israeli-weed-industry-is-changing-american-pot-w499117

[7] See Caulkins, Jonathan P., Angela Hawken, Beau Kilmer, and Mark Kleiman's book,
   Marijuana Legalization: What Everyone Needs to Know, for more details on marijuana research.

[8] The full text of the American Medical Association resolution can be found here: https://assets.ama-assn.org/sub/meeting/documents/i16-resolution-907.pdf

[9] The full list of 259 conditions can be found here: https://medicalmarijuana.procon.org/view.background-resource.php?resourceID=001393

CHAPTER 7.

REGULATING MEDICAL MARIJUANA

Dr. Larry Wolk, M.D. is the Executive Director of the Colorado Department of Public Health and Environment (CDPHE), and he might have one of the most difficult government jobs in Colorado: he is charged with oversight of all things health, environmental, vital records, public records, and laboratory services. Within each of those departments there are dozens of specialties, studies, and reporting requirements, and people who care deeply about any decision the CDPHE makes. As if that weren't enough, he also is responsible for managing six rulemaking boards and another thirty-four boards and commissions that range from the Assisted Living Advisory Commission to the Pollution Prevention Advisory Board, and everything in between. He also inherited a largely unregulated medical marijuana program.

I first became acquainted with Dr. Wolk in September 2014, at a Colorado Board of Health meeting during which the Board members were debating making several regulatory changes to the existing medical marijuana process. The issues under debate included:

1. Medical marijuana registry identification cards (Red Cards),
2. A process for determining debilitating conditions,
3. Requiring a waiver for caregivers that serve more than five patients,

4. Patient responsibilities, and
5. The medical marijuana research grant program.

The meeting was held in the Old Supreme Court Chambers at the State Capitol and was nearly filled with young families, with children in wheelchairs, babies crying, and people in the audience making catcalls and yelling at the Board Members, in particular, the woman sitting directly behind me. Pandemonium reigned, and I leaned over to speak with my younger sister, Bente, who covers lots of hearings in her role as a reporter with Rocky Mountain Community Radio and asked, "Is this normal?"

"No," she responded. "Not at all. The Senators would never let a meeting like this get out of hand. They would know that it's a sensitive issue, an emotional issue, and they would be prepared to be more sympathetic and understanding."

The issue at hand causing so much consternation? Number 3 from above, the proposed limit on caregivers to serve no more than five patients without receiving a waiver. The CDPHE has been pursuing caregiver limits on number of patients since 2004 when, in a closed meeting, the Department created a regulation limiting caregivers to five patients. A lawsuit was filed against CDPHE and in 2009 the Honorable Judge Naves called the limit a "capricious decision." Because the meeting was conducted in private it violated the Colorado constitution and the caregiver limits were disallowed. In 2009, in a public meeting, CDPHE again addressed the issue but decided there would be no limits on caregiver patients and the Department changed the definition of "caregiver" to be a person who only had to provide medicine to a patient. Later in 2009, CDPHE reversed itself on the definition of caregiver and expanded it to include a person with "significant responsibility for managing the well-being of a patient." Some examples include transportation, preparing meals, or house cleaning. Once again, a lawsuit was filed against CDPHE and once again Judge Naves ruled that CDPHE broke the law in changing the definition of caregiver and called the action "invalid and void."

Finally, in 2010 the Colorado General Assembly took up the issue and passed a comprehensive bill (HB-1284)—the Colorado Medical Marijuana Code—and limited caregivers to five patients, except in "exceptional circumstances." The Medical Marijuana Code also created regulations and licenses for medical marijuana centers (dispensaries), cultivation, and infused product manufacturers (edibles), and became the working regulatory framework for how Colorado would regulate recreational marijuana.

The framework that the Colorado General Assembly created was the first of its kind in the world and is a model that is followed by other medical and recreational marijuana regulators in other states. Colorado's framework included a seed-to-sale tracking system where each marijuana plant would be tagged with an RFID and would subsequently be weighed at harvest, weighed again after it has dried, weighed before transportation to a dispensary or marijuana infused manufacturer, weighed at the dispensary or manufacturer prior to sale, and weighed at the end of the business day. All of those weights, for each plant, are reported back to the inventory tracking system operated by the Marijuana Enforcement Division.

The impetus for this highly regulated marijuana tracking system? The October 2009 memo by United States Deputy Attorney General David Ogden sent to the states with medical marijuana laws. In short, Ogden indicated that, as long as businesses and individuals in States with medical marijuana laws followed State law, Federal enforcement resources would not be devoted to raids or prosecution of those businesses or individuals. However, Ogden outlined eight criteria that would lead to Federal prosecution but three in particular impacted and shaped the Colorado Medical Marijuana Code:

1. Preventing the diversion of marijuana from states where it is legal under State law in some form to other states,
2. Preventing the distribution of marijuana to minors, and
3. Putting measures in place to prevent illicit marijuana trade that funds criminal enterprises.

The Board of Health, the Marijuana Enforcement Division, state Regulators, law enforcement, and others firmly believed that caregivers and medical marijuana patients were a source of diversion to other states and fueled the black market. The evidence strongly suggests that either or both of these were the case.

Along with a significant increase in medical marijuana registry patients after 2009, Colorado's caregiver system allowed physicians to recommend higher than six marijuana plants for patients—whatever the physician deemed was "medically necessary"—and some patients had hundreds of plants, none of which were tracked by the Marijuana Enforcement Division through the seed-to-sale tracking system. It was a system fraught with loopholes and loose ends and one that regulators wanted to tighten and strictly control.

At the Board of Health meeting in September 2014, it was clear that some of the people in the room had been involved in a decade-long battle with CDPHE over caregiver limits, but for others it was their first exposure to CDPHE, most notably, the families who moved from Georgia, Illinois, Minnesota, Utah, and other states in order to provide medical marijuana for their children. The children of these families have diseases like Dravet Syndrome and Lennox-Gastaut, an intractable form of epilepsy, Crohn's disease, and other debilitating and life-threatening neurological conditions. The children were in attendance at the Hearing, many of them in wheelchairs, lying across several chairs with their heads on their mothers' laps, or being held by a relative in the back. One woman, Janea Cox, moved from Georgia with her daughter, Haleigh, when her doctor said that Haleigh would not live to her fifth birthday and would never talk. At eight months old Haleigh started having 200 seizures a day, but by providing Haleigh with a marijuana oil, those seizures declined to fewer than three a day. Today Haleigh is five years old and talking. The large contingent of people at the Hearing were supporting the Flowering Hope Foundation and its founder, Jason Cranford, who is a Boulder caregiver.

Before public testimony, there was a short introduction from Dana Erpelding, Interim Director of CDPHE's Center for Health and Environmental Information and Statistics.[1]

"The rules regarding caregiving," Ms. Erpelding began, "in statute and in the Constitution specify that you can only have one primary caregiver at any given time and the parent of a minor patient must be the primary caregiver." She went on to state that, of the 357 minor patients in the medical marijuana registry in Colorado, all had a parent listed as the primary caregiver. "Parents, therefore, based upon statute and the Constitution, obtain their product through a licensed marijuana center, not a caregiver."

Dr. Larry Wolk stood up and interjected. "I want to follow up on that point," he stated, "as a caution to the parents that are here. Obviously, information we receive at the registry is kept confidential. But if a parent is incorrectly using another caregiver for their child...this is a public proceeding and you may be putting that person at risk if you're going to testify that you're using somebody other than yourself as the caregiver. So I want to be clear that the way that the Constitution identifies it, that the parent is the only legal and correct caregiver for your child."

The moderator then called the first person to testify. "So, this is the first one. Wendy Turner?"

There was absolute silence in the Chamber. Who would testify now? Every parent in the room had already identified themselves as the primary caregiver for their child, and they were just informed that not only was that illegal according to the state Constitution, but that they were in a public forum and at risk for incriminating themselves and their caregiver.

"Wendy Turner?" The moderator asked again. "Wendy Turner do you want to testify?"

Again, there was silence.

"No?"

A woman, presumably Wendy Turner, looked at Jason Cranford who nodded his head to indicate that he was fine with her testifying and the consequences he might incur.

"Alright," the moderator continued, "may I move on to Matthew—oh, you will testify? Thank you."

Wendy Turner, a mother in her early thirties, moved to Colorado from Illinois. She walked to the microphone to testify before the Board of Health. "My name is Wendy Turner, my son is Coltyn Turner. He is a patient and he has Crohn's Disease. We go through the Hope Foundation for our medicine and we really support the fact that we can go through someone. I'm going to be really blunt here: I don't know how to grow this stuff. I rely on the Hope Foundation to give us the quality medicine that we receive for my child. I would be lost without Jason Cranford. I wouldn't know what to do. And I think I can say that for all of us that are here today, we would absolutely be lost.

"We're parents of sick children," she said with a sigh of exasperation, "the last thing we need to worry about is to grow a whole bunch of plants. It's difficult…it's a new situation for all of us and I really believe that Jason does an extremely good job of taking care of all of us. He's always available. I can get a hold of him any time, and he is giving us quality medicine."

The audience, the Board Members, were silent after Wendy's testimony, and there were no questions by the Board of Health for Wendy Turner. Kirk Anderson was called up next. "My name is Dr. Kirk Anderson," he began, "and I am a Board Certified Physician with a background in chemistry and psychology. I worked with Pacific Islanders with an organization in New

Zealand and I learned that plant science is just as important as pharmaceuticals. There are many island nations that maintain their health quite well with plants." He shifted from side to side, uncomfortable with the formality and large audience acutely focused on him. "I became aware of Jason earlier this year and learned that he has a good product that is available right away, while others have waiting lists that are months long. Jason's product is effective, reliable, predictable, and he talks regularly to the patients and communicates with the doctors.

"Not everyone can grow this strain of high CBD required for medicinal purposes, and my concern is that people will get it off the internet from dubious sources. Also, I think it's unusual for a professional that does what they do really well to have less than ten clients. Most professionals I've worked with have over a thousand patients." He looked up from his prepared statement, and to the Board members stated, "I see the dilemma you're facing about the diversion, but with something that is not psychoactive? It seems like it's less of a concern that it's being diverted, in my opinion...in my experience."

County Commissioner, Jill Hunsaker-Ryan, spoke after Kirk Anderson sat down. "Just as a follow-up, Jason's been referenced twice and I'm not familiar with who that is. My understanding is that if he's providing this to children he needs to be registered as a center, and therefore wouldn't fall under the caregiver rules. Am I understanding that correctly?"

Larry Wolk responded to her question. "My understanding is that he's both licensed as a center and is a caregiver as well."

Another Board member asked, "Can a person be both a licensed medical center and a caregiver?"

"Yes," stated Larry. "There's nothing to prohibit participating as both."

Board President Laura Davis continued. "I'm going to go ahead and ask," as she looked up and scanned the audience, "Jason

Cranford, since you are the topic of discussion, can we have you come up and talk?" The audience broke out in laughter, and Jason Cranford stood up and made his way to the microphone.

JASON CRANFORD, FOUNDER OF FLOWERING HOPE FOUNDATION

Jason Cranford is the founder of Flowering Hope Foundation and the dozen or so families at the Board of Health hearing were there in support of Jason and the work he does, as Wendy Turner and Kirk Anderson testified earlier. Jason became involved in medical marijuana in 2009 when a father approached him for help with his four-year-old daughter who had terminal brain cancer. Jason created a 1:1 CBD:THC oil and the child overcame the cancer. Since that time he has donated medicine to hundreds of children with cancer, epilepsy, Crohn's disease, and a number of neurological disorders. All of the families at the Board of Health hearing were there in support of Jason and since he is providing medicine to minor patients and only the parent can legally do that, he is in the cross-hairs of the Board of Health.

The conflict between large-scale caregivers and the CDPHE involves both a narrow definition in the state Constitution of caregiver, and also a state audit report indicating that caregivers are largely unregulated and most likely the source of marijuana being diverted out of Colorado. Despite the seed-to-sale tracking system created by the Colorado Medical Marijuana Code, the caregivers in the state remain a mystery. Since only registration is required by the state of Colorado, and not licensing, the caregiver market carries a lot of risk to the State, and the activities of caregivers are largely unknown to CDPHE and State regulators. The Hearing in September 2014 was meant to reign in the black market and to put a halt to diversion out of Colorado. Larry Wolk moved from a seat in the audience, where he had been stationed, to an empty chair with the Board. "You can't be there," the woman behind me shouted, "you're not a member of the

Board!" Her shouts were ignored and as Larry Wolk moved to a Board seat, Jason took the microphone. The following exchange between Jason and the Board of Health members indicates just how difficult it is to design and implement a regulatory system without any gaps and without harming people who need help.

"My name is Jason Cranford," he began. "I'm a registered caregiver in the state of Colorado and I'm also a licensed dispensary owner. I have one question. Would these patients that you keep speaking of have to go into my medical marijuana center to pick up their medicine or can they pick it up from me, as their caregiver?"

Larry Wolk responded, "If they're minor patients they would have to go through your center. You cannot act as the caregiver for anyone other than your own child."

"Ok," continued Jason. "So, I've been approved by the CDPHE as a caregiver for many minor patients. How am I getting approvals on these Red Cards if it's a violation of the rules?"

"We don't approve caregivers," stated Larry, "they're entered into the registry. We're just looking for parents to be listed as the primary caregiver for minor patients and for caregivers to be registered through the registry. We don't tie the two together."

"Ok," Jason replied. "So I have another question. I read a rule recently where a caregiver can assist another caregiver—not in cultivation—but in actual medicine and care of the patient. So if the parent is listed as the caregiver on the paperwork and I'm a registered caregiver, am I still allowed to give that parent medicine for their child?"

There is a private discussion between Larry and Board Chair Laura Davis, and then Larry turned his microphone back on and stated, "I'd probably refer that question to the Attorney General because it's more of a legal question. We'll take that under consideration and get back to you."

"Ok. Well let me explain to you the problem in the State. There are only two providers in the State who have taken the time to breed low THC high CBD strains. The other provider in the State has up to a one year waiting list. I provide medicine immediately. I've got around 80 patients that have signed me up as their caregiver. Many of them are sitting here right now," he said as he looked back at the large contingent of Hope Foundation supporters. "So if I'm supposed to choose which patients I can no longer give medicine to, I'm not going to be able to do that. These are life-threatening illnesses and these children will die."

He looked directly at Larry Wolk. "Are you willing to pick which patients I have to send to the streets because there are no dispensaries that provide this medicine? Me and one other organization are the only two in the State that provide this low THC, high CBD medicine. So where are these patients supposed to go besides the emergency room?"

"Can I ask a question for further clarification?" asked Larry. "Tell us, practically, the difference between providing for those patients as a caregiver versus as a center."

"With a dispensary," responded Jason, "they're going to be charged sales tax, and there's a Department of Revenue rule that we can't sell lower than what our neighbors are selling at. These parents can't buy the medicine, so I donate the medicine when the parents can't provide the money for it. They're not going to find the medicine in a dispensary model anywhere in the State. There is no access. It's me and one other organization in the State that have these genetics and it took me six years to breed these strains. So what you're asking these parents to do is to sit on a one-year waiting list or go without their medicine that's stopping their child's seizures. They're going to end up in the emergency room, or worse. So as a Department of Public Health you're turning your back on the public health by enforcing this rule."

"I'd like to take this back to the sales tax issue," responded Larry. "My understanding is that there is no sales tax on the product."

"That's not true," Jason replied.

Larry looked up, surprised. "Is it a county sales tax?"

"It's a municipality tax and there's a state sales tax and those costs are pushed onto the patient."

Larry leaned forward in his chair and looked directly at Jason. "So there's a cost difference in what you would charge as a center compared to what you charge or donate as a caregiver?"

"Absolutely. There's a massive difference. In my licensed medical marijuana center, I'm not allowed to donate medicine. Everyone has to pay full price. I can't donate to anyone. And a lot of the parents can't afford the medicine. They've moved here from other states and the pharmaceuticals that they've been on for years and their medical bills have tapped them out. They're dry and they can't afford the medicine so we have to donate it."

"I'll ask the same question I asked earlier," Larry said. "Is there something you're doing in your role as caregiver that you could teach others so that they could be caregivers to these patients? Because based on the definition of what the caregiver has to provide it seems unreasonable to put the burden on you as a single individual. Is there something you can do to teach others to cultivate on behalf of patients?"

"Yes," Jason replied. "I've tried that and nobody's interested because this is a non-intoxicating cannabinoid that I'm cultivating. It doesn't get you high, there's no high associated with it. And like I was saying, a lot of parents can't afford the medicine and these caregivers are not going to do this for free. Luckily, I make money in my dispensary and the profits go back into giving out this medicine for free as a private caregiver. So, yes, I've approached several caregivers about helping me do this and they're just not interested."

"And the parents as well?" Larry asked. "Because, again, as the only legal caregiver for their children, are you able to teach the parents?"

Jason turned and looked back at the parents, who laughed at the question. "These children are in wheelchairs, do you not see this? Do you think they have time to sit in a garden and grow marijuana and then learn biology and chemistry, and learn how to do extractions and infusions? It's impossible."

"I understand," Larry responded sympathetically. "I'm just trying to work with the language in the Constitution and what's defined in statute."

"I put in about 80 hours a week. Every single week. This is my life. Parents of special needs children are not going to be able to manage a garden, cultivate, do extractions and infusions and then make a standardized dose of a non-intoxicating substance."

"I understand," Larry stated again. "So then the question is, to ensure the safety and the quality of the product, wouldn't they be better served obtaining it through a center?"

Jason raised his voice in exasperation. "Did you not hear what I just said? There are no dispensaries in the state providing this—"

"I've heard every word of what you're saying," Larry quickly broke in.

"There's no money in it," Jason continued. "These centers are profit driven. There's no money in what I'm doing. If the dispensaries were going to have it…. They've had four years now since 2010 with HB-1284 to get these CBD strains going. They're not doing it. They're not interested. These kids are left in the cold. I saw a serious situation in the State and I stepped up and did something about it. And, just to be blunt and frank: you can pass this rule all you want today. I'm not going to stop doing what I'm doing."

In a dramatic moment Jason raised his arms above his head with his wrists together in a shackled position and proclaimed, "If I have to put handcuffs on and go to jail then you'll have to find a D.A. that's willing to prosecute me. If you do find a D.A. that's willing to prosecute me, I'm going to ask for a jury trial and we're going to try for jury nullification and set a precedent."

Board Chair Laura Davis interjected, "Ok."

"And that's just the way it is," said Jason. The audience erupted into a standing ovation with cheers, clapping, loud whistling and shouts of "Yeah!"

Laura Davis continued. "Are there any questions for Jason? Sue?"

Board Member Sue Warren spoke into the microphone. "I'm not understanding this very well. Before we came here today I didn't realize you owned a dispensary. I thought you were just the caregiver of all these patients. So, I'm not understanding, if the parents are the caregiver of these kids they can then buy their product at a dispensary. Can you just explain that again to me what your dilemma is, because I'm not getting it."

"For the third time," Jason continued with mild frustration, "my dilemma is that these dispensaries do not provide the type of medicine I provide. I provide a low THC, non-intoxicating, non-psychoactive compound called cannabindiol—"

"I get that," she said.

Jason continued. "The dispensaries are not interested in cultivating this. They've had four years to get these types of strains in their rotation and they haven't done it."

"I understand that part. The part I'm not understanding is when you talked about expense and taxes and why you have to donate, that's the part I don't understand."

"With a dispensary, if you read the 77-page rulebook the Colorado Marijuana Enforcement Division put out, it says in the rulebook that we are not allowed to donate, everything has to be sold at market rate. I can't even undercut my neighbor. If one of my neighboring dispensaries were to come up with this strain of cannabis and provide it to the patients for, say, $50 per gram, then I'm required to sell it for the same price as them. I can't undercut anybody, and I can't give away anything free. I have to charge full price and I have to charge sales tax and a lot of these parents can't afford it."

Board Chair Laura Davis weighed in. "So there's one thread from what you said that I don't want to lose sight of, and we need to get clarification from the Attorney General's office, but there may be a potential solution to this, and that is, as a caregiver, can you provide product to another caregiver? I think that would be a pathway for you to continue to do what you're doing and keep it legal."

"Ok," Jason replied, "that would be acceptable and I'm sorry for being blunt and frank but what you're asking me to do is put children's blood on my hands and I'm not willing to do that."

Laura Davis: "What I want you to understand is that we as a Board understand that, and we're not trying to be confrontational, we're not trying to create an adversarial environment. We're trying to work through this issue with you."

"Ok. I would ask, please, please Colorado Department of Public Health, stall your vote today until we can research this a little further and figure out a solution before we create a problem we can't reverse."

Laura Davis called on Board Member Rick Brown.

"Thank you Mr. Cranford for that clarification. The part I'm trying to understand is that you said this product is not available to anyone else on the market, so at this point in time, any price you set would be the price that's out there. And if someone else develops this medicine and it becomes more widely available, they would have to sell it at your price. That's the part I'm trying to understand, one, and two, I'm hearing it's a cost differential issue and you have this proprietary product."

Jason responded, "The problem is it took me six years and hundreds and hundreds of lab tests and countless hours of my time to breed these strains and I did it in a caregiver model. I'm not allowed to take my clones or genetics and enter them in to a dispensary model. It's illegal in this State because the Marijuana Enforcement Division requires that all your clones, seeds, and genetics come from another licensed source. Since a caregiver is not considered a licensed source it's impossible for me to take these genetics and enter them in to a commercial model. I would have to start from scratch all over and put in another four or five years to create these low THC medicines. So it's impossible for me to bring my genetics into a medical marijuana dispensary model."

Rick Brown continued. "Madam Chair, just a follow up, that might be a question for the Attorney General, to just clarify if legally there's a mechanism whereby your proprietary medicine could be available through your center."

"Ok," Laura Davis responded. "Any other questions for Jason? Dr. Stanley?"

Board Member Dr. Christopher Stanley responded. "Yes. Thanks very much again for being here. For those patients that you feel you are the caregiver for them, are you regularly providing activities of daily living assistance for those individuals, or is it really more providing them with this unique strain and unique medication?"

"I do both. I've set up online support groups where all the patients can ask me freely. We've set up dosing calculators for the patients where they can see how many milligrams of cannabinoids they're giving per pound of body weight. We align their doctor's visits. We have cookouts at my farm where we allow patients to come over. So, yes, we provide other service than just handing over a bottle of medicine."

Dr. Stanley: "Any instances where you're provided regular transportation for them, where you've done shopping for them?"

"No, because they haven't requested that and I leave it up to the patients, but I have provided transportation to doctors' offices."

That was the last question for Jason Cranford and he returned to his seat. After a short break the Hearing reconvened and one by one, mothers of children with debilitating diseases spoke to the CDPHE of moving to Colorado, the sacrifices they have endured, and that Jason Cranford changed their lives. Said one mother, "My child would not be alive without Jason's help." Said another mother in a tearful testimony, "I can't grow enough marijuana for my child. It takes one pound of marijuana to get one ounce of oil, and I can't get that with three plants. It takes six months to get that much and I don't know how to grow the plant and I'm busy 24 hours a day taking care of my child. None of us can do this without Jason."

Other people testified that limiting caregivers to five patients was unreasonable and would never be contemplated with physicians, who can have thousands of patients. Moreover, requiring caregivers to spend hours with patients is not a standard that physicians are held to and many physicians might spend only fifteen minutes a year with patients. "Where did you get that number?" one person asked. "There's not enough help here now and you are restricting it further. We need *more* caregivers. The system you've come up with satisfies the needs of the Department of Revenue and law enforcement, but not the patient. The regulated market is unaffordable and not consistent. My caregiver grows for me, and knows me."

In the end, the Board of Health passed two motions. One motion excluded Recommendation 3, the waiver for caregivers to serve no more than five patients, and one motion dealt solely with Recommendation 3, by removing the line, "Where waivers apply, caregivers will be allowed to serve a maximum of ten patients at a time." But the parents, caregivers, patient advocates, and others in attendance left the Hearing without clarity on the future. Could parents delegate to Jason Cranford the caregiver responsibilities for their children, or were they in violation of the Constitution in doing so? Was Jason Cranford at risk of prosecution because he donated medicine to children in need? It's unlikely that CDPHE can do anything about the current situation other than pass motions. "We're not an enforcement agency per se," said Larry Wolk. "Nor do we receive any funding to do enforcement. It's very confusing," he continued, "We have a confusing system."

But the Colorado General Assembly can do something to provide clarity to the caregiver issue for parents and patients, and guidance to law enforcement on how to deal with the caregiver-patient system. They did that in 2015 when legislators passed

Senate Bill 15-014 which clarifies what a caregiver is and what "significant responsibility" entails. There was no change from the original definition of caregiver based on Amendment 20 of the Colorado Constitution, which stated that a "primary caregiver" is a natural person, other than the patient or the patient's physician, who is eighteen years of age or older and has significant responsibility for managing the well-being of a patient with a debilitating medical condition. However, the Senate bill further clarified various roles caregivers may have beyond age, including:

- A parent of a child and anyone who assists that parent with caregiver responsibilities including cultivation and transportation;
- An advising caregiver who advises a patient on which medical marijuana products to use and how to dose them and does not provide, cultivate, or transport marijuana on behalf of the patient;
- A transporting caregiver who purchases and transports marijuana to a patient who is homebound;
- A cultivating caregiver who grows marijuana for a patient.

So, the state legislature created a more finely-grained definition of caregiver that appears to solve the problem of parents who move to Colorado to obtain medicine for their children from a caregiver, like Jason Cranford, who can be the person that "assists the parent." But the Colorado General Assembly went one step further in defining "significant responsibility." The bill states the following: "Significant responsibility for managing the well-being of a patient means that the caregiver is involved in basic or instrumental activities of daily living. Cultivating or transporting marijuana and the act of advising a patient on which medical marijuana products to use and how to dose them constitutes a significant responsibility."

Governor Hickenlooper signed the bill on May 18, 2015, fifteen years after Colorado legalized medical marijuana, and the law finally provides guidance and structure to what has been a highly unregulated market. There are still some loopholes in the system, however, including the lack of testing of medical marijuana for pesticides, THC and CBD levels, and contaminants. And caregivers are not required to place an RFID tag on each plant and track the plants they are growing from seed to sale. Whether those loopholes are closed in the future remains to be seen, but for now the caregiver system appears to keep at bay the Federal government, and the DEA in particular, from prosecuting medical marijuana businesses, caregivers, and patients.

DR. LARRY WOLK, EXECUTIVE DIRECTOR COLORADO DEPARTMENT OF PUBLIC HEALTH AND ENVIRONMENT

I met with Dr. Larry Wolk in June of 2015, well after the September 2014 Board of Health meeting, and after Governor Hickenlooper had signed the bill to further regulate caregivers. I was impressed with his willingness to speak with me, and his openness during our conversation. I merely sent his assistant an email explaining my project and asked for some time for an interview. I heard back within hours of sending the email and was on his calendar within two weeks. After introducing myself and explaining what I had learned so far, he began.

"My personal evolution into all of this started long ago, in 1988. I was a pediatrician and counseled adolescents on the ills of marijuana, but in September of 2013 I became the Executive Director of CDPHE, so I have had to rethink things a bit. You're familiar with the history of Colorado's medical marijuana program, right?"

"I'm fairly familiar with it," I responded.

"Well, we've had a medical marijuana program since 2000, but it really got a kickstart in 2008 or 2009. That's when the Attor-

ney General said, 'We'll leave you alone, go forth and multiply.'"
He raised both arms spread wide, as if to indicate the growth of
the medical marijuana market. "The number of dispensaries that
opened, and the number of Red Cards that we handed out grew
significantly. We have that data on our website but you'll never
find it. Our website is complex," he stated with frustration. "Let
me know if you can't find it and I'll send you that data."

"I think I have the information. It was something like five
thousand Red Card patients in 2009 and then over a hundred
thousand by 2011."

"Yes!" he exclaimed. "Just exceptional growth since the memo."

"But there's really nothing you can do about that, if I understand your role correctly, is there?"

"Correct. Our role is basically to manage the registry, the
application for Red Cards, and physician records. We don't have
any enforcement capability."

"But obviously," I stated, "You have the ability to influence, like
with the caregiver bill."

"Yes, we worked with legislators to help craft that bill. The language of the original caregiver term prevented those kids who
needed help, and the caregiver bill is a step in the right direction."

"So, what has been the transformation for you personally, that
you mentioned earlier, from pediatrician basically opposed to
marijuana, to your role now with significant responsibility?"

"I did what you would do: the first month I looked at all of
our data. We have boxes and boxes of data and I had them all
brought up here to my office and I looked through each one. I
really wanted to understand what's going on. Calling marijuana
'medicine' is incorrect. Yes, there is precedent that some plants
are medicine, that plants have medicinal value, but with marijuana it hasn't been proven yet. It's mostly anecdotal."

"And by anecdotal you mean...?" I clarified.

"I mean that we don't have pharmaceutical-based scientific
evidence to establish marijuana as a medicine. The criteria for

marijuana, in terms of dosage, amount of active components like THC and CBD, are not stated. We don't have any information based on controlled, double-blind studies."

"Are you saying that marijuana is not medicine?"

"It's not a matter of whether I believe that marijuana is a medicine, it is a matter of Colorado's State Constitution stipulating that it is. It's not about the practice of medicine, but the regulation of it. What I am really seeking is parity for marijuana. I want the same rules that we have for other medicines to apply to marijuana, and to do that we need to have scientific-based research."

"Would you be surprised if marijuana was in fact a medicine?"

"Not at all. It's heterogeneous. Not the plant, but you can characterize the plant components like THC and CBD. We already have medicinal marijuana, synthetic extractions with one hundred percent THC like Rubinol and Marinol. But we can't get parity for marijuana, we can't hold it to the same standards as medicine. I would like to be able to take the plant and figure out the active ingredients in terms of potency, dosage, and side effects, but the State Constitution dictates to us the standard dose."

"I don't know if people understand that you're trying to take a scientific approach to medical marijuana," I stated. "I first became familiar with you at the September Board of Health meeting and frankly, I was ready to write an article, 'Colorado Board of Health Proposes Genocide.'"

"Ugh," he groaned as he leaned back in his chair and grimaced. "We knew it was going to be like that, and I told the Board to prepare for it, but you saw what happened."

"Yeah, I did. And it surprised me, especially when Jason raised his hands above his head and mentioned going to jail."

He shook his head. "It's always the same every time we have a meeting having anything to do with medical marijuana, or caregivers. They come out in full force with kids in wheelchairs, people from rural communities who say that we're trying to shut them down and will harm their patients and communities."

He shifted in his chair and asked, "Are you familiar with the Stanley brothers?"

"Aren't those the guys down in Colorado Springs who have developed a Charlotte's Web?" ("Charlotte's Web" is a strain of high CBD, low THC hemp oil used in the treatment of childhood epilepsy, and can be in a 24:1 CBD:THC ratio.)

"Yeah. Have you seen their interview with Diane Sawyer? You should watch that."

"Whoopie Goldberg, I think."

"Yes, that's right. If you haven't seen that you should watch it. They do an absolutely beautiful job of creating their position. You can't watch that without getting a tear in your eye. That's what we're up against every single meeting involving medical marijuana."

"The same thing is true with the pro-fracking crowd," I responded. "They always have a commercial showing a beautiful farm with green grass and a rabbit and lamb playing with each other, but they never show the 30-foot structures and all the trucks driving back and forth and the noise and—"

"Yes," he broke in, "it's just like that. It's the same thing with medical marijuana. The activists know what they're doing, and they bring out the propaganda…and it works. My question has always been, we only hear about the kids who respond to the medicine, not those that don't. And we don't hear about purity. As a Health Department, we know that every medicine has positives and negatives, but with marijuana we never hear about the negatives.

"The other thing," he continued, "it was very clever to have a Constitutional Amendment focused on plant count. How much marijuana can you get from one plant? We don't know. You can get an ounce or a pound from a plant," he stated as he shrugged his shoulders. "We have no idea what the actual yields are, how much actual marijuana is out there. That was clever."

"Along those same lines," I continued, "in terms of clever approaches, there's an argument from the pro-marijuana crowd that no one has ever overdosed on marijuana—"

"That's true, to my knowledge," he interjected.

"And that alcohol is far worse than marijuana in terms of negative health effects and social costs. What is your thinking on that?"

"It's tough to answer that because we haven't done the research that allows a true comparison. If you compare alcohol and marijuana equally, what does that mean? One glass of wine compares to, what, 100 mg of THC? The dosage and the purity make a difference for marijuana, in terms of potency and effect, and we haven't been able to do that research yet. There is a lot of data that we're missing. I've been looking at the DUI data and right now we have five or six roadside tests that we're working through in the pilot phase. The problem is that, historically, when a law enforcement officer pulled someone over the first test they did was for alcohol sobriety, and if that was positive they stopped testing for other substances. They even stopped testing if it wasn't positive. So, we don't have any historical data on driving under the influence of marijuana. We'll get that data, but it will take a couple of years."

"One of the things I'm interested in, now that marijuana has been legal for eighteen months, are some of the negative, or unintended consequences of legalizing," I stated. "Has anything cropped up that you didn't expect?"

"Yes. We did an interim survey on kids and marijuana use and we found that there is no change in either marijuana use, in terms of frequency, or in the amount that kids are using. In fact, the numbers are down a little bit for adolescent use. And who knows? Adolescents are testing limits, that's what it means to be an adolescent and now that marijuana is legal, we might see marijuana use go down."

"I heard Frank McNulty speak at a panel discussion last fall and he stated that since legalization of marijuana our numbers for homelessness have increased dramatically, that we are now the preferred place for homeless people to live. Do you know anything about that, or know if that's true?"

Larry waves his hand and thought for a moment before answering. "With homelessness...there's lots of other factors besides legalizing marijuana that can lead to an increase. I would be surprised if marijuana alone was the only factor contributing to homelessness. But you know, as a sociologist, just how difficult it is to understand the dynamics of that population. It's hard to do a census on them."

"Well, Frank mentioned some sort of survey that had documented that but when I asked him for the data he couldn't track it down. I'll probably just talk to the homeless shelters and see what they have to say."

"Yeah, that will work."

"I only have a couple more questions," I stated. "What surprised you most about the cannabis industry and how it has played out so far?"

"The edibles piece is huge," he exclaimed, with renewed enthusiasm. "There was a lot of carelessness on their part, in terms of packaging. We remedied that, but they're still creating products that appeal to kids and by kids, I mean two, three, four-year olds. The other thing is that, now that they have a foothold, the marketing and revenue side of the industry is taking over. It's big business, with a lot of money."

"If you had a blank slate and could start all over again, what would you do differently, if anything?"

"I'm much more comfortable with the recreational market versus the medical market. I believe that it is the right of the individual to choose, it is their freedom to choose whether or not to use marijuana. We should really treat this like cigarettes: we inform people, we educate people, but we let them make their own decision. There is nothing in the medical literature that says marijuana is a medical necessity and by starting with medical marijuana we created a lot of problems. The whole caregiver market…there's just so much opportunity for abuse and misuse.

Even in the physician-patient relationship there is opportunity for abuse and misuse. There are probably three thousand doctors in Colorado and 99 percent are like me. We occasionally have a patient for whom marijuana makes sense and we recommend that to them. There are another hundred or so people that recommend marijuana to lots of their patients, like the people you've spoken to in Boulder and Denver, but for them it is a spiritual belief as well as a medical belief. They believe fundamentally in the healing properties of the plant. I have no problem with that second group of people. And then there's a third group of physicians, probably not more than twenty-five or thirty people, who are basically recommending marijuana to anyone that will pay them $250 for a Red Card. I have a big problem with that group since they're not seeing the patients after they recommend medical marijuana and they are just making money. They're not focused on the well-being of the patient."

"Anything else?" I asked.

"One thing," he continued. "You don't realize how important the FDA is until you don't have them. For us, in Colorado, we have cannabis legal at the State level and it still remains illegal at the Federal level. You don't appreciate the protection of Federal regulations until you do what we're doing, which is to start from scratch and create all of our own regulations, testing requirements, dosage, purity levels, packaging. It's a lot of things to think about, a lot of things to get done in a short time, and we don't have any help or guidance from a Federal level. This is truly a cottage industry and we are pioneers in regulating it."

Notes to Chapter Seven

[1] The following is based on an electronic recording of the Hearing. All conversations are verbatim responses by participants of that public forum.

CHAPTER 8.

THE RHETORIC OF MARIJUANA

People have strong opinions about marijuana legalization. I have yet to speak with someone who says, "I'm mostly opposed to marijuana legalization," or "I'm partially in favor of it." No, there is very little ambivalence about marijuana legalization and the lines are drawn between advocates and opponents. Advocates typically have an intimate experience with cannabis—they use it, they grow it, they cook with it, they share it with friends, they subscribe to magazines devoted to cannabis and participate in online forums and discussions. They are part of the cannabis culture. Opponents, on the other hand, are largely clueless about cannabis culture, and they are not users and typically, don't know all that much about the plant, its effects, or the experience. Opponents are therefore more susceptible to the rhetoric and propaganda surrounding cannabis since they have no logical way to refute anything they see and hear.

The general ignorance about cannabis by non-users became apparent to me when I spoke with a Commissioner of the San Diego Superior Court about similarities and differences between California and Colorado from a law enforcement perspective. Initially, I contacted the Commissioner to determine if marijuana arrests were a profit center for law enforcement, if the mere arrest of someone for possession increased revenues for a jurisdiction, through fines, for example, but we ended up speaking more broadly about cannabis.

"I would be *shocked* if marijuana was a revenue maker for the courts," she stated, with an emphasis on the word *shocked*. "If you get arrested for marijuana possession, or intent to sell, you're not entitled to a court appointed lawyer, the tax payer doesn't pay for that."

"But," I asked, "if the person charged with either possession or intent to distribute marijuana is not entitled to a court appointed attorney, wouldn't they have to pay for an attorney themselves?"

"They rarely hire an attorney," she stated, "they almost always represent themselves. There is really no revenue for law enforcement or the DEA for a marijuana arrest, and in California, possession of marijuana is an infraction. So, for a lot of these people, it's no big deal. They don't go to prison for marijuana possession."

"Ok," I responded, "What do you know about marijuana legalization in Colorado?"

"Well, we're all watching it very carefully. I know there are a lot of drug cartels coming to Colorado."

That's news to me! I have been following nearly all that's been written about marijuana and Colorado for the past two years and I can't recall one article stating that drug cartels are *coming* to Colorado. In fact, Brian Vicente, author of Amendment 64 and a leading marijuana reform activist, told me in an interview that "the cartels have a much lesser role now, they've moved underground." But it is an important point: what has happened to the black market since Colorado legalized marijuana? I address this issue later in the book.

"Do you see a lot of marijuana-related cases in your court?"

"It's rare that I see someone who is only using marijuana, they're always using other drugs. Everybody knows that marijuana is a gateway drug. The cops are not looking for marijuana, but usually somebody gets caught for doing something else—stealing a bike, shoplifting, fighting on the beach, a traffic violation—and they have marijuana on them. I never see a 60-year-old on a marijuana charge. Everyone I see in this court is always in their twenties. All these people using marijuana are young."

"It seems like you're against legalization, is that true?"

"Yes. I think all drugs should be illegal. If you legalize them then everyone will use them, and that's bad for society. They say that marijuana use is a victimless crime, but there's never a victimless crime. These people are stealing to get the money to get drugs, or they're having health problems, and that costs the taxpayer."

"Well," I stated, "marijuana is legal here in Colorado and I don't use it, and neither does my wife, or our neighbors, or the people at our church. I don't think everyone will use drugs because they're legal."

"If we lowered the drinking age to eighteen, don't you think more people would try it?" she asked me.

"Maybe," I responded, "but I don't think it's all too difficult for an eighteen year-old kid to get his or her hands on alcohol now, is it?"

"Are you saying 'Hey, let's make cocaine legal and then educate kids about that?'"

"I don't know anything about drugs like cocaine or heroin, or meth. But I do know that here in Colorado we haven't seen a situation where everyone is using marijuana now because it's legal."

COMMON BELIEFS ABOUT CANNABIS

There are four ideas expressed in my conversation with the Commissioner that are commonplace for most Americans and that are part of the rhetoric surrounding cannabis:

1. The idea of a "gateway theory" in which marijuana use leads

to more dangerous drugs like heroin, cocaine, and methamphetamine;

2. The belief that marijuana users are primarily young;

3. The idea that there is a strong link between marijuana use and crime, and

4. The idea that by legalizing cannabis, demand for the drug will increase dramatically ("if you make it legal, everyone will do it").

Although I am primarily interested in the social and economic changes in Colorado after cannabis legalization, these general perceptions about marijuana expressed in the conversation with the Commissioner of San Diego Court are important. What are the facts and myths of the cannabis plant?

THE GATEWAY HYPOTHESIS

The "Gateway Hypothesis" has been a part of the American discourse on drug prohibition since at least 1951, when Congress sought to change mandatory sentencing laws for narcotics violations. In 1937, when the Marihuana Tax Act became law, people received five years and / or a fine of $2000 for violating each provision of the law. But by 1951, in response to a spike in heroin use, Congressman Hale Boggs (D-LA) argued that the increase in heroin use resulted from mild sentencing. Representative Boggs suggested increasing prison terms to 2-5 years for a first offense, 5-10 years for a second offense, and 10-20 years for a third offense. Many members in Congress believed in a direct, causal link between marijuana and heroin use, believing that marijuana was the stepping stone to heroin. Henry Anslinger, first Commissioner of the U.S. Treasury Department Federal Bureau of Narcotics, testified before the committee stating, "Over 50 percent of those young addicts started on marihuana smoking. They started there and graduated to heroin; they took the needle when the thrill of marihuana was gone." [1]

What Congress didn't pay attention to were landmark studies contradicting Anslinger's testimony. In 1944, New York Mayor Fiorello LaGuardia asked the New York Academy of Medicine to conduct a study of marijuana use in the city. The resulting report found that smoking marijuana did not lead to addiction in the medical sense of the word. Additionally, the researchers concluded that the use of marijuana did not lead to morphine or heroin or cocaine addiction, that marijuana was not the determining factor in the commission of major crimes, that marihuana smoking was not widespread among school children, and that juvenile delinquency was not associated with the practice of smoking marihuana.

Yet, since the 1950's the Federal government, along with a vast majority of the American public, have subscribed to the view that marijuana is a "stepping stone" to harder drugs and it is a dominant ideology that is espoused today. For example, during the 2016 presidential election campaign candidates made the following remarks:

Ben Carson: *"Marijuana is what's known as a gateway drug. It tends to be a starter drug for people who move onto heavier duty drugs -- sometimes legal, sometimes illegal -- and I don't think this is something that we really want for our society."*

Chris Christie: *"Marijuana is a gateway drug. We have an enormous addiction problem in this country. You want to elect somebody else who's willing to legalize marijuana and expose our children to that gateway drug and the effects it has on their brain?"*

Hillary Clinton: *"I think the Feds should be attuned to the way marijuana is still used as a gateway drug."*

Martin O'Malley: *"I've seen what drug addiction has done to the people of our state, the people of our city. And I also know that this drug and its use and its abuse can be a gateway to even more harmful behavior."*

Scott Walker: *"I oppose legalizing marijuana use... It's a gateway drug."*

This confidence in the "gateway hypothesis" by politicians and others is most assuredly unwarranted since even the best researchers in the world, spanning forty years of work, do not agree that marijuana is the "gateway drug" to hard illicit drugs like heroin and cocaine. Serious scholarship on a causal link between marijuana and other drugs like heroin and cocaine was first investigated in a seminal article by Kandel (1975) in which she postulated that there are developmental stages to drug use. "I find that drug use does not begin *de novo* with marihuana, but with legal drugs: beer or wine at first, and cigarettes or hard liquor subsequently" (Kandel, pg. 912). Kandel based her conclusion on two longitudinal surveys of randomly chosen high school students (N=5468) in eighteen schools in New York. "Drug use starts with legal drugs, which are a necessary stage between nonuse and illegal drug use. A direct progression from nonuse to illegal drug use practically never occurs" (Kandel, pg. 913).

Despite the conclusion that adolescents progress from beer and wine, to cigarettes, to marijuana, and then to heroin or cocaine, she notes in a commentary on Ferguson et.al., "While the initial formulation (of my work) emphasized the full developmental spectrum of drug involvement, ranging from drugs that are legally available for adults, such as tobacco or alcohol, to the most serious illicit drugs, such as heroin, the Gateway Hypothesis has been invoked subsequently most often in the link between the use of marijuana (cannabis) and subsequent use of other illicit drugs." That is, researchers, policy makers, and the general public ignored the full spectrum of developmental drug use and focused solely on the link between cannabis and other illicit drugs. [2]

Kandel further notes, "In the absence of experimental manipulation, the search for ultimate causes in the development and maintenance of human drug-use behavior is elusive. We believe that the next great advance in understanding the Gateway Hypothesis will be made through collaboration between epidemiologists, behavioral pharmacologists and molecular biologists" (Kandel, 2006, pg. 471). Toward that end Kandel conducted an investigation with Nobel Prize-winning neurologist Eric Kandel, using laboratory mice to test whether use of one substance (e.g. nicotine) "primes the organism for use of another substance (e.g. cocaine)" (Op. cit. pg 471). With mice, of course, the competing explanations of interaction with drug-using subcultures, or interactions with drug dealers, are irrelevant and the researcher can focus on the biological and pharmacological impact of the drug. Kandel and Kandel found that nicotine is the gateway to illicit drugs like cocaine, not cannabis (Kandel and Kandel, 2014).

Is cannabis a "gateway" drug or a convenient ideology held by uniformed people? Sophisticated research over the past forty years has not confirmed that cannabis is a gateway drug, and the controlled experimental animal research by Kandel and Kandel (2014) suggests that nicotine may be more influential as a gateway drug than cannabis. Moreover, Kandel's original research from 1975 strongly suggested a developmental pathway that started first with legal substances like beer, wine, or cigarettes, followed by cannabis, and then other illicit drugs like heroin or cocaine. But beer, wine, and cigarettes are never invoked in the "gateway hypothesis," only cannabis. Beer and wine, and to some extent cigarettes, are legitimized, consumed in public with no moral outrage, and with no backlash or repercussions to the consumer. People drink alcohol at sporting events, at the intermission of a symphony concert or other performances, in front of their children, at family gatherings, and in a wide range of public venues. In short, beer and wine are legitimized and institutionalized in American society, and as a society we accept both the right of others to use those substances and the consequences of the misuse of them as well.

Alcohol and tobacco are also mature, enormously profitable industries. According to Wharton School Professor Jeremey Siegel, a dollar invested in 1900 in an average industry would yield about $38,000 in 2006. That same dollar invested in the food sector would generate over $700,000 over the same time span. But a dollar invested in the tobacco industry would return over $6.3 million dollars. [3] The legitimacy and institutionalization of the alcohol and tobacco industries, along with the vast resources accumulated over decades, provides companies within these industries opportunities to shape—even control—policies and regulations in their favor, opportunities that have been denied the cannabis industry for nearly eighty years. As sociologist James Coleman stated in the forward to Edward Laumann and David Knoke's *The Organizational State* (1987), "There are actors that shape (political) events, but the actors are not persons at all. They are corporate actors: firms, trade associations, federal agencies, trade unions and professional associations, and others. These actors do not represent *persons;* they represent *interests"* (1987; xiii).

Within the cannabis industry there are only a few trade associations and they are small and nascent: NORML (National Organization for the Reform of Marijuana Laws) founded in 1970; the Marijuana Policy Project founded in 1995; the Drug Policy Alliance founded in 2000; the National Cannabis Industry Association, founded in 2010. As these organizations mature and gain traction they will be able to influence policy and perhaps work to alter the image and the common perception of marijuana as a "gateway" drug. But for the past 80 years the legitimate industries of alcohol and tobacco have been able to shape and control the ideology of American drug use in their favor, while the cannabis industry has been omitted from participation in any policy-level discussions and decisions.

AGE AND MARIJUANA USE

A second common perception is that marijuana users are predominantly young but surprisingly, it is difficult to determine the age of marijuana users. In the past, the primary way to understand the age of marijuana users was to present a survey and have the respondent answer a question like "Have you ever used marijuana?" and then tally the responses by age. But even with a guarantee of confidentiality and anonymity, those answers are unreliable because they involve self-report, and there is no reliable way for the researcher to ascertain whether the respondent gave a truthful response (Lewontin, 1995). Further, since marijuana is an illegal substance one could imagine the task of determining the age of users to be even more daunting than that of other, legal behaviors.

In Colorado, of course, since marijuana is legal it's easier to gauge the age of cannabis users and one has to merely go to one of the two hundred legal dispensaries and see what customers show up. If you were to do that, as I have, you would find that customers are not predominantly young, but range in age from across the age spectrum, as Eric told me when he said, "It's everybody."

Eric's response of "everybody" is not a new perspective on marijuana users. In 1972 a highly regarded but largely ignored report by the National Commission on Marijuana and Drug Abuse, referred to as the "Shafer Commission" after its Chairman former Republican Pennsylvania Governor Raymond P. Shafer, concluded that contemporary marijuana use is pervasive. Marijuana use occurs in all segments of the population, across all races, religions, socioeconomic groups and occupations. There is slightly higher use among wealthier and better-educated users, but nearly equal proportions of use in males and females in younger populations. In short, the Shafer Commission states, "No valid stereotype of a marijuana user or non-user can be drawn" (1972:36).

The Colorado Department of Health and Environment tracks age and gender within the medical marijuana market through patient registrations and in 2009 the average age of males was 40 and for females, 43. By 2015 the average age of men was 41.2 and 44.9 for women, and in 2018, the average ages were 43 for men and 46 for women, hardly what anyone would consider "young."[4] Over the last forty-five years, starting with the well-documented findings of the Shafer Commission and continuing to the present, cannabis users defy categorization.

CRIME AND MARIJUANA

Perhaps the most strongly held belief about cannabis, and all illicit drugs, is that drug use increases crime. For instance, Nancy Grace, a legal commentator, television host, television journalist and former prosecutor Tweeted after Colorado legalized marijuana, "I guess I should say congrats Colorado, b/c/you're setting yourselves up for one of the biggest crime waves you've ever seen! #PotShortage." And President Donald Trump along the same vein stated at the 2015 Conservative Political Action Conference, "They've got a lot of problems going on right now in Colorado, some big problems."

But, according to drug policy expert and Harvard economist Jeffrey Miron, drug use does not increase crime, prohibition does. "Prohibition causes most ills typically attributed to drugs, and prohibition's ability to reduce drug use is modest" (2003:1). The "ills" of prohibition are well-documented by Miron (2003), including that because of prohibition, black market participants can't use the legal or justice system and disputes are typically solved through violence; that prices of illicit drugs are higher under prohibition and consequently theft, prostitution, and other illegal money-generating activities are engaged in by consumers; that corruption by law enforcement, prosecutors and judges is fostered (ACLU – Texas, 2003); and that significant wealth ($21 billion in 2003) is transferred to criminals. In addition, operators in the black market evade government taxes (income tax, social security tax, excise taxes), government regulations, environmental laws, employment discrimination laws, child-labor laws, antitrust laws, occupational health and safety laws, and avoid the scrutiny of watchdog groups such as consumer and employee advocates for quality and safety.

The idea behind prohibition is that drug use encourages crime and violence and if societal drug use is reduced, there will be a corresponding drop in crime and violence. There is ample evidence that drug use and criminal activity are highly correlated and extensive research to document that association. According to the Center on Addiction and Substance Abuse at Columbia University, alcohol or drugs are implicated in an estimated 80% of offenses leading to incarceration in the United States such as domestic violence, driving while under the influence, property offenses, drug offenses, and public-order offenses (1998). But the causal link between drug use and crime, like the gateway hypothesis, is difficult to prove. As Miron (2003) notes, "The fact that many criminals are also drug users shows merely that drug use is correlated with criminal behavior. The methodology used in these analyses would also demonstrate that consumption of fast food or wearing blue jeans cause criminal behavior" (2003:14).

Moreover, alcohol and drugs are often used interchangeably as leading to criminal behavior, but alcohol and drugs impact people in vastly different ways. Researchers Valdez, Kaplan, and Curtis (2007) conclude, "Studies have found that alcohol is consistently linked to aggressive and violent behavior. In contrast, research on drug use and violence generally concludes, contrary to popular conceptions, that these relationships are unsystematic and / or weak" (pg. 595). Similarly, Fagan (1993) concludes that "several reviewers have concluded that alcohol is the substance most likely to lead to psychopharmacological violence," although "there is some evidence that cocaine, barbiturates, amphetamines, phencyclidine (PCP), and steroids also have psychopharmacological properties that can motive violence" (1993: 68).

Beyond the individual response to alcohol, drugs and the roles of these substances in criminal behavior, empirical evidence suggests that enforcement of drug laws has a direct impact on increasing criminal activities, not the use of alcohol or illicit drugs. Several studies are noteworthy here. First, Miron (2003) studied the relation between homicide and the enforcement of alcohol and drug prohibition laws over the past century in the United States and also that same relationship (homicide and prohibition enforcement) in countries other than the United States. Controlling for factors such as the age composition of the population, the incarceration rate, the use of the death penalty, per capita income, the unemployment rate, support for marijuana legalization, or gun ownership, he found that in both cases "the evidence provides no indication that prohibition reduces violence; in fact, enforcement is consistently associated with higher rates of violence" (2003:43). Further, the estimated impact of enforcement on homicide suggests that eliminating drug prohibition would reduce homicide in the United States by 25-75 percent (Miron, 2003: 51).

A second set of studies have concluded that drug arrests, and marijuana arrests in particular, do not lower criminal activity but may actually increase crime (Harcourt and Ludwig, 2007). These researchers looked specifically at the New York City Police Department and its vigorous enforcement of laws prohibiting smoking marijuana in public. They state, "In 1993, the year before broken-windows policing was implemented, a New York City police precinct made, on average, 10 arrests per year for smoking marijuana in public; by 2000, the police precincts were averaging 644 arrests per year—almost two arrests per day per precinct" (Harcourt, 2006:1).

This incredible increase in enforcement of smoking marijuana in public resulted from the "broken windows" theory of policing implemented by the New York City Police Department in 1994. The Broken Windows theory is the idea that strict police enforcement of relatively benign social disorders—graffiti, loitering, vandalism, public drinking—creates an atmosphere of lawfulness, preventing more serious crimes from happening (Wilson and Kelling, 1982). As carried out by the New York City Police Department, the policy mostly targeted African-Americans and Hispanics disproportionately for both their use of marijuana and their representation in the resident population. "Although both groups (African Americans and Hispanics) each represent about 25 percent of New York City residents, they compose 52 and 32 percent of smoking marijuana in public arrests, and they fare worse in the criminal justice system: they were more likely than their white counterparts to be detained before arraignment (2.66 and 1.85 times more likely, respectively), convicted (both twice as likely) and sentenced to additional jail time (4 and 3 times more likely, respectively)" (Harcourt, 2006:2).

Studies in other parts of the United States confirm that police enforcement of drug crimes increases other crimes. Classifying crimes into Index I crimes—murder, forcible rape, aggravated assault, robbery, burglary, larceny, and motor vehicle theft—and Index II crimes (all crimes except Index I offenses and minor traffic violations, including simple assault, narcotics, vandalism, vice, fraud, and major traffic violations), Benson analyzed enforcement and crime in Florida and found that for every ten additional drug arrests there were an additional seven Index I (violent and property) crimes (2001).

And an analysis by Shepard and Blackely of New York state law enforcement tactics found that rising numbers of drug arrests resulted in a significant increase in assaults, robberies, burglaries, and larcenies. They report that a 10% increase in marijuana sales arrests was accompanied by an additional 800 larcenies in the state (2005). In short, the empirical evidence on crime and drug use, both historically, by looking at alcohol prohibition, and more recently, by analyzing drug prohibition, points to increased police enforcement as a major driver of increased violent and property crimes. As Benson states, "Given the reality of scarce police resources, getting "tough" on drug crime meant getting soft on Index I crime, and getting softer on drug crime apparently allowed police to get tougher on Index I crime" (2001:97).

Of course, all these studies analyzing the impact of police enforcement policies on crime were conducted under a regime of prohibition for cannabis and other illicit drugs, but what has happened in Colorado with respect to crime, since cannabis has been legalized? Is Colorado experiencing the "biggest crime wave ever!?" and is the state dealing with "big problems?" The clear-cut start date for marijuana legalization in Colorado, January 1, 2014, allows us to make comparisons of crime activity in Denver and Colorado across prohibition and legal regimes.

According to the Denver Police Uniform Crime Report, between 2013 and 2014 the following changes took place: burglaries declined 10 percent, robberies declined 3 percent, and burglaries at a licensed marijuana facility decreased 20 percent. Driving under the influence of drugs (DUID) was not tracked before 2014, but in 2014 there were 5,546 total driving under the influence violations, and marijuana-only violations totaled 354, or 6 percent. In the state of Colorado, according to the Colorado Bureau of Investigation, vehicle thefts increased 1 percent, but homicides decreased by 12.8 percent, robbery by 3.7 percent, and burglary by 6.6 percent. So much for the "biggest crime wave ever."

And about those "big problems" that President Donald Trump mentioned? Colorado does have some big ones. It is ranked first nationally in the following categories:

- "Best State for Labor Supply" (*Forbes*),

- "Fastest Growing Economy" (*Business Insider*),
- "Most Economically Competitive State" (*Business Insider*),
- "Denver: Best City for Job Seekers" (*Forbes*),
- "Denver: America's Best Place to do Business" (*Forbes*),
- "Denver: U.S. City Most Popular to Move to" (*Pew Research*),
- "Lowest Monthly Energy Cost" (*WallHub*),
- "Boulder: Strongest Housing Market" (*MSN Real Estate*).

Colorado ranked second nationally in another seven categories, including best place to start a business, best state for entrepreneurship and innovation, and most highly educated state. The popular perception that legalizing marijuana will lead to a dramatic increase in crime is not supported by academic research nor by the actual crime statistics over prohibited and legalized regimes in Colorado. In fact, it is just the opposite: crime *decreases* when cannabis is legalized.

EVERYONE'S SMOKING POT

Finally, there's a strong belief by a lot of people that legalizing marijuana will lead to a vast increase in consumption and that "everyone will be doing it." Even though my personal experience with cannabis didn't change after legalization, maybe I'm the outlier—the only person in the state who hasn't taken up cannabis consumption. The empirical evidence points to flat demand, however, which means that my experience of not starting a cannabis habit is shared by a lot of Colorado residents. It is also well-known by regulators and marijuana policy experts that demand for cannabis is flat. Andrew Freedman, Director of Marijuana Enforcement in Colorado stated, on the issue of demand, "Everybody who was using marijuana before is using it now and we see no increase in demand." And Governor Hickenlooper said essentially the same thing, "Everybody who was using before is still using, and everybody who was not using before is still not using. Within the industry," he said to me with a wry smile on his face, "it's a fight for market share."

The demand study, commissioned by the Colorado Department of Revenue, states that there are 485,000 adult regular marijuana users who consume marijuana at least once a month, about nine percent of the total state population. Also, 201,000 people report at least one use in the past year, which is 3.8 percent of the state population (2014:2). However, controlling for age of consumer, the Marijuana Policy Group states that, "23 percent of marijuana users claim to consume marijuana near daily (26-31 times per month), compared to 17 percent in the United States overall. Colorado has a larger share of users (that consume high amounts of marijuana) compared to the national average and a smaller share of users (whom consume less marijuana)" (Op. Cit.:12). Additionally the majority of marijuana demand emanates from the regular users—and in particular from the heavy users who consume marijuana on a "near-daily basis" and this group (21.8 percent of users) account for 66.9 percent of the demand. Rare users—the nearly 80 percent of people consuming less than once a month—account for just 0.3 percent of total demand. The legal cannabis market is driven in large part by the heavy users.

Visitors to Colorado are another story. The Marijuana Policy Group found that visitors to Colorado accounted for 44 percent of Denver metro retail sales and 90 percent of retail sales in heavily visited mountain communities such as Crested Butte, Telluride, and the towns near Breckenridge in Summit County, home to four world-class ski resorts, Keystone, Arapahoe Basin, Copper Mountain, and Breckenridge. Not only are visitors driving most of the demand in the mountain communities, but they're paying much higher prices: 50-100 percent higher, most notably in small quantity purchases. For example, a gram of cannabis in the Denver metro area will cost $7 while a gram of the exact same strain will cost $14 in the mountain communities. The impact of tourism is felt state-wide and the Colorado Tourism Office, in a release of several reports, showed that a record 71.3 million visitors spent $18.6 billion in Colorado in 2014, generating $1.1 billion in state and local taxes. However, the Tourism Office did not attribute any of the record-setting growth to marijuana and Al White, director of the Colorado Tourism Office, stated, "This isn't about marijuana, this is because we are doing a good job in Colorado. Is marijuana beneficial? Marginally, yes, I think it may be a decision influencer for some people coming."

In a poll of visitors conducted by the Tourism Office about whether marijuana played a role in their decision to vacation in Colorado, sixty-five percent said marijuana didn't make a difference, while 16 percent said they were more likely to visit because of legal marijuana, and 18 percent said they were less likely to visit. "So it's a double-edged sword," said White. "We have had records for the last four years in a row, and three years of those marijuana wasn't even legal. It may be a modest benefit to us, but it is not the reason we are seeing great records." So, it's not the case that "everybody in Colorado is smoking pot," as some would believe, but maybe everybody who smokes pot is coming to Colorado.

The technical report by the Marijuana Policy Group, as precise as it is, misses a key demographic for marijuana use, people under 21 years of age. By design, the researchers only conducted the survey on marijuana demand for persons age twenty-one and older, the people who can legally purchase and use marijuana. But one of the major concerns about legalizing marijuana is that it will be diverted to adolescents, a group for whom marijuana is still illegal. To understand this demographic, the Colorado Department of Health and Environment conducts a biannual survey of high school and middle school students, the *Healthy*

Kids Colorado Survey, about a range of attitudes and behaviors concerning their health, including several questions about marijuana use.

Two questions in particular are also asked by the *Youth Risk Behavior Survey*, a national assessment, which provides a comparison between cannabis use in states where it is legal and in states in which it remains illegal. That is, one can determine to some degree if marijuana legalization impacts use for adolescents. One question asked students, "During your life, how many times have you used marijuana?" and the possible responses range from "0 times" to "100 or more times." A second question asked, "During the past 30 days, how many times did you use marijuana?" but in this case the possible responses range from "0 times" to "40 or more times." The first question is referred to as the "lifetime use" question and the second question, the "current use" question.

Contrary to the expectations of opponents to legalization, the responses by Colorado students are 4 points lower than the national average for both questions. The percentage of Colorado students who have ever used marijuana is 36.9 percent (versus 40.7 percent nationally) and the percent who have used marijuana in the past month is 19.7 percent (versus 23.4 percent nationally). This is not to imply that the differences are statistically significant, but the percentages are in the opposite direction of what many had predicted: there has not been a dramatic increase in adolescence use of marijuana since marijuana was legalized, but a reversal, with lower usage among adolescents within Colorado. One other telling question asked by the Colorado Department of Health and Environment in the *Healthy Kids Colorado Survey* was "If you wanted to get some marijuana, how easy would it be for you to get some?" and the responses provided were "very hard, sort of hard, sort of easy, very easy." Nearly 55 percent of the students (54.9%) responded that it was "sort of easy" or "very easy" to obtain marijuana.

The four beliefs raised by the San Diego Commissioner are just that—beliefs, but they are common and widespread, especially among the people who are not cannabis users. Without actual experience, without knowledge of the research undertaken, we are left with more rhetoric than reality on cannabis and the impact that legalization might have on society. Is cannabis a gateway drug? No one knows for sure, but research indicates that nicotine is most likely the gateway to illicit drugs. Are cannabis users young? In the medical marijuana registry in Colorado they average 43 and 46 years old for men and women respectively. Does cannabis lead to violent crimes? The empirical evidence suggests that it doesn't, and the experience in Colorado so far is not a spike in crime, but a drop in nearly all of the major categories: homicides, burglary, and robbery. And finally, is everyone using cannabis now that it's legal? Clearly not, and even in Colorado it appears that roughly 20 percent of the users, the heavy users, are making 80 percent of the purchases.

Notes to Chapter Eight

[1] This quote is found in Ernest Abel's *Marihuana: The First Twelve Thousand Years* and can be accessed in its entirety here: http://druglibrary.org/schaffer/hemp/history/first12000/abel.htm

[2] In the commentary of *Addiction* (101, 470:476, 2006) the world's leading researchers on drugs weighed in on an important article by David M. Fergusson, Joseph M. Bowen and John Horwood in which they claimed that marijuana is the gateway drug. That causal link between cannabis and other illicit drugs is difficult to prove and requires, at a minimum, establishing a fixed sequence of use between substances and an increased propensity

to use a second drug having initiated a first one. Beyond that, the issue of self-selection to use cannabis or other illicit drugs would need to be controlled, as would age, since researchers have found that neurobiological changes that are age-dependent impact an individual's likelihood to experiment with drugs such as alcohol, tobacco, and marijuana (Dahl, et. al. 2004).

Notes Hall (2006), "One of the most robust findings in adolescent drug use over the past 30 years has been that almost all adolescents who have tried cocaine and heroin first used alcohol, tobacco and cannabis, and the more regularly adolescents use cannabis, and the earlier the age at which they begin, the more likely they are to use other illicit drugs" (2006, pg. 472).

Noted researcher MacCoun, commenting on the same Ferguson et. al. research, highlights the complexity of the gateway hypothesis between cannabis and hard drug use. "On my scorecard, four candidates are still in the running: (1) a spurious association due to a common propensity for drug use, (2) a biochemical influence of cannabis on the propensity to use other drugs, (3) contact with hard drug-using subcultures or (4) contact with hard drug sellers" (2006, pg. 473).

[3] The full article can be accessed here: http://www.fool.com/investing/general/2015/02/13/the-extraordinary-story-of-americas-most-successfu.aspx

[4] Data on the history of the medical marijuana program, including patient counts, age, gender, condition, number of plants, and caregivers, can be found at https://www.colorado.gov/pacific/cdphe/medical-marijuana-statistics-and-data

CHAPTER 9.

OPPONENTS TO LEGALIZATION

When Colorado passed Amendment 64 in 2012 there was, understandably, considerable media attention focused on the first jurisdiction in the world to legalize the sale and possession of marijuana, and since that time there has been a steady stream of media attention—positive and negative—about Colorado's social "experiment." But the voters in 2012 didn't overwhelmingly pass Amendment 64. The margin was 55 percent in favor, 45 percent opposed. There is no shortage of opponents to marijuana legalization, but even so, I asked the people I interviewed—who are all intimately involved in the cannabis industry—"Who are the people opposed to legalization, do you know?" And they all had their list of ideas.

Representative Jonathan Singer: "Elements of law enforcement. The religious right in Colorado Springs. You know, the Focus on the Family people. Smart Colorado. Treatment providers, but they will tell you that there is a sampling bias. The substance abuse people would love to get rid of alcohol. That's the big problem."

Rav Ivker, M.D.: "Pharmaceuticals are highly threatened, and alcohol and tobacco. They're probably already feeling the effects."

Senator Pat Steadman: "Law enforcement. The religious conservatives, like down in Colorado Springs. People that worry about children."

Amendment 64 Author Christian Sederberg: "Most opposed to legal marijuana?" he confirmed. "Just follow the money trail. The private prison industry is against drug policy reform. They've been putting a lot of money into California to stop it there. Traditional law enforcement and the DEA are resistant to reform since their career is based on arresting users. Pharmaceuticals are opposed. Big tobacco could either be for it or against it, it's too early to tell," he stated with a shrug of his shoulders. "Alcohol producers will definitely fight it because marijuana is a substitute for alcohol. Addiction specialists will be opposed, but they see the worst of the worst, so they're biased. But, still, they're opposed."

Surprisingly, no one answered that the Federal government was opposed. But throughout the past 80 years—since 1937—the U.S. Government has pursued numerous policies to curtail the production of marijuana, educate youth on the perils of marijuana use, and incarcerate persons for the possession, manufacture, or distribution of the substance. The war on drugs—and that's not just semantics, it really is a war—is the longest war in the history of the United States and since Richard Nixon, every president has used local law enforcement, the Federal Bureau of Investigation, the Central Intelligence Agency, the military, the Drug Enforcement Agency, and the military and police forces of other nations to fight this war. And the U.S. Government has co-opted obscure, 200-year-old laws, like civil forfeiture, to apply in this long-running war. Additionally, the Supreme Court has upheld every challenge to the Constitution when it comes to drugs, especially marijuana. But how did the United States come to this point, to a point where the most innocent of infractions leads to a lifetime of imprisonment?

A SHORT HISTORY OF THE
WAR ON DRUGS

It is well-documented that the United States passed the Marihuana Tax Act in 1937, making illegal any and all aspects of
cannabis possession, manufacture, distribution, or use. But the
fascination with drugs in America started long before that. In
1804, German scientist Friedrich Serturner was the first person
to isolate an alkaloid from any plant when he extracted from
opium an alkaloid he termed "Morphium," after the Greek god of
dreams, "Morpheus." Morphium was so intoxicating that by the
1830's morphine was a staple in the home of nearly every American medicine chest, and at the end of the Civil War it was estimated that over 400,000 soldiers were addicted to morphine. In
fact, so common was morphine addiction that it was called the
"soldier's disease."

By 1875 opium addiction had increased dramatically, especially in California and, coinciding with a large immigration of
Chinese, San Francisco passed the first city ordinance against
possession or smoking of opium. A number of cities followed as
well with similar ordinances banning opium and morphine. By
1882 anti-Chinese sentiment was so great that Congress passed
the Chinese Exclusion Act, prohibiting Chinese laborers from
entering the United States for ten years. In retaliation, China
placed an embargo against American manufacturers. However,
by 1908 President Theodore Roosevelt sought to open up rela-
tions with the Chinese in order to sell to the Chinese market
and he orchestrated an international convention under the guise
that the United States would help China with its opium problem,
which was significant.

The only problem with Roosevelt's plan was that opium was
not illegal in the United States nor, in fact, were any drugs since
the United States Constitution makes no provision for the Federal government to regulate drugs. The only powers Congress

have are to regulate interstate commerce and impose taxes. But in 1914 Congress passed the Harrison Act, which became the framework for all future drug regulations and is still evident today, over one hundred years later. Congress decided that it was possible to regulate opiates by having pharmacists dispensing narcotics register with the Bureau of Internal Revenue and pay for a tax stamp. The Bureau of Narcotics was then created within the Bureau of Internal Revenue to oversee the tax collections, but zealous bureaucrats expanded the scope of the Narcotics bureau from oversight to enforcement.

By the time Harry Anslinger became Commissioner of the Bureau of Narcotics in 1930, the Bureau of Narcotics had orchestrated a public media campaign against marijuana, the remnants of which are still touted today. For example, newspaper articles started to proliferate detailing accounts that marijuana users were violent, that marijuana use caused people to become insane, that its use would lead to sexual promiscuity, and that schoolchildren were targeted by unscrupulous peddlers. In fact, cannabis got caught up in a wave of anti-everything that was happening in the United States in the early 20th century: Americans were anti-alcohol, anti-Black, anti-women's right to vote, anti-jazz, and anti-Mexican, among others.

Anslinger, for his part, did not initially see marijuana as a menace to society and distanced the Bureau of Narcotics from proponents of marijuana prohibition. It was not because Anslinger was sympathetic to drug use, because he was a hard-liner against alcohol and drugs. For instance, Anslinger suggested that people convicted of purchasing alcohol a first time be fined $1,000 and serve six months in jail, and for a second conviction, receive a fine between $5,000 to $50,000 and two to five years in jail. Adjusted for inflation, that's $13,651 in fines for a first conviction and $68,000 to $682,000 for a second conviction—and that's just for purchasing alcohol. But the reason Anslinger did not pursue marijuana prohibition stemmed from more practical concerns. First, the Federal courts had limited jurisdiction to prosecute alcohol or drug offenses. Amendment Eighteen prohibited the manufacture, distribution, and sale of alcohol, but not the purchase or possession of alcohol, and prosecution was left to the states, with widely variable results. Second, the Harrison Act was primarily a taxing measure on pharmacists, but did not prohibit possession, and therefore did nothing to stem the use of drugs. And third, there was no way to prosecute under Federal law anyone who possessed or consumed marijuana because the Harrison act only applied to drugs not grown in the United States, like opium.

But Anslinger changed his mind about prohibition of marijuana for several reasons. First, Prohibition ended in 1933—that is, Amendment 18 was repealed through Amendment 21—and second, the Great Depression was impacting the budget of the United States government. The Bureau of Narcotics saw $200,000 cut from its budget that resulted in payroll losses and Anslinger believed that the Bureau was in a fight for its very existence. He turned to a tactic that worked before with alcohol by launching a media campaign indicating that marijuana was the menace of society. Anslinger provided information to community service clubs and the popular press about the atrocities of marijuana. According to one source, only two articles detailing issues within marijuana use appeared in the American popular press between 1920 and 1929. After 1930 they began to appear in a steady stream, and in every major newspaper in the country (Abel: 48). Anslinger's tactic worked and in 1937 the Treasury Department proposed to Congress to outlaw marijuana. The Treasury Department called as a medical witness Harry Anslinger, who was not a physician nor trained in a medical field, yet he was allowed to offer his own medical opinion on marijuana. Understandably, Anslinger's testimony was one-sided on the horrors of marijuana.

In the legislation the original definition of "marihuana" excluded the mature stalk and its compounds and manufactures, in order to appease the rope and cordage industries, which used the stems to manufacture their products. But the seeds were included in the definition and that brought an outcry from the paint and varnish industries, as well as from the birdseed industry. In fact, the birdseed industry used millions of pounds of cannabis seeds. As a compromise to these industries, the legislation was rewritten to exclude seeds from the definition of "marihuana," as long as the seeds were sterilized thus preventing the growth of any new marijuana plants. In the popular press the passage of The Marihuana Tax Act went largely unnoticed, with the *New York Times* stating on August 3, 1937, "President Roosevelt signed today a bill to curb traffic in the narcotic, marihuana, through heavy taxes on transactions."

From that inauspicious start, the Marihuana Tax Act has become one of the most significant pieces of legislation any Congress has passed. It has impacted the United States for eighty years as well as nearly every country in the world. Throughout the successive decades since its passage, the United States Federal Government has escalated the reach and scope of anti-drug legislation. In the 1950's Congress passed laws increasing mandatory sentencing for minor cannabis violations. In the 1960's the United States agreed to the Single Convention on Narcotic Drugs, which was an international treaty to prohibit the production and supply of narcotics. The treaty included cannabis along with manufactured drugs like cocaine, heroin, and morphine. President Kennedy's Ad Hoc Panel on Drug Abuse concluded, counter to the treaty and Congress, that the dangers of marijuana have been exaggerated and that harsh sentences for the occasional user are poor social policy. President Johnson's Committee on Law Enforcement and Administrative Justice went one step further in stating that under the law marijuana and opiates are treated equally, but the abuse of the two have nothing in common. Opiates lead to higher usage and dosage, marijuana does not.

Nevertheless, in 1970, during Nixon's Presidency, Congress passed the Controlled Substances Act and included marijuana as a Schedule I drug, which meant that it has a "high potential for abuse, no currently accepted medical use in treatment in the United States, and a lack of accepted safety for use of the drug or other substance under medical supervision" (United States Code, Title 21, 1970). Congress overlooked early medical research indicating that cannabis had a positive impact on the treatment of glaucoma (Hepler and Frank, 1971), childhood epilepsy (Davis and Ramsey, 1949), and in the alleviation of symptoms such as vomiting and nausea brought out through cancer chemotherapy, in relieving acute appendicitis, in reducing stress and depression, among others. But, contrary to the hardline approach by Congress, they must have realized that marijuana differed from hard drugs like heroin and cocaine because Congress set up a commission, known as the Shafer Commission to study marijuana and other drugs further. The Shafer Commission studied thousands of pages of transcriptions from formal and informal hearings, solicited opinions from all points of view, surveyed district attorneys, judges, probation officers, health officials and others, and undertook more than fifty projects (Gardner, 2012). Shafer concludes:

"[T]he criminal law is too harsh a tool to apply to personal possession even in the effort to discourage use. It implies an overwhelming indictment of the behavior which we believe is not appropriate. The actual and potential harm of use of the drug is not great enough to justify intrusion by the criminal law into private behavior, a step which our society takes only with the greatest reluctance."[1]

The Shafer Commission recommended decriminalization for personal use and possession of small amounts of marijuana and that "the use of drugs for pleasure or other non-medical purposes is not inherently irresponsible; alcohol is widely used as an acceptable part of social activities" (Drugs and Social Responsibility, DrugLibrary.org).

Yet Richard Nixon, adamantly opposed to marijuana, stated, "As you know, there is a commission that is supposed to make recommendations to me about this subject, and in this instance, however, I have such strong views that I will express them. I am against legalizing marijuana. Even if this commission does recommend that it be legalized, I will not follow that recommendation.... I do not believe that legalizing marijuana is in the best interests of our young people and I do not think it's in the best interests of this country" (Quoted in King, 1972:101). Nixon ignored the Shafer Commission recommendations and instead created the Drug Enforcement Agency, escalating the war on drugs even further, and primarily focused the DEA on marijuana possession.

In 1972, for instance, there were 292,179 arrests for marijuana possession and in 1973, 420,700 possession arrests. The number of marijuana arrests have increased since then, to 749,825 in 2012, mostly for possession of small amounts of marijuana. For example, in Illinois, researchers found that 97.8 percent of all marijuana arrests were for possession, and Blacks eight times more likely to be arrested than whites (Kane-Willis, Aviles, Bazan, and Narloch, 2014).

In the 1980's the tax code was changed and section 280E was added to the U.S. Tax code. 280E states that taxpayers trafficking in controlled substances get no deductions for many expenses, like marketing, advertising, utilities, rent, payments to selling personnel, legal and accounting fees, and others. The only real deduction is for cost of goods sold—the actual cost of making or buying a product. In the cannabis industry 280E plays out for companies differentially, based on where a company is in the production chain. Growers get to write off all the expenses associated with growing cannabis—soil, nutrients, materials, rent, labor, water, electricity. Dispensary owners, on the other hand, only get to write off the cost of purchasing cannabis from growers, and not much else. 280E only applies to industries, like cannabis, that are selling controlled substances but other industries that cause social harm, like alcohol and tobacco, are free to advertise, and to write off those and all other expenses.

In the 1980's President Ronald Reagan ratchetted drug enforcement even further, extending an obscure maritime law used to seize assets of pirates, the Civil Forfeiture Law, to the drug wars. Originally, civil forfeiture was designed to apprehend pirates who were not physically present by allowing authorities to seize the assets of the pirate, and under Reagan the law was resurrected to confiscate any and all assets under suspicion of illegal drug use. So, under civil forfeiture law enforcement may bring charges against the property rather than the person who committed a crime. And, unlike criminal forfeiture, civil forfeiture does not require formal criminal charges against a person or a criminal conviction—it doesn't necessarily involve the judiciary, and it is an "administrative" procedure.

In many states law enforcement can, with mere "probable cause," seize any and all property and cash they see fit and the burden of proof lies with the individual to prove that they are not guilty. In 1986 the government seized $93.7 million through civil forfeiture, but by 2014 the seized assets had soared to over $3.7 billion. In fact, the Institute of Justice reports that civil forfeiture revenues grew over 4,000 percent since its inception and that between 2001 to 2014 revenues of forfeiture funds were nearly $29 billion. The Inspector General, in an annual audit of fiscal year 2014, notes that forfeiture has generated over a billion dollars annually over the past nine years. Critics of civil forfeiture have suggested that police agencies are engaging in forfeiture practices to maximize revenue generation, rather than to curb the drug trade. Academic studies concur that the policing-for-profit allegation is true (Worrall and Kovandzic: 2008, 219-244).

The U.S. Supreme Court is complicit in civil forfeiture, concluding in several cases that one's constitutional rights are not violated when police, or the IRS, or one of another dozen Federal or State agencies confiscates your money, car, house, jewelry, or any assets you possess prior to a formal charge, or any charge at all, for that matter. That's a good thing for the budget of many law enforcement agencies, since in 85 percent of civil forfeiture cases, the property owner is never charged with a crime. But it's not so good for the individual who happens to get ensnared in the civil forfeiture process. The original intent of the civil forfeiture law was to reign in the assets of drug kingpins, but according to former Deputy Chief of the Los Angeles Police Department, Stephen Downing, "The average seizure is $8,000, so that means that the little guy is losing his car, his house, whatever cash he has. And the government is not charging them with a crime. The little guy doesn't have the resources to fight this. Just to get an attorney to fight an asset seizure will cost you $25,000 up front. Most of these little guys walk away from it" (www.Leap.cc).

In the 1990's the first inkling of a backlash towards the war on drugs began to emerge. In 1992 Dan Baum wrote an article in *Nation* that was highly critical of the war on drugs, and especially critical of the Regan and Bush administrations, the amount of funding devoted to drug enforcement, and the terrible human cost. Baum noted that, by 1992, more Americans were in federal prison for drug crimes than people in federal prison for all crimes in 1980, and that the female prison population had doubled since 1986. Baum found that the incarceration rate for black American men is five times higher than in South Africa, that over half the prison population is black yet blacks are less than an eighth of the U.S. population. He also found that there are more American black men in prison than in college. In fact, Baum noted that there are twice as many people arrested for possession than for dealing drugs, and that treatment and prevention programs receive half the funding of enforcement. He states, "The goal is simply to lock people up."

Baum discovered that the Justice Department started looking at cases where people were convicted and served time in a state drug case and then the Justice Department tried, convicted, and sent them to prison under federal law for the same crime. The plight of fifty-year old Donny Clark is a relevant example. Convicted in 1985 for growing marijuana on his farm, Donny served a one-year prison sentence meted out by the state of Florida. But when federal agents found a drug ring near his farm six years later, they charged Donny again—for the exact same crime—and he was sentenced to life in prison with no hope of parole. Clark's saga was not an anomaly in the early 1990's and the Justice Department had a term for the policy, "Project Trigger lock." Justice spokesperson Doug Tillett said, "The intent is to get bad guys off the street with apologies to none."

Evidently, Americans in the early 1990's were perfectly happy with that approach because, as Baum found, Americans were more afraid of drugs than unemployment or the deficit, and drug enforcement was something people said they were willing to pay higher taxes for. As Baum states, "The consensus crosses racial, gender, class, ideological and geographical lines, so it's sometimes hard to tell the difference between the antidrug rhetoric of, say, Jesse Jackson and George Bush" (Baum, 1993:1)

It's not surprising then, that the Supreme Court followed suit and made every accommodation to the hardline approach to drugs. As Baum states:

"The Supreme Court, meanwhile, is steadily eroding the protections against police excess promised by the Fourth, Fifth, Sixth, Eighth and Fourteenth Amendments to the Constitution. The Court during the past decade let police obtain search warrants on the strength of anonymous tips (Fourth and Sixth Amendments). It did away with the need for warrants when police want to search luggage, trash cans, car interiors, bus passengers, fenced private property and barns (Fourth). It let prosecutors hold drug offenders without bail (Eighth). It permitted the confiscation of property before a suspect is charged, let alone convicted (Fifth). It let prosecutors imprison people twice–at the state and federal levels–for the same crime (Fifth). It let police fly as low as 400 feet over houses in their search for marijuana plants

(Fourth). It allowed the seizure of defense attorneys' legal fees in drug cases (Sixth). It allowed mandatory urine testing for federal employees (Fourth). And in a Michigan case last year, it let stand a sentence of mandatory life without parole for simple drug possession (Eighth)" (Baum, 1993).

Along those lines, Eric Schlosser (1994) followed up Dan Baum with a two-part article in the *Atlantic Monthly* entitled "Reefer Madness," in which Schlosser detailed the power that U.S. attorneys wield in marijuana cases. Prosecuting attorneys can determine the jurisdiction in which to try a case (local, state, or federal), as well as what charges to bring. 38 year-old Mark Young provides a chilling example of what can happen. Young introduced buyers to the growers of over 700 pounds of marijuana in rural Indiana. He didn't manufacture the marijuana, didn't distribute it, didn't transport it, didn't possess it, didn't even touch the plant; he merely introduced the buyers to the sellers and based on that action, Mark Young received life imprisonment—at Fort Leavenworth Penitentiary, a maximum-security prison—with no chance of parole. To put Mark Young's punishment into perspective, his life sentence is more draconian than punishments for the most violent criminals in American society. An armed robber can expect to spend five years in prison, a rapist, twelve years, and a murderer, eight years, eight months, on average. But the amount of prison time for a first-time offender involving marijuana is often far longer. Schlosser exposed the cases of others like Mark Young:

- A first-time offender received twelve years for unloading hashish from a boat.
- Another first-time offender received eight years after the truck he rented was used by a friend to transport marijuana.
- A 66 year-old woman and first-time offender received eight years for selling ditchweed (no psychoactive properties).

In the 2000's Jon Gettman published an article listing the top producing states for marijuana: California, Tennessee, Kentucky, Hawaii, Washington, North Carolina, Florida, Alabama, West Virginia, and Oregon. Gettman used data of marijuana seizures supplied by the DEA Domestic Cannabis Eradication / Suppression Program, and a conservative estimate of black market value for the cannabis to determine cash value of the seized cannabis (2006). He found that marijuana was the top cash crop in twelve states, one of the top three cash crops in 30 states, and one of the top five cash crops in 39 states. At $36 billion dollars annually, marijuana is not only the largest crop in the United States, but more valuable than wheat and corn combined.

Estimates on the value of marijuana in Kentucky, for example, are $4.5 billion dollars, and if Kentucky were to tax that value at the same rate as Colorado (a 15 percent excise tax), the state would have generated $675 million in tax revenues. And that's based on an estimate of *seized* marijuana in Kentucky—who knows how much cannabis is not seized? What could the state of Kentucky do with an extra $675 million dollars in its budget each year?

In a 2015 follow-up article, Gettman summarized the state of cannabis cultivation in the United States. "Here's what we learn from these eradication statistics—marijuana is grown throughout the United States. It is grown in large and small fields outdoors, and it is grown in large and small sites indoors. Over three decades of eradication activity has failed to curtail the domestic cultivation industry, and it is so decentralized now that it cannot be controlled by law enforcement."[2] The United States is now one of the leading cultivators of cannabis world-wide.

Eradication didn't curb the cannabis trade, civil forfeiture didn't stall it, the "Just Say No" campaign and D.A.R.E. education program didn't stop people for using cannabis, the 280E taxing scheme didn't prevent the industry from flourishing, mandatory minimum sentencing didn't quell cannabis use, nor sentences with no parole or life imprisonment. The War on Drugs has failed on every single measure except for one: it has benefitted enormously a select group of people who have been able to monetize the criminalization of cannabis.

OPPONENTS TO LEGALIZATION IN 2018

Despite polls indicating that 61 percent of Americans are in favor of cannabis legalization for recreational use, 91 percent in favor for medical use, and twenty-nine states and the District of Columbia that have legalized medical marijuana, there are a number of significant opponents to legalization.[3]

Federal Agencies. The DEA, for example, has received over $50 billion in funding since its inception in 1973, and its 2017 budget request was $2.1034 billion. If cannabis were to be rescheduled from schedule I to II, there would most likely be a reduction in the DEA's budget and number of employees. In fact, that's beginning to happen. In 2015, for instance, there were eight amendments involving cannabis and the Republican-led House of Representatives voted in the affirmative on seven of those. Notably, the House voted to protect state medical marijuana and hemp laws from federal interference; it voted to cut DEA funding for marijuana eradication in half ($9 million); it took another $9 million from the DEA budget and put it toward police body cameras; and it cut another $4 million from the DEA budget for testing rape kits. These cuts didn't make a dent in the 2015 $2.4 billion DEA budget, but the fact that they passed, and that some of the bills passed with only a voice vote, indicate that the Congress was willing to curtail the scope and reach of the DEA.

Private Prisons. The United States can aptly be characterized as the democracy that embraces mass incarceration, since the U.S. has more people in prison—per capita and in absolute numbers—than any other nation in the world, including repressive nations like Russia, China, and Iran. Incarceration rates have soared since Nixon's presidency, and the biggest beneficiary is the private prison industry which, between 1990-2009, saw the number of prisoners increase 1,600 percent. The two largest companies in the private prison industry, Corrections Corporation of America ($1.7 billion annual revenues) and The GEO Group ($1.6 billion annual revenues), state in SEC filings that "[A]ny changes with respect to the decriminalization of drugs and controlled substances could affect the number of persons arrested, convicted, sentenced and incarcerated, thereby potentially reducing demand for correctional facilities to house them."[4] Both companies have extensive lobbying activities and work at the State level to ensure that minimum mandatory sentencing is enacted, that sentencing alternatives like electronic monitoring never come to fruition, and that Truth in Sentencing laws, which require inmates to serve 80-90 percent of their sentence before being eligible for parole, are passed.

At the turn of the century compassionate voices emerged decrying the for-profit prison system. The Catholic Bishops Resolution (2000), the Presbyterian Church USA (2003), the United Methodist Church (2000), and the Episcopal Diocese of Newark (2002) raised serious concerns about private prisons stating that the "profit motive may lead to reduced efforts to change behaviors," and that there is a "fundamental conflict with rehabilitation" and the profit motive. Further, they stated that the "warehousing of prisoners" so that a company can "profit from the punishment of human beings" is wrong. Those pleas made no impact with State and Federal correctional facility authorities, nor with Congress, which has oversight of the penal system. Today the private prison industry remains robust and profitable, due in large part to marijuana-related arrests.

Local Law Enforcement. In determining opponents to cannabis legalization, it would seem that none would be more obvious than law enforcement given the sheer number of cannabis arrests (about 690,000 annually), but that would be incorrect on several fronts. First, law enforcement officials are not the policy makers in the United States, they are the enforcers of policies and laws that others create. The reason for the high number of cannabis arrests stems in large measure from the Reagan and Bush administrations who essentially bribed local law enforcement to pursue the war on drugs. On the one hand, these administrations cut funding and general assistance to local police, and on the other hand, offered large drug-enforcement grants. The Department of Justice also enticed local police by offering to split the loot collected through civil forfeiture—cash, property, houses, cars—and local law enforcement took the bait and now collects over a billion dollars annually.

Second, every large group is diverse, and law enforcement personnel are no different in that regard. There is a non-profit organization, Law Enforcement Against Prohibition (LEAP) that advocates ending prohibition on drugs, especially cannabis. One member, Joanne Naughton, provides a narrative on how she came to oppose prohibition. Naughton was an undercover narcotics officer in the New York City Police Department and eventually retired as a Lieutenant. She then got a law degree and practiced as a criminal defense lawyer, defending many people that were similar to the people she had arrested as an undercover police officer. "That put a human face on so-called 'drug dealers'" she stated, "They were really small-time drug users selling to support their habits, for the most part." Naughton also taught criminal justice at a local college and stated, "When I spoke to my students about the Constitution, about the War on Drugs, what we're doing—not just in this country but in this world—to combat this so-called 'drug problem' is wrong. Just wrong. It's unfair. It's un-Constitutional. And, it hurts people. It doesn't help them, it hurts people. There's just no upside to it. It doesn't work." [5]

Another member of LEAP, Russ Jones, had a different experience than Naughton, but came to the same conclusion. Jones was a retired DEA Task Force Agent and during the course of that career had an opportunity to work closely with narcotics officers in Russia. "By the time I left the DEA I was pretty discouraged with what the nation was doing to itself with the war on drugs. I pulled it all together after my trip to the Soviet Union, and it was still the Iron Curtain, still the Soviet Union. I worked on the streets with their narcotics detectives, we seized a meth lab, I saw drug dealing on the streets, went to their rehabilitation clinics and spoke to recovering addicts, and when I got home, the question that kept running through my mind was, 'If the Soviet Union, still behind the Iron Curtain, as controlling of its citizens as it was, if they were unable to control drugs through prohibition, then how were we, a free people, how were we going to do that?' This is not a problem that we're going to arrest our way out of. This is a health problem, not a law enforcement problem."

Smart Approaches to Marijuana. SAM is a non-profit that "Envisions a society where marijuana policies are aligned with the scientific understanding of marijuana's harms, and the commercialization and normalization of marijuana are no more. Our mission is to...decrease marijuana use and its consequences." The organization has alliances with other like-minded non-profits including Parents Opposed to Pot, the American Society of Addiction Medicine, and the National Association of Drug Court Professionals. In addition, SAM has affiliate organizations in a number of states, including Colorado, Hawaii, Maine, Massachusetts, Minnesota, Missouri, New York, Vermont, and Washington.

RACHEL O'BRYAN, SMART COLORADO

I contacted the Smart Colorado group after hearing one of their speakers at the panel discussion in September of 2014. The person who eventually connected with me was Rachel O'Bryan and we met at a coffee shop to discuss her perspective on cannabis legalization. I explained to Rachel that I was conducting research for a book on the newly legal cannabis industry, and also that I had a client for whom I had written a business plan. Rachel became visibly alarmed at that.

"I don't think I can speak with you."

"What?" I asked, "Why not?"

"Because you work for the industry, and that's exactly who we are fighting."

"Well," I responded, "I don't work for the industry, I just had the one client and understood his operations, and became interested in the development of the whole industry. I'm taking a broad view of the industry and speaking with people from all different segments—people who are growers, retailers, law enforcement, regulators. I thought it would be good for the book to have someone from your organization who is opposed to cannabis, that's all."

"I will give you some background information," she finally stated, "for your book, and since I've driven here. But that's it."

"Ok, great." I responded. "What is your involvement with Smart Colorado?"

"After Amendment 64 passed Governor Hickenlooper created a task force to study all the angles of legalization, and I wrote him a letter and asked to be on the task force. There were six committees, but the task force was dominated by industry people. There were no average citizens on the committee, no doctors, no parents. Really, they were all industry people. And when we took a straw poll on various issues the task force ranked health and safety last.

"During the next several meetings it became clear to several of us, all mothers, that there were not protections in place for kids, and the industry wasn't interested in protecting kids. So we formed a non-profit and aligned with Smart Approaches to Marijuana. One of our founders has a background in law, one has a public policy background and is focused on local control, and one is a tax attorney. Smart Colorado was founded to represent the non-industry, the parents and kids, and to put protections in place."

"And how are you going about doing that?" I asked.

"We pushed for child-proof containers and got that implemented. The industry didn't want to do any special packaging and we're now battling the edibles manufacturers about making edibles clearly identifiable. You've seen the news and reports of people going to the hospital because they either accidentally ingested a marijuana-laced edible, or they overconsumed the edible, right?"

"Yes, I've seen those reports."

"One hospital has already reported that nine children have been to the emergency room because of ingesting a marijuana-laced edible—and that's just the first three months of sales. If you extrapolate that there could be hundreds of children who have been exposed to marijuana edibles. The problem is that the State opened stores before there was adequate education about the safety of the product, and the safety of children."

"Do you know if schools are tracking any data on marijuana?" I asked.

Rachel shook her head, "It depends on the principal. My kids go to a local Denver high school and the principal doesn't track it, but at another school it is tracked. But that's really a big problem for us, the tracking of data. We don't have a baseline for a lot of things. Colorado Department of Health does have a Youth Risk Survey, but they don't have any data for 2013. We don't have any data on DUI's since legalization, or even before. When police officers made a stop and suspected something they tested for alcohol—if they found it, they stopped, and if they didn't find it, they stopped. We're not tracking the residuals that are found in marijuana—we aren't testing for them at all. So, we're really lacking a lot of important information."

"Do you see that changing anytime soon?"

"It's hard," Rachel replied. "The medical marijuana people are very influential in how the recreational market is playing out. We're fighting fourteen years of people thinking that this is a wellness product. So kids think that it's healthy."

Rachel and I spoke for several hours that afternoon, and I don't know if she withheld any information, but she answered every question I asked. Six months later, in March of 2015, I circled back to Rachel to get her perspective given eighteen months of legalization.

"So, Rachel, here are the things that I'd like to talk with you about," I stated as we sat down at an outdoor restaurant. "Your perspective now that we've had eighteen months of recreational marijuana, the pros and cons of legalizing, and what you'd do differently knowing what you know now. That is, with perfect hindsight, what would you change up?"

"Ok," she stated. "First, I'm not with Smart Colorado anymore...."

"Really? Why not?"

"Well, you know, we just are going in different directions. I'm focused on the edibles part of the market, and we decided that I should do that if that's what I'm motivated by. And, I'm going to Oregon later this month to talk about edibles, so overall it's a good move for me. I'm still not making any money though," she said with a laugh, "but the work is important."

"Why the edibles, and not the kids?" I asked.

"They're related. But the big problems are with the edibles. They are hard to control. There's not a consistent reaction in people who ingest them, like there is for alcohol. Honestly, you'd be better off buying a joint if you want to try marijuana. Otherwise it's just so inconsistent, and there are no standards on potency."

"What are the pros and cons?" I asked. "Are there any 'pros' from your perspective?"

"Yes, only one pro," she stated. "I'm struck by the innovations" she said as she sat up in her chair, "by the amount of innovation in the industry, and by the things that are being innovated. I am just stunned by that, and also by the number of people that are innovating in the industry. I mean, there are people who are creating new lighting for the industry, moisture controls, security…you name it, it's everything."

"How about the tax revenues," I asked. "Are the tax revenues a pro?"

"No, not really," she replied. "Yes, the money goes back to the people, but it's really insignificant. It just looks good on paper. Amendment 64 was drafted to give the appearance of rights to the people, but the cost to regulate is high."

"And how about the cons," I asked.

"The cons?" she repeated. "The cons are significant. We failed to understand edibles, how important they would be to consumers, and how difficult it would be to control them. We failed to understand that the marijuana industry doesn't want the comparison to tobacco, because tobacco, to get consumers, starts pitching to people when they are young. Tobacco wants to get people hooked early and keep them for a lifetime. That's why the marijuana industry says, 'regulate marijuana like alcohol.' But why do they put marijuana into a gummy bear? What's the point of that? It is hugely attractive to children and really is not a very good experience for the adult who wants to consume marijuana."

"What are the issues moving forward for you?" I asked.

"I think we're going to have to reconcile medical and recreational marijuana. Medical is so loose, it's really a moral hazard. Medical marijuana is based on how a person uses it, not on the problem or affliction that they have. It's the same product for medical and recreational marijuana. The same product. So for one person it's an experience and for another person it's a medicine? The medical marijuana industry is very influential in this state. They basically came in as policy makers."

"So," I asked, "given the eighteen months since legalization, what is your perspective now?"

"I'm more discouraged now," she responded with resignation. "The State doesn't have the will to fix medical…you get entrenched interests and it's tough to get rid of them. So we're pretty much stuck with the system that we have, and it was basically crafted by the medical marijuana people."

"And if you had a blank slate and could do things over, would you change anything?"

"I would go back to 2000," she said with renewed enthusiasm. "I would have paid more attention to what was happening when we legalized medical marijuana. We came in after medical dispensaries had been open, but the medical marijuana industry really created what we have now. People thought that medical would disappear when recreational was created. But that is clearly not happening. I would also do a better job of tracking the important data. We didn't track data and now we don't ever get to see a fully clear picture of what legal marijuana looks like, because we never had a baseline to compare it to. I think those are the important things. Pay more attention to how medical starts and collect better data to track where things are compared to where they were."

THE END RESULT

Eighty years of intense tactics to wipe out drugs—and cannabis in particular—have come to naught. Stiff penalties like minimum mandatory sentencing, truth in sentencing, hefty fines, civil forfeiture, combining State and Federal forces to locate and eradicate cannabis and to incarcerate Americans for mere possession, has really done little to curb the manufacture, distribution, and use of cannabis. It's estimated that there are over 19 million regular users (on the low end) to over 24 million regular users (on the high end), and cannabis grows in every state in the union, in nearly every soil condition, in nearly every environment imaginable. The legislators in Colorado recognized that "the smoke is out of the bottle," but that's not unique to Colorado or to other medical marijuana states; that's true of every state in the union. Cannabis is widespread, easily obtainable, and easily grown for personal consumption, and anybody who wants it—the grade school kid, the high school or college kid—can find and purchase cannabis.

The fiercest opponents to cannabis legalization are the people and organizations who have been able to monetize the persecution of cannabis users, either through forfeiture of assets, through fines, or by creating long and lucrative careers rooting out the menace of cannabis. The fact that none of the supposed evils of cannabis legalization have materialized—there has not been an increase in black market activity and organized drug cartels, nor an increase in crime, nor an increase in youth or adult use—is summarily dismissed by opponents. It's too early to tell if the experiment is working say the experts, such as Mark A.R. Kleiman, a New York University professor and a leading expert on cannabis legalization. It will take "10 years" to understand the impact of legalization he reported in an interview. But, is 80 years enough time to determine that prohibition doesn't work, or is it still "too early to tell?"

That ten-year time frame is arbitrary—why is ten years the amount of time to determine if a social experiment is working? But over the first four years of legal cannabis in Colorado none of the predictions by opponents—none of them—have materialized. Instead, prices have dropped, quality has improved, sales have generated taxes for schools, communities, and the State of Colorado, demand has remained relatively flat, and drug cartels have ceased to be a problem. In a perfect, utopian world, all drugs would be absent, but drugs exist in both natural and manufactured forms. For the people that say, "all drugs should be illegal," one response is, "Have you ever had a glass of wine or a beer? Do you tough out your headache or pain, or use aspirin, Ibuprofen, or another drug? When you go to the dentist do you say, 'no anesthetic for me?' If you have open-heart surgery, do you tell the medical staff, 'just give me something to bite down on, I don't believe in drugs?" I suppose most people use some drugs in their life.

The question for the "all drugs should be illegal" crowd is, "What is your proposed alternative?" 80 years of intense prohibition, with incentives to law enforcement, to district, state, and federal attorneys to prosecute minor marijuana infractions to the fullest extent of the law, along with Constitutionally illegal DEA eradication programs, has done nothing to quell the cultivation and distribution of cannabis. Cannabis is grown in every state in the union, in every environment. What is the alternative to regulating, testing, and taxing?

Notes to Chapter Nine

[1] For the full Shafer Report, see http://www.druglibrary.org/schaffer/library/studies/nc/ncmenu.htm

[2] See Jon Gettman, "DEA Statistics Reveal Cultivation Trends," in *High Times Magazine*, June 22, 2015. Accessed at http://www.hightimes.com/read/dea-statistics-reveal-domestic-cultivation-trends

[3] For a list of states with medical marijuana laws, year passed, how the measure was passed, and possession details, see https://medicalmarijuana.procon.org/view.resource.php?resourceID=000881

[4] ACLU, "Banking on Bondage: Private Prisons and Mass Incarceration," May 10, 2012. Accessed at https://www.aclu.org/banking-bondage-private-prisons-and-mass-incarceration

[5] Ms. Naughton's work, interviews, and videos can be accessed here: https://lawenforcementactionpartnership.org/?s=JOANNE+NAUGHTON

CHAPTER 10.

BLACK MARKET ENTREPRENEURS

The Ogden memo of 2009 was explicit about the conditions under which the federal government would enforce marijuana laws in states that have medical marijuana establishments. One such stipulation was that, if states were unable to ensure that marijuana was not being diverted to the black market—either within the state or across state lines—the federal government would step in, raid, seize assets, and prosecute any persons involved in those activities. Colorado's legislators took that point seriously and instituted a number of safeguards to lessen the chance that legal medical marijuana would be diverted to the black market, including:

1. Seed-to-sale tracking,
2. An onerous application process with significant background checks for owners and employees,
3. Requiring that all recreational establishments be licensed to existing medical marijuana operators, and
4. Requiring participants in the legal marijuana industry to be people who have at least two years of residency in the state.

This last stipulation should help to prevent outsiders, cartels, and large-scale businesses from participating in the industry.

With the start of legal recreational sales some of the most pressing questions are, "What has happened to the black market? Has it become smaller? Has it transformed into something different? Has it led to an increase in cartel activity?" Those are difficult questions to answer because most of the transactions that take place in a black market are hidden; in fact, the entire production chain from seed to sale is largely unknown. Even so, researchers from the Marijuana Policy Group, using sophisticated demand methodology, determined that in 2014 the total demand for cannabis in Colorado was 130.3 metric tons, only a portion of which was supplied by the regulated market. They concluded that 53.3 metric tons were supplied by people outside the regulated market, including home growers, caregivers, medical marijuana patients themselves, and black market operators—that is, people with no ties to either regulated market–medical or recreational.

A consortium of Federal, State, and local agencies operating under the auspices of the Rocky Mountain High Intensity Drug Trafficking Area (RMHIDTA), pays close attention to the impact of marijuana legalization in Colorado, and they concur that the black market is still thriving. In their annual report on the effects of marijuana legalization in Colorado, RMHIDTA provides a comprehensive overview of various areas that are impacted by legalized marijuana including the following:

- Impaired driving,
- Youth marijuana use,
- Adult marijuana use,
- Emergency room and hospital marijuana-related admissions,
- Marijuana-related exposure, treatment,
- Diversion of Colorado marijuana,
- Diversion by parcel,

- THC extraction labs,

- And a catch-all "related data" category that covers crime, revenues, homelessness, suicide, environmental impact, THC potency, and other topics.

On "diversion," RMHIDTA reports over sixty cases involving interdiction of marijuana obtained in Colorado and destined for other states, and twenty-two cases involving marijuana diversion to youth. In 2014 there were over 360 seizures destined for thirty-six different states, the most common destinations were Kansas, Missouri, Oklahoma, Illinois and Florida.

A majority of the cases reported by RMHIDTA involve people from outside of Colorado purchasing marijuana and transporting it back to their own state to sell, and the numbers are fairly small: thirty-two pounds to New Mexico, thirty-eight pounds to South Dakota, seven ounces to Wyoming, fifteen pounds to North Dakota, twenty-four pounds to Kentucky, thirty-six pounds to Florida. The list of marijuana flowing to other states from Colorado goes on, but the numbers are essentially the same: the amount of marijuana crossing state lines is the amount that a person could conceivably conceal in a car or truck.

But, assuming $2000 per pound for marijuana, the actual value of cannabis transported out of Colorado is well under $100,000 per transaction, not really enough to constitute a huge black market. The numbers for diversion by parcel are similar to diversion by driving across state lines and the RMHIDTA reports that between 2010 and 2014 seized packages increased from fifteen to 320, and pounds of marijuana seized increased from 57 to 470 pounds. At least forty states were recipients of packages containing some form of marijuana, but typically in small numbers: seven pounds to Chicago, nine pounds to Texas, sixteen pounds to New York, thirty-seven pounds to Florida, 1.2 pounds to Maryland.

But not all the seizures are small and there are several high-profile diversion cases that have emerged since Colorado legalized marijuana. For example, police in Nashville intercepted 425 pounds of marijuana. In Colorado, 1,100 plants were confiscated in a home in Lafayette and another 2,630 plants were confiscated on public land in the White River National Forest. In a substantial drug bust, police confiscated 4,600 pounds, 2,000 plants, and $1.4 million in cash from a "caregiver" in Denver who had 13 warehouses and had laundered millions of dollars. And the largest illegal drug bust so far involved 20,000 plants, six grows and 660 pounds of dry marijuana being diverted to the black market by Mexicans and Cubans, some of whom were illegal aliens. The 20,000 plants could fetch roughly $60 million dollars on the black market, especially if the growers were intending on selling outside of Colorado.

Law enforcement officials have finally figured out what Eric, the established cannabis operator, told me in the summer of 2014: illegal growing operations are located right next to Colorado's sanctioned growing operations, as Colorado Attorney General Cynthia Coffman confirmed, stating, "Illegal drug dealers are simply hiding in plain sight, attempting to use the legalized market as a cover." I also heard from an informed source that once Colorado legalized marijuana, growers from California started renting and buying warehouses in Denver to shift growing operations to Colorado, to be closer to the east coast markets and avoid driving through Utah. But the evidence clearly points to illegal drug trafficking from a number of people, either U.S. citizens or people from other countries.

Frankly, I had zero interest in penetrating the large-scale drug trafficking organizations from California, Mexico, Cuba, Russia, or various other places, and I didn't even try to become acquainted with that segment of the cannabis industry. I had heard from Derek, the financier, about his experience with cartels and I wasn't prepared to take a risk for what would assuredly be a large-scale version of smaller scale illegal operations. Derek told me that he went in to a recreational dispensary to inquire about whether the owner would be interested in capital for expansion and the "budtender," the retail clerk, not only responded in a very thick Russian accent, but pulled out a handgun and placed it on the counter as he said so. Penetration of large-scale, illegal drug trafficking organizations is a task best left to Federal agencies, in my opinion. But I was interested in the far more common "black market" operator, the small-scale, neighborly operation that is found throughout the United States and I was able to find all sorts of people that operated illegal marijuana businesses on a smaller scale.

SMALL SCALE BLACK MARKET OPERATORS

It wasn't all that difficult to find people who were selling marijuana on the black market. Once people figured out I was writing a book, that helped to open doors, and as I have mentioned before, there is an openness about speaking publicly about marijuana now that it's legal. I met five people who were selling to the black market and they were all the opposite extreme of drug trafficking cartels: they were lone entrepreneurs growing in their home or in a small garage, they were selling to people they knew, and all but one of them were looking for ways to participate in the legal market rather than the black market. I normally met these black market operators through introductions from people I met in the industry.

For example, I was introduced to Ezra by a person I met at a symposium, John. I met John at the University of Colorado symposium on cannabis organized by Students for Sensible Drug Policy. I had arrived at the symposium early and when I got to the auditorium John was the only one there, sitting in the second row with his feet casually draped over the first row of seats. John was in his early seventies and he was both a consumer of marijuana and looking for opportunities to participate in the industry. He told me that he was a millionaire and that he was now living a hippie lifestyle, living out of a camper that he parks in his ex-wife's driveway. John was looking for something that his twenty-nine year-old son could do. "He lives at home with his mother and he likes to smoke pot," John told me, "so I figure that maybe there will be something for him to do in the industry. So, I'm here just to figure out what the industry is like and what might work for him."

Several weeks later John invited me to meet him at a bookstore in Boulder. "There's someone I want you to meet," he said, and when I got there he introduced me to Ezra. Ezra is in his mid-twenties, he has a slight build and is wearing jeans, a button-down shirt, and tennis shoes. He looked like one of the many college students at the University of Colorado. He was sitting at a table with his laptop working out some numbers for John.

"What are you working on?" I asked.

"He's just putting together some numbers for me," John replied. "I'm thinking my son should just grow marijuana in the basement and Ezra is putting together a list of equipment and prices to do that. Ezra works in the black market and I thought you might want to talk with him about your book."

Ezra looked up from his laptop in shock after John mentioned his black market activities.

He quickly corrected John. "I *used* to be involved in the black market," he emphasized, "but the numbers aren't good anymore. Me and my buddy are going into the hemp market."

"That's a good idea," I stated. "There are a lot more opportunities in the hemp market than in marijuana, that's for sure."

"Yeah," he replied. "But if you want to know something about the black market I can share some stuff with you."

"Great," I responded, and several days later I sent an email to Ezra to suggest meeting for coffee and talking about his experience. Unfortunately, I received the following response: "Hey Pete, I won't be able to give you the information you are looking for (*vide aude tace*), but I would suggest speaking with any of the grow tech's working at your clients' dispensaries." I never get an email response with Latin phrases, but Ezra's response says it all: *see, hear, be silent*. And, it was also helpful advice on Ezra's part to suggest I seek out the employees at existing growing operations because that could easily be a source of supply to the black market. The grow houses have hundreds, up to thousands, of plants and the cannabis plants are about five feet tall and bushy. It would be easy for a worker to snip part of a plant, stick it in a pants or shirt pocket, create a clone, and no one would be the wiser. Or, it would be easy during the trimming process to find a seed and start with that. As it turned out, I didn't need to speak with either Eric or Johnny's employees because people kept lining me up with black market operators that they knew.

For instance, Scott, the athletic club owner from the introductory chapter, had mentioned to me that his brother-in-law was in the black market, and I contacted and met with him and his two partners over lunch. Chase, his brother-in-law, was in his early twenties, as was another of the partners, Jason. But the ringleader, Matt, was in his late thirties or early forties and had been growing marijuana for several decades. He owned a liquor store, grew marijuana in the basement, and sold it to his liquor store customers. Matt wasn't just the oldest person in the group, he also had expertise growing marijuana hydroponically, had contacts to sell to, and was the key to their future success in the legal marijuana market.

"I got started in this a long time ago," Matt told me as we sat down at a restaurant. "After the Eric Holder memo that marijuana was a low priority, it was a lot easier to sell marijuana. I had, literally, hundreds of clients as a caregiver. I remember one time I was driving down to Denver to deliver some 'medicine,'" he stated as he held up two fingers in each hand to make the quote sign with the word 'medicine,' "and I was pulled over by a cop and I had, like, twenty pounds of pot in the car. The cop comes up to my window and looks around and sees all this pot and asks, "What are you doing with all this pot?' 'It's legal,' I say, 'I'm a caregiver,' and I shuffled through a folder in the front seat and handed it to him, 'Here's all the people I'm growing for,' I told him, and the cop looked at everything and let me go," Matt said with a laugh and a shrug. "I mean, what could he do? I had all the documentation, I had all the Red Cards with the names and amounts. But that's what it was like in the early stages of this. That is what we had to deal with…both the caregivers and the police. It was the black market. The cops knew it and I knew it, but they couldn't do anything about it."

"So, how did you get into this?" I asked.

"I learned from an old guy," Matt replied. "He was probably in his late sixties and he had been growing for a long time. He was a mean guy, and I'm not just saying that. He was a guy that no one wanted to deal with, but he liked me, and he decided that if this was going to continue he would need to transfer his knowledge to someone younger, and that was me," Matt stated with a laugh. "He used hydroponics to grow pot, and that was unique at the time. When I first started, it was so difficult that I basically ruined half of the crops for the first five years. It's hard. It takes a long time to understand hydroponics. I'm ok now, but…man! I ruined a lot of crops!" he laughed.

"And what's your plan now?" I asked.

"Well, we're going to Commerce City. You know that a lot of growers are out there and there are a lot of warehouses to choose from. So, we're going out there and we'll be growing several hundred thousand feet. My ultimate plan is to sell to RJ Reynolds. Those guys are interested in the business and have the money to invest and they're just waiting on the sidelines. But I want to have a state-of-the-art facility where they just come in, look at it, and say, 'Yep. We'll take it'. I expect them to start buying in five years, and we want to be set up for that."

"What's happening with the black market now, do you know?"

"It's still going. The prices would have to come way down before you'd put much of a dent in it. But I think there are a lot of people like me who were caregivers and selling to the black market and are now going legit. I tell you, though, the people that really have it rough are the Mexicans. Not the cartels, the regular people that live here in town. Some of those guys would go down to the border and get a backpack full of marijuana, like twenty or thirty pounds, bring it back here and sell it. You used to make good money, you know? Like $50,000 to $60,000 cash. But now it's tough. You're not making much."

I met a third black market operator through a relative, who was excited to have me speak with Dave, a guy in his neighborhood whom he had been buying marijuana from for years and years. I finally met Dave at a party and although I never went to his grow house, I did sit down and speak with him for a bit. Dave is older than all the other black market operators, probably in his mid-fifties and he's been growing for a long time.

"I have a nice little business. I just grow for people I know, people at work, people in the neighborhood. It's pretty low-key and laid-back. All I really want to be able to do is sell about $200 dollars' worth of marijuana a day. I don't want to get any bigger and honestly, $200 a day is just fine with me. I would be very happy with that."

It sure would be a nice business. $200 a day would total over $70,000 in tax-free cash a year and at such a small scale, Dave is unlikely to pop up on anyone's radar screen. In fact, when I mentioned Dave's business to some of the regulators I interviewed they were quite dismissive and responded similar to Jonathan Singer, who said, with a wave of his hand "That's not the black market that the Federal government is worried about. They're concerned about cartels and drug trafficking, not a small-time guy selling to his neighbors."

ZANDER AND JACK, BLACK MARKET ENTREPRENEURS

The people I spent the most time with—nearly ten months—were Zander and Jack, two guys who contacted me through the same website that Eric and Johnny had used. I met with them at a coffee shop outside Boulder—Zander had a trim beard and button-down shirt, and Jack had tussled hair, and was wearing a t-shirt and jeans. They were closer to Ezra and Chase's age—late twenties or early thirties, but unlike Chase they were college educated. They grew up in Kalamazoo, Michigan, and became good friends during college and migrated to Colorado when Amendment 64 was passed.

Both Zander and Jack had a holistic, spiritual view of cannabis, and they believed in the efficacy of the plant to alleviate all sorts of pain and ailments. In fact, when I asked Zander and Jack to list their vision and mission for the business plan several weeks later, Zander sent me an email with the following response:

Our vision is a world where people live in harmony with nature, and in peace with one another. And our mission is protecting the diversity of life through contributions made possible by providing the most consumer-safe, medically-beneficial, and highest-quality cannabis concentrates possible, helping establish an industry standard of excellence in ethical and ecologically responsible practices.

They are both caregivers and ultimately were seeking to help people with a range of medical ailments.

Zander studied acupuncture in China and learned about medicines and Eastern religion while he was there, and Jack worked with the Department of Natural Resources in Michigan prior to moving to Colorado. They are bright, articulate, and motivated to get started in the cannabis industry. The only problem is that there are moratoria and outright bans on new growing facilities and dispensaries, and there are no start-up opportunities for Zander and Jack. That didn't matter to them because they were planning on setting up shop in Oregon which, in the spring of 2015, did not have a residency requirement and had unlimited licensing opportunities for medical marijuana.

"You know," Zander started out, "the thing that really swayed us to go with you is that you have already consulted in the industry. That's important to me and Jack. We need to work with someone who understands us and the industry."

"Well, I understand the industry pretty well. What are you trying to do?"

"We're making concentrates," Zander responded.

"Oh, I don't know much about that."

"We'll get you up to speed on that," he replied, as he opened his backpack and pulled out a soft-bound book put out by Marijuana Business Daily, *Marijuana Business Factbook 2015: Exclusive Financial Data For Cannabusinesses & Major Investors.* "This will get you started," said Zander. "It's got a lot of industry level information, and it's known in the industry for having reliable data."

"Yeah," responded Jack.

"Oh, this will be really helpful for the background and growth of the industry and helpful to investors. But I will also need your numbers that are specific to your extractions."

"Sure, we'll get that to you in a day or so," said Jack, "but I can give you a little background now. What we're doing is more art than science, with the concentrates. We make a shatter that has nearly 90 percent THC concentration, and virtually no smell, no solvent residue, and no chemicals."

"Wow, 90 percent?" I asked, surprised.

"Yeah," said Jack. "We get that consistently and our products can be used the way they're made, or transformed and infused into edibles. But we also use the shatter for a starting material that we create called 'raw' and the 'raw' consistently gets 92-96 percent THC levels—it's nearly pure."

"I know there are some people who demand higher and higher THC levels, but would anyone really want 96 percent THC in a concentrate?"

"Well, the infused manufacturers do. If I have a gram of our raw product that is, let's just say, ninety percent pure, that's nine hundred milligrams and the manufacturer can make nine

100-mg candy bars. If I sell them the gram for $25, and each candy bar sells for $25, they'll make $200 dollars on that one gram."

"That sounds like a pretty good business, for both you and the infused manufacturer," I replied. "How much equipment do you need, and how big of a facility does it take to do this?"

"We'll have to price out the equipment," Zander responded, "but the space we need is what," he asked with a look to Jack, "about 2,000 square feet?"

"Yeah, or maybe a little less."

"So, you could basically do this in a strip mall, I mean, if the building was zoned for that?" I asked.

"Yeah," said Zander.

"Well that makes finding real estate a lot easier. Let me ask a question, though, why Oregon? Why not produce here in Colorado?"

"First," Zander responded, "there are not any licenses available in Colorado. Second, there are already some really good companies making extracts here but third, we think Oregon will be a better market in general. Oregon has higher adult use of marijuana, they don't have any limit on medical licenses, and they don't have a residency requirement. We think if we can get into the Oregon market quickly we can establish our brand and get more market share than others."

"Ok, that makes sense. Why don't I take a look at this industry data, and you guys send me some numbers on what your costs and expected selling points are and I'll start putting together a financial model and then we can see where we're at."

"Great!" exclaimed Zander with enthusiasm. "Thanks, Peter."

As we got ready to leave Jack asked, "How much is your rate?" and he pulled out some cash from his jeans pocket. I told him, he paid me, and we parted ways. Like Eric and Johnny, Zander and Jack never carry any debts to vendors, they pay as soon as they get the service, they pay in cash, and they don't ask for an invoice or any paperwork. In small companies in America, ones with owners that are people and not shareholders, payments for services are nearly as quick as the cannabis operators, just never in cash, and never without an invoice. But in corporate America, in the global corporations and the Fortune 500-size companies? Good luck getting paid timely. You'll have to submit a detailed invoice and then wait ninety days for your payment, if ever.

Several days later I received the numbers from Zander and Jack on their extractions business. In an email they told me that they were going to purchase ninety pounds of raw cannabis flower as their starting material on a weekly basis. In Colorado that would set them back $180,000, but in Oregon wholesale cannabis is $1,400 per pound, so only $126,000 per week, or a little over half a million a month. Still, that's over $6 million a year in cost of goods sold, before rent, labor, taxes, shipping, marketing, or any other business expenses. They were expecting to sell their concentrate for $25-35 per gram wholesale, leading to revenues of $207,000 per week and leaving them with a little over $80,000 before operating expenses, per week. Only eighteen percent of the raw cannabis flower could be converted to concentrate and the rest, I assumed, was wasted during the process.

When I met with Zander and Jack the next time, I had already learned that concentrates and edibles were the fastest growing segment of the cannabis industry and were expected to be the fastest growing segment for the next five years. I also learned that concentrates had the highest profit margin within the category. At this early stage of industry growth the typical infused marijuana product manufacturer was small, with fewer than ten employees and a facility less than two thousand square feet. As the industry matures, I expect that larger companies with economies of scale will enter the market and force out the small, mom-and-pop edibles manufacturers. And, I expect that other extraction companies will emerge, and through economies of scale, force out guys like Zander and Jack. But for now, the market was ripe for these guys to get going and make good money.

We met at the same coffee shop a second time. "I've done a little research on the extracts industry," I started off, "and I think you guys are in the right segment of the cannabis industry, but purchasing ninety pounds a week of cannabis flower is expensive, and risky."

"Once we get started," Zander stated, "it won't be hard at all."

"Yeah," I replied, "but you guys don't have any contacts in the industry in Oregon, right? You'll have to create some extracts and then go to dispensaries and see if those guys will put your product on their shelves."

"That's what we're planning!" Zander stated with excitement. "Jack is moving out to Oregon in a month and he's going to start meeting with people and get some orders lined up."

"Or," I stated, "maybe you get the dispensary owner to purchase the cannabis flower, you create the extract for them, and they sell it. They'd probably want to put their own label on it, though."

"No," Zander broke in, "we're not interested in that. The whole thing is that we want to create our brand not someone else's brand."

"I understand that, but to get going you're either going to need about a million dollars, or you'll have to get someone to buy the cannabis flower for you. And honestly, I think it's going to be hard for you guys to get a million dollars."

"Ok," Jack spoke up. "Let's just work the numbers a couple of different ways and see where we're at."

"No problem. How confident are you in being able to process ninety pounds a week? And why do you have to process so much?" I asked.

"We're totally able to process ninety pounds a week," Jack stated, "that's not going to be a problem. We can process thirty pounds in three days, from raw cannabis flower to finished product, so we think we can do ninety pounds a week."

"That's how fast you can convert raw cannabis flower to saleable product?" I asked. "Three days?"

"Yeah," Jack responded matter-of-factly.

"Ok, why don't you walk me through the process so I understand how this works. If I don't understand it, very few investors are going to understand it and that's a big number for an investor to come up with if they don't really know what's going on and what the process is."

"Sure," stated Jack. "Most people making edibles create an extract out of the leaves and trim, which is a worse starting material—it's called food grade. That's why a lot of edibles taste weedy, but we're starting with the flower, and we're processing it in a different way that makes it tasteless and odorless. First, we make something called 'shatter' and we use a closed loop process with butane for that, although there are other ways to do it. You've seen all of these accidents where people get burned trying to make hash in their kitchen?" he asked me.

"Yeah, I've seen that in the news."

"Well, they are basically trying to make shatter, but it's dangerous if you don't know what you're doing. Our system is a closed loop system so there's no chance that a spark or something will ignite. It's totally safe.

"So, once we have the shatter we use that as the starting material for something we call 'Raw.' We take the shatter and we refine it in a process called 'winterization,' in which we remove the waxes, fats, and lipids. Then we do a second refinement step called 'decarboxylation,' and it's a heat and pressure process that removes any remaining impurities or residual solvents. The decarboxylation process activates the THC, the same as when marijuana flowers are ignited with a flame. After that second refinement process the extract is ready to be consumed, inhaled, ingested, or used topically. Our extract always has 90-96 percent THC. The other thing is, the decarboxylation process burns off any terpenes so the weedy flavor is gone, and our Raw product is tasteless and odorless, perfect for an edible."

"And you don't need much space to do this?" I asked.

"No," responded Jack. "We can do it in 1,200 square feet, and that's with an office and some storage for both cannabis flower and finished product."

"Ok," I responded. "I think I have enough information to write your business plan. Once it's done if you want I can introduce you to a couple of people who are investors, although I don't know how interested they will be in Oregon. But, they do understand something about the industry, and they'll be good people to speak with."

GETTING STARTED IN THE BLACK MARKET

I met with Zander separately once to understand how he got started in the black market. By all outward appearances both Zander and Jack look like any other twenty-somethings in America. They both play in soccer leagues in Boulder, they hike and ski, they both have regular jobs. They just happen to also grow, manufacture, and sell cannabis.

"Originally, I started selling so I could get my marijuana for free," Zander told me. "I would buy from street dealers, and once they found out I was going to college they hooked me up. College kids have money and as long as people can't smell it in your dorm, you're good to go."

"And how would you find people to sell to?" I asked.

"It's easy," said Zander. "Word of mouth, really. Once people know you've got stuff to sell then they come around to buy some. But I would only sell to people that I knew, or a friend of a friend," he said with some thoughtfulness. He hesitated bit and reflected. "Yeah, you'd have to be friends. You can't inspire loyalty, and that's what you need in the black market. You need people that can keep a secret. One time a buddy of mine got caught with some weed and he spent two weeks in jail—and it was stuff he bought from me! But he never revealed anything, and when he got out I hooked him up. If you are friends with someone then they're emotionally invested in you, and they see you as a good guy. So, really, you're only as good as your connections. It's about people you know, and it's about people you trust. At a certain level, there's some fear, too. I mean, if you turn someone in for selling pot, you don't know what they're going to do, right? There's a little fear there. But I always figured if people respect you and like you they won't turn you in. If they don't like you, they'll turn you in."

"Do you know much about where your marijuana came from?"

"Not really," Zander replied, "I was too low level for that, and I really didn't want to know. The guy who sold to me was a hustler from Detroit. He had the connections. But I guess he'd send guys down to Arizona and Texas and they'd load up their car and drive back to Detroit. They would always distribute from a big city like Detroit. And my connection would look for someone to sell to in the ghetto, the suburb, the private school, the college. He also had a legitimate business and my guy owned a couple of those bouncy castles that you set up at kids' birthday parties. I don't know, I guess it's easier to deal with the money and a business like that, it's all checks and cash."

"And is there a typical buyer?" I asked.

"No, not really," Zander stated. "All sorts of people buy, and on the college campus it's just as many girls as guys. Girls actually are the best customers. They're more generous, they don't argue about price. Guys are stingy. If I could sell to only women I would."

"Do you ever have issues, like with the quality or the quantity?"

"Oh, yeah, stuff comes up, but when you're dealing with your friends, or the friend of a friend, it's pretty easy to solve. I always told people the first time they bought from me that the quality is the quality. I do my best to make it high quality—I remove the seeds and the shake, but beyond that it is what it is, and the price is the same. Sometimes the quality is great, and sometimes it's lousy, but I can't control that, and they have to buy what I have. They can't, you know, go to another dealer because they don't like what I have. People rarely take advantage of you. Sometimes I'll get a call back and a guy will say that he weighed his stuff and it's less than what I told him and I'm like, 'What? Are you saying that my scale is different than yours?' If it happens a second time I'll tell the guy to find another dealer.

"For a first-time buyer I'll weigh it up a little fatter. The prices are always flexible. I would usually get fronted a pound and the price was half a pound, so once I sold half a pound the rest was all profit for me. That gives me a lot of flexibility on the prices. There are a lot of opportunities to be a nice guy. I can take care of people, I can smoke with them, hang with them. It's like a brotherhood, you're all doing something illegal, and you're doing it together. I've had some great sessions."

"What? What's a session?" I asked.

"Oh," Zander laughed, "that's what we call it when we smoke together, a session."

That term, "session" reminds me of the music scene and of jazz in particular, when any practice or live music venue is called a "session," and it reminds me of the seminal work by sociologist Howie Becker, who immersed himself in the jazz scene of Chicago in the 1950's.

"So now you're out of the black market and you and Jack are growing, right? So you don't have to buy marijuana from anyone?"

"Yes. We're incredibly excited. This is an opportunity that could potentially really help out my current family and allow me a foundation to have a wife and provide for children of my own one day possibly. It's life changing!" Zander said with enthusiasm. "And the same is true with Jack. Our dedication runs deep. So anyway, we decided to grow on our own. We have more control, and the quality is a lot better, too. We started with some seeds from Amsterdam. It's pretty easy to find on the internet. The only problem is that you have to pay up front and then sometimes your shipment comes through, and sometimes it doesn't and you're just out that money."

"How do they send it to you?"

"Oh, lots of different ways. One of the common ones is to remove part of a book binding and slip the seeds in there. The seeds are really small, so that's not a problem, and you can send books cheap. So that's what those guys would do, is slip the seeds into a book binding."

"And how did you learn how to grow, did you learn that on the internet too?"

"No, Jack and I had a friend who had an older brother that grew. That's how most people learn, from someone's older brother or a cousin, someone like that. But this guy was growing legally because he was a medical marijuana patient. Anyway, Jack really took to it. He enjoyed it, thought about it, improved it. Jack learned a lot, and he's still learning. We're doing totally organic growing—no pesticides and no fertilizers. Jack has figured out that certain plants, like mushrooms, when they biodegrade provide fertilizer to the marijuana plants. So we have a system where we put plants into the soil and specific plants into the planters to help the marijuana plants."

"Why aren't you going to grow out in Oregon?"

"We could," Zander replied, "but we'd rather focus on the concentrates. Let the growers grow, let the dispensary guys sell. We just want to make the best concentrates and only do that, at least for now."

FINDING MONEY FOR ZANDER AND JACK

I liked the business that Zander and Jack were setting up. It didn't require a lot of space, it was difficult to replicate what they were doing, and the two of them along with a master extract maker could operate the whole thing. When I finished with the plan I suggested that they meet with Derek, the finance guy who tried to work out a deal with Johnny but could never do it. I knew that Derek would not be all that excited about a $300,000 deal, since there's just not that much upside. He told me that he and the consortium of investors he worked with liked to be in the $2 to 5 million dollar range, but I thought at the very least that Zander and Jack could use the meeting with Derek to understand how an investor would look at their business and what sorts of questions they needed answered.

We met at a coffee shop in Boulder. Derek rode his bike and showed up very casual—t-shirt, shorts, hat and sunglasses—and I did the same, since I rode my bike.

"So, you're Pete's guys?" he asked as he pulled a chair up to the table.

"Yes. I'm Zander."

"And I'm Jack."

"Good," replied Derek. "Nice to meet you. Pete told me a little bit about what you guys are doing. I actually have an investor that lives in Portland and I'll shoot off your executive summary to him to get his thoughts. But why don't you tell me what you're doing?"

"Ok," responded Zander. "We're making extracts for the Oregon market—"

"Where are you going to be located, do you know?" Derek broke in before Zander could finish.

"Portland," said Jack.

"Yeah, that's good. It's kinda tough to finds real estate though. It's really crowded in Portland. You'll have to pay top dollar to get something."

"We don't need much space," said Zander, "only about 1200 square feet."

"That's it?" Derek asked in surprise. "I don't know if any investors will be excited about that. When the industry first became legal investors were willing to loan hard money in a 40 for 40 deal—40 percent interest over forty months, but I haven't heard of anything like that recently, and most of the investors are looking for a real estate play. The problem with a small building is that there's really no play there for investors. That's what the investors are really looking for is a real estate play, something that if the Feds come in and they send the marijuana business packing, the investors can repurpose the building for something else. But, like I say, I have a guy I work with who lives in Portland and he'll know the market for real estate and for marijuana pretty well. And, we'll let you know."

"So anyway," Zander continued, "me and Jack are working with an extractor who won the Cannabis Cup for best CBD extract and we're going to start in medical first, since there are no limits on licenses, and then we'll wait to see what happens with recreational. But ideally we'd like to be in both the medical and recreational markets."

"Yeah, of course," said Derek, "you have to be in both. What kind of money are you looking for, and what's your timeframe for getting started?"

"We think we need $300k, and Jack is heading out within a few weeks to figure out the building and get some things going with dispensaries. So, as soon as we get the money we can get a building and buy the equipment."

"Ok, let me run this by Jay, my buddy in Portland, and see what he thinks."

After Derek left Zander and Jack looked at each other, and Zander commented, "Can you believe that Derek never once took off his sunglasses?"

"I know!" said Jack. "What's up with that? Who does that? Who has a conversation and never once looks at the other person?"

Zander laughed, "If he didn't ride his bike here I would have thought he was blind."

A couple of days later I heard from Derek. "So, I heard back from Jay. He's skeptical about these guys. He thinks that if they're not a part of the local scene they'll never be able to make it work. I know it looks promising to go to Oregon because of the licensing thing, but Jay seems to think that the market is already locked up and these guys won't be able to get anywhere. Without Jay on board I won't be able to get anyone else interested."

"Ok, well, that's pretty much what I figured. But it's crazy that these guys can't even get $300,000."

"Yeah, well that's the market now. A year ago they would have had no problem, but now investors are savvier about the industry, they're leery of what's happening, all the hype but no real payoff. I'll let you know if I run across anyone who might be interested."

"Ok, thanks."

I relayed Derek's response to Zander and Jack, but I also told them about another investor in Boulder, Julie, and that Julie's investors might be a better fit.

I met Julie at a Boulder Cannabis Meetup several months before and tried to get her investors to consider Johnny's business. Julie told me that her investors, Patrick and Dave, were interested in edibles, but that they weren't interested in just investing in an edibles business, they had ideas on creating their own line of edibles. They wanted a work space, and they needed the knowledge on how to create an edible. It seemed to me that Patrick and Dave could maybe work out something with Zander and Jack, and I approached Julie about that.

"I'll run it by them," she replied when I told her about Zander and Jack. "I haven't spoken to them in awhile, so I don't know if they're even still interested in the space, but I will let you know. They're hard to track down."

"Ok, great."

I sent Julie the executive summary of Zander and Jack's extraction business but after two weeks hadn't heard anything back. Zander and Jack were getting worried. "These guys are high-powered and super busy," I told them. "Why don't I set up a face-to-face meeting with the three of us and Julie and maybe after she meets you she'll be more motivated to push things forward."

We did that and Julie got more excited about their business, but couldn't believe that there were unlimited licenses in Oregon for medical marijuana. After another two weeks we still hadn't gotten anything going with Julie's contacts and I suggested to Zander and Jack that they contact Julie with a cash offer to get things moving. Once they did that Julie pushed things forward and we had a conference call with Patrick.

Julie gave me a little background on Patrick and Dave. Patrick was a successful trader and Dave was a real estate developer. They are in their late fifties or early sixties, and are only interested in the edibles segment of the cannabis industry. They are also part of a consortium of investors that includes a former U.S. Governor, a best-selling business author, and other high networth people. After introductions, Patrick started the conversation.

"Do you guys have all the permits and licenses to operate?"

"We don't need a license for medical marijuana in Oregon," Zander replied.

"Really?" asked Patrick, surprised. "I didn't know that."

"Yes, that's the way the law is written at this point. For recreational you'll need a license but right now it's illegal to sell recreational marijuana. But for medical there are no license restrictions."

"That's good," Patrick responded. "We've talked to a lot of people that have good ideas and business plans, but they don't have the license and without that you just can't operate. But I'd like to hear more about how you make your edibles. The problem that we're running in to is that the food processing is unstandardized, and the taste of the edibles is awful."

"Right," agreed Jack. "For most of these edibles the only reason that you eat them is because they have cannabis in them, not because they taste good, but our process produces an extract that is 90 to 96 percent pure THC, and it is tasteless and odorless. So, it's the perfect way to infuse an edible, because you get the THC but not that weedy taste. And also, because we know exactly what the THC levels are, we can standardize the dose."

"I did meet with an entrepreneur in California who has a cannabis-infused water, and it tasted just like water," Patrick stated. "There was no cannabis taste or smell. He uses nanotechnology for that—is that what you guys are doing?"

"No," Jack responded. "We start with cannabis flowers, not the leaves or trim, so our starting material is higher quality. Then we make something called shatter in a closed loop system. And then we take the shatter and refine it further through a heat and pressure system. Once we do that the THC is activated, and all the impurities and terpenes that produce that weedy taste are gone. So, we use a two-stage process to create our extract."

"One of the things that we're finding in the current market," Patrick began, "is that these edible companies are just spraying existing candy, like gummy bears. We don't want to do that. We don't want to buy something that's a children's product and spray it with marijuana. Our ultimate goal is to be the McDonald's of the edibles market. We want to make our candy to market specs where we label it in milligrams per serving, and we want to be compliant with all the food labeling laws. The companies that spray have a really inconsistent product, and you can't build a strong brand if you have inconsistent products.

"Let me ask you guys, who is the biggest end-user of the edibles?"

"Definitely the thirty to forty-year-old female," Zander responded. "Edibles are both the fastest growing segment of the industry, and they're expected to be the fastest growing for the next five years."

"Yeah," I broke in. "I went to a cannabis symposium earlier in the year and one of the speakers was an infused manufacturer and she said that one of the appealing things about edibles for women is that you can go to a concert at Red Rocks, enjoy yourself, and never have to get up and wait in line for the bathroom. There are a lot of upsides to the edibles market, plus a variety of products, like the water product you mentioned, Patrick."

"Nearly half of the recreational market in Denver was concentrates," Jack stated. "We think that will be true in Oregon, too."

"Well, let me ask you this," Patrick continued, "if you were going to make edibles, what would you make?"

Zander was the first to respond. "I would make a high-quality infused coconut oil, or a high-quality peanut butter. With the coconut oil you can use that in so many ways in your own cooking. Why buy an edible when you can cook with a THC infused coconut oil? And with our extract we can infuse either the coconut oil or the peanut butter and both will taste like regular foods, not like cannabis infused food."

"Interesting. Well, you have to start somewhere and find out what's working. We would like to be able to experiment with creating some edibles. We have ideas on what we'd like to do, so maybe there's a way where we could work together—you can do your extractions and we can set up a kitchen and experiment."

"Sure," said Jack enthusiastically. "We would definitely be up for that."

"Ok," said Patrick. "I am in New Jersey right now and I'm going to Washington to speak with some people there and look at some businesses. Let me get back to Dave on this and see what he's thinking. Where are you guys, in Oregon?"

"No, we're in Boulder," said Zander, "but Jack is heading out to Oregon in a few days to scout around and look for some real estate."

"I'm just thinking that I would like to meet with you in Boulder," Patrick replied. "Maybe do a tour and find out who's good in the edibles space. We want to be in ten states as soon as possible and we see this as a branding problem right now, and the first company to create a strong brand will be able to dictate the market. I'll talk to Dave and circle back."

Several weeks later we still hadn't heard back from Patrick. Zander and Jack were upset that there was no response since the conversation went so well but I reminded them that it was

August and a lot of people take vacations and might not be around. Anyway, I texted Julie to ask about Patrick, and she got back to me a couple of hours later.

"Yes, so when I talked to Patrick he said getting the investors to sign off on anything was like herding cats. He sent the executive summary around and there was no interest. He said that they were all in a lot of investments right now and were spread too thin. So, Zander and Jack are going to have to wait, or find a different way to get their business going."

"Ok, well, that's too bad. I thought it might work since Zander and Jack have the skills and Patrick and Dave need the help."

"Yes," she responded. "I thought so too. I can check back in a month or so and see where they're at. But I have a colleague in Chicago who can provide a revolving line of credit to Zander and Jack."

"Really?" I asked. "Even with no real business and everything just a guess?"

"Yes. The way he works is he sends a pre-application and based on that tells you how much money you can expect. He takes 8 percent right off the top of the total amount, but for the other funds you don't pay interest on them until you actually use them, and the lender gives you 8-12 months grace period before you have to start paying back."

"That sounds too good to be true, but these guys don't have any assets or collateral for a loan, just an idea."

"Evidently that's all you need," she responded. "They decide how much to give you based on your credit score. All you need is a DUNS number and to be registered as a company. Zander could do an application and so could Jack, and maybe together they would be able to get the $300,000 they need."

"Ok, why don't you send me the application and I'll get those guys going on that."

I gave the application to Zander and Jack and we set up a phone conversation with Mark, who was in Chicago, and who arranged the financing. He was ambivalent about the nature of

Zander and Jack's business as long as they had generic names for their companies. He needed the Dun and Bradstreet number for each company, the articles of incorporation, and the credit scores for both Zander and Jack. The whole process took thirty days and was basically a solution for Zander and Jack to the banking problem plaguing the cannabis industry—not only is it near impossible for cannabis companies to put money into a bank account, it is impossible to get a loan for a cannabis business from a bank. Mark's company would shoot the pre-application to over two hundred community lenders who would use the personal credit scores to determine how much money they were willing to lend. After the pre-approval Jack received an offer of $60,000 and Zander got $40,000, for a total of $100,000 between them.

Unfortunately, Zander and Jack priced out the equipment for their extraction business and the money they would get from Mark's lender was short by $200,000. Zander and Jack thought it would take $100,000 to convert a commercial space into a world-class extraction lab, and another $150,000 for the closed loop system and the ovens. And they didn't include any operating capital for salaries, rent, utilities nor, most importantly, the money needed to buy the cannabis flower for the extraction. On top of that, Mark, the person putting together the financing for Zander and Jack, took 8 percent off the top of the total amount awarded. The actual lender would give Zander and Jack twelve to eighteen months with no payments, but Mark collected his 8 percent as soon as the transaction closed between the lender and Zander and Jack. This was a problem for Zander and Jack because if they never used any of the money awarded by the lender, they would still have to pay back the $8,000 to Mark.

They were both hopeful that Jack could get something going in Oregon and Jack was out there doing his best, but he was struggling. Everyone he met was open to buying the extract, but not to providing the cannabis flower—they wanted the finished product. He even met with a company where the owners were his age, they reportedly had the highest revenues in the state, and they owned 85 acres of land that would be ideal for Zander and Jack to put up a building for their extraction lab. But they wanted to sell Zander and Jack's extract exclusively in their lone dispensary, effectively making Zander and Jack employees of the company.

In September I got a desperate call from Zander. "Pete, we don't know what to do. Jack hasn't been able to get anything going with anybody and our rent check is due. It's the last money we have."

Their only real option was for Jack to come back to Colorado, which he did. Zander and Jack started growing cannabis again in the basement of their rented home. I recalled that Julie once asked if I knew a buyer for a growing operation and dispensary, so I called her to see if those were still available.

"Yes," she said. "The client has been growing in a 15,000 square foot facility and has a dispensary in Boulder."

"Ok," I stated. "Do you know how many lights they have and whether they are growing in soil or hydroponics?"

"Good questions," Julie responded, "I'll ask."

She sent me a document later that day. The business was 15,000 square feet of space, including 320 lights, but the grow was hydroponics and Zander and Jack only knew how to grow in soil. But it was a turnkey operation and included the grow house, a dispensary, and the transfer of all licenses, for the asking price of $2.32 million. The seller listed $26,000 in rent for both the dispensary and the growing facility, but no other expenses like taxes, labor, utilities, or cost of goods sold. Using a rule of thumb of four pounds per light per year the total volume would amount to nearly 1,300 pounds and at a sales price of $1500 per pound, the gross revenues would be $1.9 million. But without knowing any of the details on the expenses it was impossible to know whether the company was even profitable at $1.9 million. Julie also told me about a grow operation in Denver that was 7,200 square feet and 200 lights selling for $1.7 million that would generate roughly $1.2 million in gross revenues. But Zander and Jack weren't even close to being serious about any of these opportunities, and they couldn't even come close to buying a MIPS license which several brokers told me would cost about $350,000.

As caregivers they could legally grow cannabis, but it was difficult to gain any traction without a lot of plants and they were limited by the size of their basement. I did have a plan for them, however. I had a college buddy, Mark, who owned five acres of land in southern Larimer County, about twenty miles north of where Zander and Jack were living. I approached Mark about erecting a pole barn on his property where Zander and Jack could grow medical marijuana. I highly doubted that Mark would be interested in hosting marijuana growers on his property, but he surprised me when he said he was really excited about it. "Let me talk to my wife, Michelle, and see what she says about it," he told me. "But you know she's kind of a hippy and open to that sort of thing."

"Sure, just make certain that she understands that what Zander and Jack are doing is legal because they are caregivers, and also that they are growing medical marijuana, for patients."

"Yeah," Mark responded, "I don't think Michelle would be all that interested in recreational marijuana."

The next day Mark got back to me. "Michelle's really excited about it."

"Wow, that's surprising to me," I said.

"Me too, but she's open to it, and would even like to learn how to grow it. So let's set up a meeting with Zander and Jack so that we can look for a good location, and we can meet those guys and get a feel for who they are."

Jack was still in the process of moving back from Oregon and unavailable to meet, but Zander and his girlfriend followed me to Mark's property several days later. I asked Zander to do some quick research on the cost of a pole barn and he came up with a figure of $15,000 for a 40 x 60 size barn. We met briefly just as Michelle was leaving on an errand but even so, she and Zander had a lot in common. They are both interested in Eastern medicine, acupuncture, holistic healing, organic food, and other alternative approaches to life and health.

Walking around on the property it was clear that the best place to put the building was just behind Mark's garage, but that was fine with him. Mark's ultimate goal was to convert the pole barn to an aircraft hangar after Zander and Jack were done growing and by locating the pole barn next to the garage, Mark had enough land to create a runway for his plane. The rent that Zander and Jack would pay Mark would get him a hangar for free. But he needed to do his own research to figure out the actual costs, the permitting, and the utilities.

"It's way more than $15,000" Mark said to me in a phone call about a week later.

"Why's that?" I asked. "It's just a metal building, right?"

"Well, I don't know where Zander got that number—maybe it's just for the building, you know, something you order off the internet and it shows up in pieces at your house. But you still have to put in a cement foundation and you have to have someone erect the building. I had a contractor come over and look at the spot. He figured it out."

"What did he figure out?"

"That I'm building a grow house. He said, after looking at the size and location, 'It looks like you're building a grow house' and I said, 'Yeah, how did you know?' And he said that he has built all sorts of grow houses over the past year, all up and down the Front Range. He's got a lot of experience with it."

"Well, that's good. What did he say?"

"He said that you want a cement floor and that it makes a big difference in insulation if it's five inches thick rather than four inches thick. And also, that we'd want to go with the highest insulation levels for the building because it will make a big difference in heating and cooling costs."

"Well, what did he come up with for a price?"

"$68,000."

"Holy smokes! Seriously? $68,000 versus the $15,000 Zander came up with?"

"Yeah, I know," Mark replied. "But I looked at all the numbers and it's about right. I also got quotes from two other contractors and they were about the same. One of them was less because he priced a 40×40 building, and the other was less because he used R19 insulation rather than R30. But really, they are all in the same ball park."

"Hmmm. Well, that changes things a bit. I think Zander and Jack can still make it worth your while, but they were thinking—maybe—$30,000 for the entire building."

"Yeah," responded Mark, "and they talked with me about taking some space in the building to create an apartment. If we were to do that, we'd have to put in a septic tank and that would add, I don't know, but probably another $10,000. And," he added, "we'd probably want a separate entrance from the side road rather than have those guys go down our driveway every day. I don't know, but the cost is adding up."

"So, if you add it all up, where are you at?"

"Realistically, over $85,000. And with cost overruns and contingencies, I think we're looking at $100,000."

"That seems like a lot."

"Yeah, and I have to start paying for college in the next year. So, it has to be a sure thing. And, truthfully, we still haven't met Jack. Michelle needs to feel comfortable with that because those guys will be there all day long, seven days a week. So, she needs to meet Jack and see where things are at."

"I agree. Jack's on his way back from Oregon. I don't think there will be much of a problem with Jack and Michelle, but they ought to meet before this goes much further."

As it turned out, there was not a problem between Jack nor anyone from Mark's group and they proceeded to figure out how to make it work. Jack and Zander were on cloud nine concerning their good fortune in working with Mark. They couldn't believe how lucky they were to be able to grow marijuana in Colorado and sell it and they wanted to ensure that everything worked out. One of the things that Jack and Zander thought would make a big difference, and one of the things they wanted to explore, was whether it made sense to bring in an engineering firm to work the numbers to maximize yield and reduce costs. They contacted a firm that specialized in cannabis growing facilities. In fact, one of the high-growth areas of the cannabis industry involves companies that have a product that they can adapt from another industry to the cannabis industry.

The so-called cannabis "Green Rush" is really no different than the actual "gold rush" of 1848: the people and companies that made all the money in the gold rush were the companies that sold shovels, pick's and axes—not the people and companies that sought gold. In the cannabis industry the same seems to be true, and the big money makers are the companies that provide services or products to the cannabis industry, like lights or other ancillary products, not the cannabis providers themselves.

Zander and Jack ran into one company that provided an analysis of a grower's space and would then recommend a particular HVAC and cooling system. They were typical of the companies vying for a stronghold in the cannabis space, with significant promises of savings and efficiencies. This particular company had three packages, which were all analytical and based on the grower's facility size, cost of utilities, and other factors specific to the location and environment. The packages ranged from $530 for the do-it-your-selfer, to $2,800 for some engineering, climate, and engineering specifications, and finally, to $8,500 for the full turnkey package including engineering, specifications, on-site visits, and discounts on equipment and installation. Naturally, Zander and Jack were smitten with the top-of-the-line "turnkey" package, but Mark said if they wanted that, they were on their own.

As time went on during the fall of 2015 the participants—Zander, Jack, Mark, and Michelle—became increasingly optimistic for the grow project, and euphoric about the financial outcomes.

Zander and Jack were convinced that the grow operation on Mark's property was a done deal, even though no formal contracts had been signed, and despite the fact that the earliest the contractor could erect a building was late February of 2016. Mark, for his part, starting thinking about ways that he and Michelle could participate in the operations. "You know," Mark mentioned to me, "when Calvin heads to kindergarten next year Michelle will have a lot of time on her hands and we've talked about her working in the growing operations. She could help out in the grow facility and learn the business."

"It will be illegal for her to just work in the growing operations," I stated. "I think she would have to also become a caregiver."

"Is that hard to do?" asked Mark.

"I don't think so. I think you just go to a government office and pay them some money, but I'll ask Jack."

Later Mark said to me, "I've been thinking that I might quit my job and work full-time in the grow operation."

Mark is an engineer and a pilot for a top-tier commercial airline.

"Hold on a second," I said. "Let's see where this goes. We don't even know if Zander and Jack are competent at growing marijuana. All we have is their word, and we can't judge the quality of anything they do."

"Yeah, that's right," Mark responded. "But maybe after I retire I can continue the operation."

The optimism for the growing operation started to wane once the reality of the cost sunk in, along with the reality of a large 40×60 building obscuring Mark and Michelle's view of the mountains. Also, the reality that Zander and Jack would be present on the property 24 hours a day, seven days a week was taking a toll. Mark mentioned to me that the building would obscure their view from a fire ring in their back yard.

"How often do you use the fire ring," I asked.

"We use it pretty often," Mark replied.

"You mostly use it at night, right?" I asked.

"Yeah," stated Mark.

"Well, you can't see the mountains from your fire ring at night, even without the building. But if it's that big of an issue just move your fire ring to where you can see the mountains."

"Yeah, you're right," laughed Mark.

"Is Michelle getting cold feet?" I asked.

"She's really concerned about the neighbors," Mark replied.

"Concerned how?"

"She's just concerned that they're going to find out. They don't come over that often, but occasionally they do and she's afraid they're going to ask about the building."

"So why does she have to tell them anything? Why doesn't she just tell them it's an aircraft hangar? I mean, look around at your neighbors. Every single person has a pole barn about the size of the one you're thinking about. Besides, people live out here on these five-acre plots so they don't have to be neighborly, they don't have to answer questions from nosey neighbors. I mean, really, it's nobody's business what you do on your own property in your own barn, is it?"

"Yeah, I know, but she's just really concerned. I mean the neighbor right there," he pointed to the house next door, "is a Mormon Bishop, and he's got people over at his house all the time and their back yard will be looking directly at the building. And they guy on the other side? He's a retired fireman and his son is a sheriff. I just think it's going to be hard for Michelle to get over the neighbor thing."

"Ok, well, I still don't have an estimate of revenues from Zander and Jack, and we still don't know what they think they're going to pay you in rent. Maybe once I get those numbers she will be willing to consider it."

"Yeah," replied Mark. "That will make it a lot easier if we know what we'll be getting in rent."

I met up with Zander and Jack a few days later and as we were walking across a parking lot to a restaurant. Zander said to me,

"Hey, Pete. We're wondering if we could not pay you a fee for this deal. But we're going to expand and we want you as our business advisor, and we'll pay you for future deals."

I didn't say anything, but that's a huge red flag. For one, it's unethical to cut someone out of a deal that never would have happened without their introducing two parties to each other. Second, it shows that Zander and Jack are greedy. And third, it shows that they are dishonest because I had been straightforward with them about my fees for putting a deal together, and they had agreed to that. Now with them going back on their word I'm concerned that they are not as trustworthy as they have said that they were.

"You guys need to put together a financial statement for Mark," I said to them. "You need to include the revenues you expect, your expenses for labor and a guess for utilities, the rent you'd like to pay, and any other expenses you expect."

"Pete," Zander responded, agitated, "you know we can easily do $300,000 a year in revenues, and that's conservative."

"I know that, but I need it written down for Mark and Michelle to look over, and we need to know your expenses and what you're paying in rent."

That conversation took place in October of 2015. By December I still didn't have a written document with expected revenues and expenses from Zander and Jack. They were increasingly annoyed with me since nothing solid was happening with Mark, and their nervousness that things might not go the way they had planned emerged in nearly every interaction. I sent an email to them with the subject line, "I might have a backup plan for you…" in which I mentioned that I had met another would-be grower, Eduardo, who along with his older brother wanted to grow marijuana. Eduardo and his brother were from Mexico, and neither one knew anything about marijuana—as consumers or as producers.

"I've decided that we should grow marijuana," Eduardo told me during our first meeting.

"What do you know about it?" I asked.

"Really, nothing," he replied. "But we come from a family of farmers in Mexico and I understand that growing marijuana is a lot like growing tomatoes, and we're good at growing tomatoes."

I suggested to Eduardo that he first focus on getting a license to operate a growing facility, because without that he's in the same situation as Zander and Jack—they have to figure out how to grow the cannabis, and how to sell it in the market. I also mentioned Zander and Jack as possible resources to teach Eduardo and his brother how to grow marijuana. Eduardo and his brother were open to that, which explained my email to Zander and Jack.

But Zander went ballistic when he saw that email. "I didn't think Mark not working out was a possibility," he stated, "especially since we changed our whole life plans based around what he told us before. We all had an understanding of how this would work a couple of months ago when we made these life decisions, numbers and all. Is Mark not a man of his word? We all have been planning on doing this. This needs to be figured out immediately. We are extremely upset about the potential for things being up in the air."

I sent an email back to Zander to calm him down. "At this point, without a done deal with Mark, we need to keep options open. Don't stress out about this. This is the way that business works...you always have another option. The worst case scenario is to be 'all in' with no backup plan. What I've gotten you is a plan and a backup plan." That seemed to calm Zander down a bit, but I reminded him that Mark took out a $100,000 home equity loan, he had begun the process of figuring out costs for different sized buildings and with different qualities and characteristics, he had identified a contractor to work with, and he was waiting for the numbers from them.

"No landlord is ever going to build a building for you guys without a business plan that shows your revenues and expenses," I said to Zander. "Who would put up a $100,000 building, that they really don't need, and not know whether the two guys who said, 'trust us, we can make a lot of money' even show up once it's built? What if you bail after six months? Mark is taking a huge risk in putting a building on his property and you can't expect him to take that risk because you're good guys, or nice guys, or because you say you'll 'be generous' to him at the end of the year. The delay in getting this going is 100 percent your fault because you guys haven't put anything together to help Mark and Michelle understand the risk they're taking. I won't let them go forward without some hard numbers."

I received an email from Zander and Jack later that day, finally, with some numbers. But now it was early January 2016—several months after Zander, Jack, and Mark had agreed, in principle, to build a pole barn for medical marijuana plants. In that email Zander and Jack said they would expect revenues of $300,000 to $400,000 and would have one-time start-up expenses of $90,000 to $110,000, operating expenses of $50,000 to $75,000, labor expenses of $10,000 to $20,000, and rent of $17,000. Every year after that was essentially the same, except for the one-time start-up costs. Zander and Jack had a business that would give them about $1.5 million in revenues over five years; Mark could expect a measly $85,000 over that time frame, which would result in a loss for him, and I would get nothing, even though it was my idea and I put the whole thing together. But I still didn't have any hard numbers from Zander and Jack, so I asked them, "How many plants are you going to grow to generate the $300,000 to $400,000 in revenues?"

"Eighty," Zander responded. "And three cycles per year. We'll keep nineteen plants as mothers and clones."

"And are you expecting to get three to four pounds per plant?"

"Oh no," Zander responded quickly. "Nobody's getting 3-4, especially if you're looking for quality. Realistically we are aiming for 1-2 but the numbers that will generate $300k to $400k in revenues reflect 3/4 of a pound to the 1.5-ish range to be safe. Going for larger numbers like 2-3 pounds per plant will decrease quality and selling price dramatically. The sweet spot is aiming for a high quality 1-2 pounds, and maintaining high demand and sale prices… Hold on a second—Pete." Zander stepped away from the phone for a moment.

"Oops, I'm totally mistaken. Jack just pointed out that we do it per light not per plant. I had a brain fart, but that's how we came up with our numbers and how we have measured it all along. So we're shooting for 1-2 pounds per light. At roughly 60 lights."

It's difficult to figure out volume of cannabis based on the number of plants because the yields can vary wildly from under a pound to well over several pounds, but the number of lights in a grow facility tells you everything you need to know to come up with an accurate estimate. I contacted Johnny to see if he had time to go over the numbers with me. He suggested I meet him at this grow house on the east side of Boulder.

"Pete! What's happening, brotha?" Johnny said to me with his usual exuberance, as I walked into his grow house.

"Remember Zander and Jack?" I asked.

"Yeah. I told those guys that they needed to make a decision and take a big risk, otherwise this industry is going to pass them by."

"Yeah, well, the Oregon thing didn't work out. They couldn't get anyone to work with them, so they came back here and I introduced them to a buddy of mine who has five acres in Larimer County. We thought about putting up a pole barn where those guys could grow. They're both caregivers and have a license to grow 99 plants."

"Cool," he said with a laugh. "Pete the cannabis broker! I love it!"

"Not really, but it could be a win-win for both people."

"Where is the property?"

"It's about twenty minutes north of here. But one of the things I wanted to run by you was what sort of volume they could do, and what sort of revenues they could expect."

"How big is the building?" he asked.

"It's 40 by 60, so 2,400 square feet. And they're going to have sixty lights."

Johnny took out his iPhone and did a quick calculation. "Let's see, they ought to do five cycles in a year. Any decent grower ought to get three hundred pounds and if they can't do that," he paused and looked at me carefully, "they don't know what they're doing. So, with three hundred pounds…I can sell a pound for fifteen hundred bucks every day of the week." He went back to his iPhone to calculate. "That's $450,000 minimum."

"Yeah, they said they'd get $300,000 in revenues, which sounds low to me. They also said that they would pay rent of $17,000 per year."

"That's super low," Johnny quickly stated. "Let me see…" as he went back to his iPhone calculator. "They should be paying $40,000 for that space. Start at $45,000 when you negotiate with them and maybe you'll end up at $40,000."

"Ok. One other thing, they don't want to pay me anything for putting this deal together."

"Pete! Dude, you have to get paid," Johnny exclaimed. "I'll do the deal. I'll pay the $40,000 and pay you a fee, too." He looked at one of his employees who was working at a counter. "That would be cool, Jason, don't you think?"

Jason turned around with a big smile on his face. "Yep."

"A little black market lab where we can experiment," said Johnny. "Think about it and text me if things don't work out with Zander and Jack. We'd have to come out and look at it. Is anybody living there?" Johnny asked.

"Yeah, Mark, his wife, a teenager and a five-year-old, but they might be moving closer to town."

"That's a Federal offense," Johnny said with concern, "to grow marijuana with children on the property. That's child endangerment. But, text me and we'll come out and take a look around the property and see if it's something we might want to do."

I left Johnny's grow house with more questions about the proposed caregiver growing facility on Mark's property than answers, and more concerns about Zander and Jack. For one, they came up with a lowball estimate of their revenues and now it looks like they'll have $2 million dollars after five years, and Mark will have just $85,000 and I'll still be stuck at zero for my efforts. But I realized that everything Zander and Jack were doing was hidden from Mark and from me. How would we know how much marijuana they grew, and even if we knew that, how would we know what price they sell their marijuana for? Do caregivers pay taxes? Do they need to have audited financials? This was a business that would be totally discreet. I told Mark in an email that we needed to be assured that everything Zander and Jack were doing was legal—that they have the permits, the licenses to grow, and that they have actual people that they're growing for. We needed to know that, if the Sheriff of Larimer County were to show up on the premises, that they would find the correct paperwork, licenses, and plant count. Otherwise, not only could the whole thing be shut down, but the civil forfeiture laws could be applied to Mark and he could lose his house and all of his property. Or, if the State determined that what Zander and Jack were doing really was child endangerment, Mark and Michelle could maybe lose their kids and have them assigned to a ward of the State.

Mark came to the same conclusion as me: this was a complex and sketchy proposal by Zander and Jack. Besides that, Mark was thinking of moving closer to town and selling the property. But the $17,000 rent didn't sit well with him, especially after I mentioned that Johnny said the going rate was $40,000.

"I just don't have the time to do this," Mark stated. "We like Zander and Jack. They're nice people, but everything they do is in the shadows. We just can't commit to this. It's way more complicated than what I thought at first. I would like to meet with those guys face to face to tell them that we're not going through with the deal. I owe them that, and I want them to understand where we're coming from. Michelle will probably run into Zander at the salt baths, and I don't want her to feel uncomfortable about going there."

"I agree. But I don't think you need me at the meeting, do you?"

"I don't need you, but you're more than welcome to come."

"Nah," I responded. "If they're not paying me I don't want to spend a nanosecond thinking about them."

"Yeah, right!" Mark laughed.

"But why don't you stop by on your way home and we can debrief? I'd be curious to hear their reaction."

"Sure," said Mark, "that would be good."

THOUGHTS ON THE BLACK MARKET

The entire episode with Zander and Jack reminded me of something Derek said after he couldn't work out a deal with Johnny. He said that in so many instances a deal between a legitimate business and a cannabis business falls through at the last minute. That's certainly the case with Zander, Jack, and Mark. They started out with a simple plan: Mark would erect a pole barn that could later serve as an aircraft hangar, he would rent the space to Zander and Jack, and they in turn would grow medical marijuana. But it quickly became an enormously complex project with a lot of unanswered questions about whether it was even a legal grow operation. And the numbers didn't add up given the amount of cannabis and number of medical marijuana patients Zander and Jack were growing for. Zander and Jack said they were growing about 300 pounds of cannabis per year, for four patients. If the patients were to divide that 300 pounds equally, each would receive nearly 34,000 grams of cannabis per year, enough to consume 92 joints per day. And, it would cost each of those patients roughly $100,000 per year to obtain that amount of cannabis. Everything seemed highly unlikely: that four people would spend $100,000 each on cannabis—per year—and that they would personally consume ninety-two joints per day. I suspected that Zander and Jack were planing to sell on the black market, or planning to ship the cannabis back home to Michigan where they could sell it there.

I don't know if the black market is thriving in Colorado—but it's highly unlikely since, in 2017, there were $125.6 million dollars of legal marijuana sales in Colorado, monthly. The black market still exists, though, just as it does in every other state in the union, and people are aware of that. Colorado Attorney General Cynthia Coffman, Eric (the established cannabis operator), an informed source of mine, and law enforcement, all those people know that large-scale black market operators are using the legal market as a cover for illegal growing. But the same could be said about the caregivers in Colorado's medical marijuana market, and there are people like Zander and Jack who grow far more cannabis than can possibly be consumed by a medical marijuana patient. Undoubtedly there are committed, honest caregivers, but there are also people like Zander and Jack who are playing the system, growing in secret locations, and keeping all the money for themselves. They are doing that under the cover of the legal caregiver role.

But, selling in the black market was not the first career choice for Zander and Jack, and they did nearly everything in their power to escape the black market and become legitimate. They created a business plan, met with interested investors like Derek, Patrick, and Johnny, and tried to work out a deal with Mark. Nearly all the people I spoke with who had been operating in the black market, like Zander and Jack, were trying to create legitimate businesses. Ezra wanted to start a business in the hemp industry. Matt and his partners were pursuing a large, legal hydroponic cultivation facility in Commerce City to position themselves for acquisition. Zander and Jack, of course, were trying to create extracts.

Even the people who had created legal businesses, like Eric and Johnny, came from careers in the black market. Eric had over 800 medical marijuana patients and thousands of plants prior to Colorado's legalization and what he was doing, in the early stages of legalization, was basically black market operations under the guise of medical marijuana. Johnny started growing when he was in junior high school and has been doing that ever since. In fact, were it not for legalization, all the people I met in the cannabis industry—save for lawyers and accountants and other vendors—all of them, were operating in the black market. Prohibition prevents any contribution to society for these people, and countless numbers of other people who provide services to the industry or are employed in the industry. With legalization, however, at least some of them are able to start legitimate businesses, follow highly regulated rules and procedures, hire employees, pay taxes, and contribute to society.

CHAPTER 11.

WINNERS IN LEGAL CANNABIS

Even though the legal cannabis industry is only several years old there are already clear-cut winners—businesses, communities, and people who have been able to capitalize on legalization. By "capitalize" I mean something more than the narrow business approach of understanding the "value chain," since that perspective refers primarily to the cultivation, transformation, and sale of cannabis, and nothing more. That is, it refers only to the value that various companies or people add to a product or service as that commodity makes its journey from creation, to sale. Obviously, those activities are important, but in understanding the cannabis industry I believe that Karl Marx, the economist and social theorist, provided a much more fruitful and nuanced set of questions, and a framework that helps us understand, with greater clarity and insight, the dynamics of the newly emergent, legal cannabis industry.

For example, in addition to understanding who owns the means of production within the cannabis "value chain," Marx would most likely expand his inquiry and ask, 'Who has the power in this industry? Who has the ability to write industry rules and regulations? Who can influence the key decision makers?' By focusing on a broader set of questions than the mere cultivation, transformation, and sale of cannabis, we can better understand the structure of the cannabis industry, we can understand the impact people and organizations have had on that structure so far, and we can begin to unveil the processes through which some people have power, are influential, and can monetize their efforts, and others cannot.

Colorado. The state of Colorado, shortly after passing Amendment 64 in November 2012, enjoyed world-wide fame as the first jurisdiction to legalize recreational cannabis, and four years later the state is still widely invoked as a model of cannabis legalization. Colorado's "regulate like alcohol" approach, along with a model to retain prohibition but decriminalize possession of small amounts of cannabis, are the two models most often cited as solutions to the failed cannabis War on Drugs. But there are a number of other models that could be used as alternatives to those two, including allowing adults to grow their own cannabis, allowing co-ops to grow cannabis for members, allowing local governments to control retail sales through dispensaries, or even allowing the government to control the supply chain, like several states have done with alcohol, such as Iowa, Pennsylvania, and others.[1]

Every lawmaker and regulator that I spoke with said that the motivating factor for repealing prohibition had more to do with individual liberties and social justice than with tax revenues, even though the impact of legalization on tax revenues within Colorado is significant. In 2014, the first fully legal year of recreational cannabis sales, direct market cannabis sales were over $700 million dollars, of which the state of Colorado captured about $76 million in tax revenues, licenses, and fees. In 2017 (the latest full year of data), cannabis sales totaled $1.507 billion dollars and the state captured $247.4 million in taxes, with $40 million earmarked for school infrastructure. In addition to taxes, Colorado has created 23,407 new jobs and 424 dispensaries, 503 cultivation operations, 173 infused manufacturers, and 15 testing labs in the recreational cannabis industry. The Bureau of Labor Statistics predicts that the legal cannabis market will create more than a quarter of a million jobs by 2022—more than the expected number of jobs in manufacturing, utilities, or government jobs. The financial impact of the legal cannabis industry for the state of Colorado is closer to several hundred million dollars—all of which would have remained in the black market were it not for Amendment 64.

In addition to the economic impact, Colorado has been a winner in court challenges to Amendment 64 from various outsiders and interested parties. In December 2015, a U.S. district judge dismissed a racketeering lawsuit by two ranchers who claimed that a marijuana cultivation facility ruined their view. A different U.S. district judge also dismissed a lawsuit filed on behalf of sheriffs and attorneys in Colorado, Nebraska, and Kansas. Another racketeering (RICO) lawsuit was dismissed involving a Holiday Inn in Frisco, CO. And the significant lawsuit filed by the state of Nebraska and Oklahoma directly to the Supreme Court, was dismissed by a 6-2 vote, with no explanation from the justices on why they refused to hear the case. Three of the four marijuana lawsuits were funded by out-of-state anti-drug organizations and socially conservative Colorado law firms, a *Denver Post* investigation revealed. Clearly, legal challenges to a state constitutional amendment are not an effective strategy for anti-marijuana forces.

Pueblo County. As detailed in chapter two, Pueblo County has generated about $1.8 million in tax and license revenues, with about $700,000 of the total coming from licenses and fees, which must be renewed annually. But the economic impact goes far beyond the tax revenues and the county of Pueblo has created 1,300 jobs and increased economic activity in the county by $120 million. Land prices have more than doubled at $10,000 an acre, and industrial property is leasing at $50 a square foot—six and a half times more than the state average. Most importantly, perhaps, Pueblo County generated $425,000 from cannabis excise tax revenue, leading to a $1,000 scholarship available to every qualifying graduating high school senior who resides in Pueblo county. Pueblo county expects 300 to 400 incoming college freshmen, who have graduated from local high schools and who will attend a local Pueblo college, to receive a scholarship.

Garden City, Colorado. At the end of my conversation with State Representative Jonathan Singer, he said, "You should talk to the people in Garden City. They legalized marijuana and I've heard that now their streets are paved with gold," with a laugh. "Oh, and also talk to Ronn Nixon—that's 'Ronn' with two n's—about Log Lane Village. Those towns have both legalized marijuana and it's making a big impact in their communities."

So, I did contact people in those towns and Cheryl Campbell, the town commissioner of Garden City, invited me to her office to talk about their experience with legal marijuana. Garden City is a small city, only twenty-six acres, or roughly an area 6 blocks by 7 blocks—with a population of 250. It sits at the intersection of two well-traveled highways, 34 and 85, and is wedged between the towns of Greeley, home to the University of Northern Colorado, and Evans. I don't know if Garden City was misnamed or if it was wishful thinking on the part of the founders, but there's not a garden in sight, no grass and few trees. It is mostly parking lots, warehouses, bars, and pawn shops. The town has a gritty, urban feel. The main street, 8th street, is five lanes wide and the most noticeable feature as you enter Garden City is the White Horse Inn, a dilapidated bar that has weathered the heat, cold, and wind typical of Colorado towns on the eastern plains. Across the street from the Inn is a strip mall with one of the town's four dispensaries. It's only 9:30 in the morning, and there are signs of life, but only at the dispensary where a steady stream of cars are coming and going.

A quick inventory of the town revealed five bars, six Mexican restaurants and a "wing shack," two pawn shops, a flea market, a loan store, and a host of auto repair shops —eleven in total. There's one franchise, not that franchising is a hallmark of advanced capitalism, but the economics of Garden City can be gleaned from the businesses there. It's a poor town, visually unappealing, with a feel of desperation, or resignation. And the data confirm my observations. The median income is $18,900 — far below the poverty level — and nearly 30 percent of the residents live in poverty, ranking 37th out of 396 Colorado communities for percent living in poverty. Since 2000 the population has declined 34 percent and housing values have declined by 35 percent. The schools perform far below the state average and are ranked 476 out of 516 schools, or the 7th percentile.

I walked over to Cheryl's office, passing two guys fixing a flat tire on a flatbed semi-truck, and past a house with a five-foot stockade fence around it.

"Hi Cheryl, thanks for seeing me," I stated as I shook her hand.

"No problem. Let's go in here to talk. It's more comfortable than my office and there won't be any distractions."

She led me through a small kitchen to the conference room. I explained my project to her, and my interest in the industry. "So, I started working with a vertically integrated cannabis business last year and found the business fascinating, and then I got another cannabis client who wanted to be vertically integrated, and I thought, I should write a book about this. Even in Colorado, so many people have no idea about the people involved in the industry, they think it's guys with dreadlocks, tattoos, and piercings."

"Yes," she said as she nodded her head and laughed.

"Since then I've interviewed and spoken with caregivers, with the authors of Amendment 64, with the top marijuana enforcement people, with lawmakers, and with lots of people in the industry. When I was speaking with Jonathan Singer recently, he said I should speak with you. He told me that the streets in Garden City are lined with gold."

Cheryl laughed and said, "Well, I don't know about that...who is Jonathan Singer?"

"He's the state representative from Longmont."

"Oh," she responded. "How much do you know about Garden City?"

"Only what I could get from your website, that a woman tried to incorporate her property after the repeal of prohibition and that after she was able to do that a lot of bars opened up here."

"Yes. It took us three tries to get incorporated and the day that happened the Sheriff in Greeley shut down two bars, and one of them came here. Greeley was dry until 1969...what is that, 35 years after prohibition ended?

"I'm not sure," I responded.

"I don't see that happening with marijuana," she stated. "Either the Feds will legalize everything, or it will go away."

"Are the people in Greeley opposed to what you're doing, with legal marijuana shops?"

"I keep track of what people are saying in the Greeley newspaper and lately I have seen a couple of letters to the editor speaking out against marijuana, but I don't know if that's just a few people or a general feeling. Greeley is dealing with the negative aspects of marijuana but they're not getting any tax benefits, so I can see that sentiment. We're just stacked in here between Greeley and Evans and when something changes in one town it makes a drastic impact in the others."

"Have there been any problems with dispensaries or their customers?"

"It's not a problem at all, and not a problem compared to alcohol. With alcohol we get fights and vandalism, and drunken driving. The Sheriff for Weld county is very anti, and so are all the commissioners, but if you ask the deputies, the ones that patrol here, they will tell you that there is a decrease in incidences. In fact, we have used the surveillance system at a dispensary to look at their neighbors to solve crimes."

It is not surprising that Greeley is opposed to marijuana sales. Dormitories at the University of Northern Colorado are less than a mile away from Garden City, and Greeley is the county seat of Weld County, a vast expanse stretching from Wyoming to the outskirts of Denver and eastward into the Colorado plains. The county has voted republican over the last five elections and the main industries are oil and gas, and agriculture. Weld County has an outright ban on marijuana but in Colorado cities and counties are independent of each other, and because of that, Garden City was able to enact regulations for marijuana cultivation and retail sales. It is the only community in the entire county that allows medical and recreational cultivation and dispensaries. But while Greeley may be opposed to marijuana, the Weld County sheriffs charged with policing Garden City do not see any problems related to marijuana. "We do not give Garden City any extra resources to help manage the stores," said Weld County Sheriff Corporal Matthew Turner. "The stores are not any more of a burden than we are used to."

I asked Cheryl how Garden City came to adopt marijuana regulations.

"Well, it started in 2008 with the Eric Holder and Obama memo, when they said that they weren't going to go after people that used medical marijuana. That statement, that one little line, changed the world. And it changed this nation, and this state, and this community. I find it really interesting that one line, *one little line*," she emphasized, "can change so much."

She reflected for a moment and then continued, "And then in September of 2009 a guy came into my office and said that he wanted to open up a medical marijuana dispensary, and I said, 'Absolutely not! And there's the door,'" as she pointed toward the exit.

"You were opposed to marijuana?" I asked.

"Absolutely! I was very anti. I didn't see any value in it at all and I thought it would cause all sorts of problems for us. Well, anyway, two months later, in November of 2009, he comes back and says, 'I've got my license.' So I knew I had to at least bring it up to the town board. They're a pretty liberal bunch and it was clear to me that my choice was either figure out a way to let this guy open his dispensary, or get a new job. But when we started it wasn't about the money, it was about personal freedoms. Our thinking was, 'Colorado voted for it and we should be respectful of that.'

"That was in 2009. We started with four licenses and at first we said, 'You can have a growing operation on your premises or a growing operation off your premises, but not both. Now we have 22 licenses, so we changed that," she laughed. "We have medical, recreational, MIPS, you know, the edibles, and growing."

"So, you have had to adapt over time?"

"Oh, yes," she exclaimed, "in 2009 the state of Colorado had nothing in place, no real regulations. I remember riding in a car with a regulator from the Marijuana Enforcement Division and telling him that it's really difficult to regulate because their rules are changing all the time. And he got angry and raised his voice and said, 'The regulations do not change!' And of course, we know that's not true because they're changing all the time. This industry is constantly changing."

"You mentioned that the motivation to allow marijuana sales had to do with the fact that the people of Colorado made a change to the state constitution, but the money is still important. I know you can't give me specifics, but do you have a rough estimate of tax revenues from marijuana sales?"

"I can tell you," Cheryl explained, "that in 2008 our monthly tax revenues were $16,000 and now the monthly tax revenues are $128,000. It's not all from marijuana, maybe half, but it has made a big impact here."

It's difficult to discern the financial impact of marijuana for any given community because the Colorado Department of Revenue has a policy of aggregating the data at the county level rather than the city level. If a county has three or fewer dispensaries then the Department of Revenue aggregates counties. In 2014, for example, Garden City had 12 months of medical marijuana revenues but only nine months of recreational marijuana revenues reported. Evidently, in April, a fourth recreational dispensary opened in Garden City and the numbers for Weld county are now publicly available and are not co-mingled with other counties.

In 2014, medical marijuana sales in Garden City totaled $5.4 million, or about $454,000 per month. And for recreational marijuana the sales totaled $8.6 million for the year, averaging $966,000 monthly. But in 2015 the revenues from marijuana sales were significantly higher for recreational cannabis and Garden City had sales of $19.6 million for the year. Along with $4.3 million in medical marijuana sales, Garden City collected $720,969 in sales taxes alone, based on a three percent sales tax. The slight decline of medical marijuana sales when recreational marijuana became available (from $5.4 million in 2014 to $4.3 million in 2015) was precisely what the Marijuana Enforcement Division had hoped (since recreational taxes are higher) although that has not happened in every county. By 2017, medical marijuana sales totaled $3,750,264 and recreational marijuana sales totaled $30,987,020, for a combined total of $34,737,284, from nine dispensaries, all located in Garden City. The 3 percent sales tax amounted to $1,042,118 in new-found money.

"What are you doing with all this marijuana tax revenue?" I asked Cheryl.

"Well, we're getting curbs, gutters, and sidewalks, for the first time ever. Even if this all goes away tomorrow for us the impact of marijuana will last another 25-50 years. And we have had a domino effect. Other business owners are fixing up their properties, and we're providing money to residents to fix their homes and landscape their property. This city will not look the same in a few years. We used some of the money to trim trees before it becomes a problem and Excel Energy said to us, 'That's the smartest thing we've ever seen a town do.'"

I picked up a copy of the town newsletter, the *Garden City Gab*, on my way out of the Board room and saw the extent of investment Garden City is making with their marijuana tax revenues. For business owners there is a 50 percent grant up to $8,000 for facade improvements, and the same matching grant for parking lot repaving. For homeowners there is a 50 percent grant up to $3,000 for new fencing, and the same amount for home improvements including exterior painting, siding, windows, and doors. Garden City also offers residents a $400 dollar water rebate per year, and a $100 dollar voucher for flowers, plants, or garden supplies.

Garden City hired a consulting company to provide ideas on how to improve the downtown and they suggested better signage, a mix of residential and businesses, creating a city park, sidewalks, curbs, and gutters, reconfigure parking, and install lighting — all of which Garden City is pursuing.

"People call me all the time and ask if there are any houses for sale," continued Cheryl, "and I have to tell them that there are not. There's not a house for sale, there are no vacant apartments, we have no open space, no empty buildings. We're paving the streets, we're trimming the trees, we're making improvements that will last for decades. I went to a seminar on marijuana regulations for city planners and the speaker was the chief of police from Erie, and he was very anti. He had all these studies saying that since marijuana has been legalized the black market is up and crime is up. The discussion got very heated between people like me who are not anti, and the anti crowd. Well, the black market and crime are definitely down here."

Log Lane Village, Colorado. I met with Ronn Nixon, who Jonathan Singer suggested I speak with, at his office in downtown Denver overlooking the grounds of the state capitol. That's convenient for him since he is an advocate for medical marijuana patients and spends a lot of time at the Capitol.

"How did you get involved in this?" I asked as we settled down.

"I grew up in Fort Morgan in the 1970's, and I would buy my marijuana in the high school parking lot, so I've been a consumer for the past five decades. But I didn't understand the medicinal benefits until my partner contracted AIDS and I helped treat him, and I learned a lot about edibles. And then in 2010 I was diagnosed with a rare disease that can't be treated with modern medicine, and I can't eat processed foods. So the only option for me is medical cannabis.

"When the first medical marijuana regulations came out in 2010, I was fascinated, and I switched gears and became more and more involved as I educated myself on the regulatory compliance issues. And that's what I do now, is work with companies to insure regulatory compliance, and I am an advocate for medical marijuana patients. Earlier this year we brought in a young man to one of the state Senate hearings and this young person was suffering from Crohn's disease. When he moved to Colorado he was in a wheelchair and in terrible pain. With medical marijuana he gets 1000 mg four times a day, and it has changed his life. Now he is happy, he is hiking, he is enjoying life just like other young people."

"I've heard so many stories like that," I said, "but when you speak with people in the medical profession they dismiss any results as anecdotal. They're all looking for a double-blind study that absolutely proves the efficacy of a drug."

"Yes," Ronn responded. "That's the fallout from a lack of research. Research on cannabis has been restricted, and it's been biased. The government, for the last eighty years, has only explored the adverse effects of marijuana. But marijuana is unique. It has a lot of positive effects."

"Right. Let's talk about Log Lane Village. Jonathan Singer mentioned Log Lane Village and Garden City to me as communities that have embraced cannabis and by doing so, have generated significant tax revenues. But, they are both in counties that have banned marijuana businesses, right?"

"Right. The way it works is, the governments have power in all of this. So the State of Colorado voted to legalize recreational marijuana, but the local community determines the time, place, manner, and number of businesses. A county can opt out, but a municipality can opt in. Jefferson County is out, but Lakewood is in. Morgan County is out, but Log Lane Village is in."

"And how did Log Lane Village get started with marijuana sales?" I asked.

"Log Lane Village has always been different from Fort Morgan, even though they are adjacent to one another. In the 1950's Log Lane Village seceded from Fort Morgan because they wanted a liquor store, and Fort Morgan was dry.

"Ed Parker is the mayor of Log Lane Village and he thought that the only way to save our infrastructure was to legalize marijuana. He started to speak with me about regulations for marijuana and I suggested we put together a question and answer session for the public."

"Now," Ronn leaned forward in his chair, "since I grew up in Fort Morgan I understand the culture and I got a couple of speakers that would fit the culture—people who were in favor of legalizing marijuana, but who also would appeal to eastern Colorado, which is conservative and agricultural. I found a former public defender to speak, and that made a big impact.

"For example," he continued, "The Sheriff of Morgan County was at the public meeting and he was sitting towards the back and I could see that he had several sheets of paper in his hand with his written remarks. After several people got up to speak I could see that he folded the paper in half. Then a few more people spoke, and he folded it in half again. And by the time he came up to speak he had folded it several more times and put it into the front pocket of his shirt. When he did speak all he said was, 'Make sure the cartels are not involved, and keep it out of the hands of children,'" Ronn said with a laugh. "But, to give the Sheriff credit, even though he's opposed to marijuana sales in the county, he does assist with the transport of the money from marijuana dispensaries. When I asked him about why he did that he said, 'because it's the right thing to do.'"

"Well, that's refreshing," I stated, "a public law enforcement officer who is opposed to something but is protecting the people and property of the thing he opposes."

"Yes," said Ronn. "Welcome to eastern Colorado. We do the right thing, the moral thing, regardless of our personal opinions."

"Has there been a big impact in the town so far?"

"Yes, and we only have one dual dispensary, with both medical and recreational marijuana, and one recreational dispensary. The tax revenues so far have been small, about five thousand dollars, but that money went into a youth program. And once higher tax revenues come in the city will use that money to repair pot holes, fix the streets, things like that.

"Also," he continued, "when I was in Log Lane Village last month I spoke with several people who had moved there from Nebraska for medical marijuana. They were happy, and grateful that they could access marijuana. So, it's early, but Log Lane Village is better off with recreational marijuana sales."

Other Industry Participants. One obvious winner since the cannabis industry has been legalized is commercial real estate—not developers, necessarily, but brokers and owners of property. And not just any property, but low-quality, dilapidated warehouses, what the industry calls class B and C properties—the owners of which are the slumlords of commercial real estate. Many of these buildings are functionally obsolete and should be scraped and redeveloped, but with twenty-year leases it's likely that the growing areas of Denver will become even more blighted than they are now. The level of growth in class B and C properties in Denver is among the highest in the country. For instance, between 2009—when the Ogden Memo came out indicating that the Justice Department would not attack, confiscate, or arrest people involved in medical marijuana businesses—and 2014, lease prices for warehouse properties increased 56 percent and currently the vacancy rate is below 2 percent. It's estimated now that in Denver one in eleven industrial buildings is a marijuana growing facility, with no slowdown in sight.

Eric told me about his plan to lease 70,000 square feet of growing space. "Right now I'm spending $300,000 a month on buying wholesale, but why spend that money?" he asked with a raised voice. "So, I had to put $2 million of *my own money in*," he emphasized that point as he raised his arms in frustration, "and borrow another $2 million to lease the 70,000 square feet. It's costing me $85,000 a month in rent and it will take about 8 months to get that up and running plus a lot more money for the build-out. And then we'll have to wait another three months to actually get product. It's hard," he stated as he sat back in his chair and reflected, "I don't know what the market is going to be like in 8 months, but why spend $300,000 a month to buy wholesale?"

"What did you end up paying in rent?" I asked.

"$17 bucks a foot."

"Holy smokes! Are you kidding?"

Eric shook his head and with resignation said, "Once they know you're growing, they jack up the prices."

That $17 rent per square foot is higher than retail prices in most major metropolitan areas. In fact, if Eric had wanted to purchase that property he would have to pay $135.63 per square foot—and that's $85 more per square foot than what he would have to pay in Chicago, Kansas City, or Minneapolis. The market for class B and C properties is so tight in Denver that the average days on market for a leased property is only 148 days, while it's 211 days in Chicago, 197 days in Minneapolis, and 180 days in Kansas City. Minneapolis and Kansas City are comparable cities to Denver in population and commercial activity, and Chicago, a city that is far larger and far more significant in commercial activities, is still cheaper and has more supply than Denver. None of those cities have marijuana cultivation, of course.

The initial lease of a warehouse for growing operations is just the first of many investments that cannabis growers must make.

All of the buildings for cannabis cultivation, whether new construction or Class B and C properties, have to be converted to accommodate cannabis operations and when I drove to Eric's growing operation the entire area near him was a hub of activity with construction contractors, HVAC contractors, electricians, security contractors and others milling about all the buildings. That's just the start of the economic impact of cannabis legalization since each growing operation will need lights, soil, nutrients, growing containers—on a scale of hundreds or thousands, and that adds up to hundreds of thousands of dollars going to vendors, for each marijuana business.

I spoke with a carbon dioxide provider who said to me,

"A typical Subway or McDonald's will buy 5,000 pounds of CO_2 in a six-month period. A cannabis growing facility? Those guys buy 12,000 pounds per month."

"What?" I asked in surprise, "why so much? What do they use so much CO_2 for?"

"The cannabis growers pump the CO_2 into their growing rooms to increase yields, and it works," said Mike. "We went to a grower that had four buildings and he was skeptical that CO_2 would do anything for him. He said, 'I tell you what, put the CO_2 into three of the buildings but leave the fourth building alone. When you come back next month we'll decide if we want to keep going or stop.' So the guy calls me a week and a half later and says, 'Put it in the fourth building as soon as you can.'"

Service Providers. There are a wide range of service providers that have emerged since cannabis legalization, most of whom have adapted their current business model to the new industry. These service providers include marketing and social media companies, consulting companies helping with traditional business plans but also with compliance and regulatory issues, security firms, accountants, law firms, and others. Perhaps no law firm has done more to take advantage of the opportunity than Vicente Sederberg. With just three employees in 2012, by 2016 the firm had grown to include an additional 13 attorneys, 6 policy and compliance employees, 7 administrators, and had offices in Boston, Washington D.C., and Las Vegas, in addition to Denver. By 2018 Vicente Sederberg had grown to 33 attorneys and opened offices in Los Angeles and Detroit. The firm also created an endowed chair at the Strum College of Law at the University of Denver, the "Vicente Sederberg Professor of Marijuana Law and Policy

Advocates, For and Against Legalization. There are a number of organizations that have emerged since 2014 that, prior to legalization, either did not exist or did not enjoy publicity on the national stage. For example, Kevin Sabet has been able to create tremendous opportunities for himself because of cannabis legalization. An obscure academic and government employee, Sabet and Patrick J. Kennedy founded the anti-cannabis non-profit SAM (Smart Approaches to Marijuana) in 2013, shortly after Colorado and Washington voted to legalize marijuana sales. Sabet thrust himself onto the center stage for all things anti-cannabis and has taken on the mantel of prohibition, with subtle nuances. He has written in the *New York Times,* the *Washington Post, Christian Science Monitor, LA Times, Huffington Post,* and numerous other national media outlets, as well as published a book with an obvious double entendre to the 1930's book, *Reefer Madness* with the title, *Reefer Sanity.* He currently has 4,500 followers on Twitter, and a full speaking schedule at high profile venues like the United Nations, the Aspen Ideas, New York Festivals, Senate hearings and has participated in hundreds of forums. Sabet has expanded his reach to Colorado, Hawaii, Maine, Massachusetts, Minnesota, Missouri, New York, Vermont, Washington, and twenty-two other states. Without a legalization movement, Kevin Sabet and SAM are irrelevant.

CanopyBoulder. Patrick Rea founded CanopyBoulder, an accelerator, in 2014. "We started in 2013 looking at the cannabis industry," Patrick told me. "We went to conferences, made connections with people and initially our idea was to create a venture capital fund in the $20 to 30 million-dollar range. But during that due diligence we learned that there weren't that many investment-worthy companies focusing on ancillary products and services to the industry at that time. So we turned our focus to early stage start-ups."

CanopyBoulder only funds companies that provide ancillary services. If you touch the plant, if you're a grower, dispensary owner, manufacturer of infused products, or testing facility, CanopyBoulder is not interested. They provide to entrepreneurs a number of services that will help them to be successful, such as mentors across a wide range of expertise, office space, networking opportunities, a venue to pitch one's business to cannabis investors, and at least $30,000 in seed capital. The program lasts sixteen weeks and over one hundred entrepreneurs apply for one of the ten available spots. "We've found that there are really three drivers for return on investment," Patrick stated, "and those are having an industry focus, research and due diligence for four weeks or longer, and active participation of the investor. This active participation has to be something that adds value beyond just giving money, like assistance in various parts of the business or networking opportunities. If you want this to work, if you want to scale it, you need a network, an ecosystem of people and businesses." In return for all the mentoring, connections, and seed capital, CanopyBoulder takes anywhere from six to nine percent in an equity stake in each business. Since its founding in 2014, CanopyBoulder has funded 80 companies, made over 100 investments in the industry, and the entrepreneurs who have gone through the accelerator have raised over $40 million in total investments.

Women Grow. Perhaps no organization in the legal cannabis industry has grown as quickly as Women Grow. The organization is focused on educating and connecting all segments of the cannabis industry, with a particular emphasis on helping women enter and be successful in the industry. Founded in 2014 in Denver, within several years Women Grow had expanded to 45 cities, claimed over 28,000 followers on Twitter and 15,000 subscribers to its newsletter. Their annual Leadership Summit in 2015 had 121 participants, but by 2016 it had over 1,300 participants and featured keynote speaker Melissa Etheridge. Women Grow is savvy in their approach to media and has been featured in *Forbes, Time, Fortune, Bloomberg, The Economist, Newsweek,* and other national publications.

Denver Post. In October of 2012 a *Denver Post* editorial titled, "Amendment 64 is the wrong way to legalize marijuana," strongly opposed Amendment 64, stating that, while the *Post* was in favor of cannabis legalization, they believed that the right approach was to change Federal policy, not State policy. Moreover, the editorial stated that they were strongly opposed to a State Constitutional amendment, rather than a statute, since any flaws in the amendment would be "baked into policy for years to come." A statue, on the other hand, could be modified by the Colorado House and Senate. But by November in 2013 the *Post* changed course on cannabis. In fact, the *Post* saw great economic opportunity in cannabis and advertised for an editor to head up an online supplement to the newspaper focused solely on the marijuana industry, called *The Cannabist*. They selected the *Post's* own Ricardo Baca, entertainment editor and music critic, to the position of the world's first "marijuana editor."

Initially, *The Cannabist* was to focus on news, features, entertainment, and reviews, but it has subsequently expanded and includes a wide range of articles and covers far more than cannabis in Colorado. For instance, *The Post* has a "strain of the day," how-to articles and recipes—like the helpful, "Your new Passover tradition: How to elevate seder dinner with cannabis"—as well as maps on where to purchase cannabis, events, a podcast, and others. *The Cannabist* even has a helpful advice column on a variety of pressing topics like, "How to get weed out of your system: Exploring the options," and "What are safe levels of cannabis use during pregnancy and breastfeeding?"

In late December 2015, the *Post* and *Cannabist* created a week-long series, "Cannabis in Colorado: Two Years After Legalization," in which the paper featured cannabis on the front page of the *Denver Post* each day with various highlights over the two-year period, like the skills needed to participate in the industry, marijuana and driving, tensions between towns that allow marijuana and neighboring towns that do not, and other special interest stories. In fact, over the course of the past two years at least, the *Post* has featured the marijuana industry on the front page several times per week. No other industry in the state of Colorado—not the oil and gas industry, not agriculture, not tourism—has received as much front-page coverage as the marijuana industry, and no industry in Colorado has its own newspaper supplement and website. And finally, to create an even greater stronghold on the "news" of marijuana, the *Post* encouraged reporters and editors to participate in the film, *Rolling Papers: A Documentary Film* that "features the cannabis culture in Colorado as told through *The Denver Post* & *The Cannabist*." In just four short years the *Denver Post* has done a complete about-face from adamantly opposed to Amendment 64, to promoting marijuana, and capitalizing on it. And the *Denver Post* did this everywhere possible—through the front page, through a separate website, through video, and by aligning with a documentarian and creating a film.

Medical Marijuana Businesses. No group of people has taken fuller advantage of legalization than the medical marijuana businesses—cultivators, infused manufacturers, and dispensaries—most of whom have been operating in a highly regulated market since 2010. But when recreational marijuana was legalized many municipalities, like Denver, stipulated that the only businesses that could be licensed for recreational marijuana had to be existing medical marijuana businesses. Several counties and cities, like Larimer County and Fort Collins still require recreational marijuana operators to be medical marijuana operators, too. Although that moratorium on new, non-medical marijuana experienced operators was set to expire January 1, 2016, the Denver City Council extended the moratorium, helping the existing recreational marijuana businesses—all of whom were medical marijuana operators—to retain their monopoly position. Consumers are harmed when producers have a monopoly position, because prices remain artificially high. For example, *High Times Magazine* lists the city, state, strain, and price per ounce of marijuana on a monthly basis and it is not the case that prices in Colorado, Washington, Oregon, and Alaska (states with legal marijuana sales) are the lowest in the nation. Instead, the prices are relatively stable at about $300 per ounce—regardless of location.

The prices in Colorado, and other legal states, should be significantly lower than prices in black market economies, but they are not. The continued high price of marijuana is counter to what economists predict, when a prohibited good becomes legal. But those predictions are based on free market principles, not monopoly or oligopoly principles. The cannabis industry has oligopoly tendencies, with limited producers and sellers of cannabis, resulting in higher prices. The quality has gone up, as predicted, because Colorado imposes strict testing procedures, but the expected price drop has not materialized.

Even without a moratorium on new recreational growing, manufacturing, or retail operations, there are systems in play that favor the existing businesses, promoting oligopoly-like markets, rather than free trade. For example, the City of Aurora had several requirements that worked against a new entrant from gaining a license because they penalized businesses that had fewer than three years of experience operating a marijuana business. Of course, only medical marijuana businesses could be awarded those points since no one else could be open that long.

Medical marijuana operators who have recreational retail locations have been able to create better financing options for themselves than new entrants. When Eric was looking for $10 million dollars, he had a serious investor within hours of reaching out to his real estate broker for help, while Johnny, Zander, and Jack—trying to create new legitimate businesses in the industry—struggled for months to get significantly less capital. The terms of Eric's deal were to pay the investors 11 percent over two years with an option to buy them out after two years. Johnny didn't have an existing location and was doing a ground-up buildout. He spent eight months looking for $1.5 million and the terms were never as attractive as what Eric was offered. In Johnny's deal the investors wanted an equity stake in the business of 15 percent plus a buyout option after five years, or they wanted to loan Johnny money at 40 percent over 40 months, which turns out to be a 22 percent annual interest rate—double what Eric would be paying, and for a lot longer time frame. Zander and Jack only needed $300,000 for their extraction business, but after a year and a half they still couldn't find any investor or group of investors to work with them and they are precluded from seeking a bank loan or SBA loan since cannabis is federally illegal.

In all respects, the power in the cannabis industry is held by the existing operators and nearly all of them were operating as medical marijuana cultivators, manufacturers, and dispensaries prior to the opening of legal recreational marijuana markets. And maybe, like Eric, Jason, and Ryan, a lot of them were operating in the black market before moving to the medical marijuana business. These operators have a chokehold on the industry that they are unlikely to give up and in the short term, at least, they will continue to reap the benefits of high prices and low operating costs, with no threat of any new businesses entering to disrupt the natural order of things.

There are more likely other people and organizations that have been able to capitalize on legal cannabis beyond the ones I have identified, like marijuana-friendly tours, marijuana-friendly bed and breakfast lodging, to name a few. And obviously, some people and organizations that have been unable to capitalize on legal cannabis, or have actually lost power since cannabis legalization. Drug enforcement agencies, whether at the state, local, or federal level, for example, ought to have budgets cut to reflect the lack of enforcement for marijuana violations. For Colorado, marijuana possession arrests dropped from 11,370 in 2012 to 5,998 in 2014, when cannabis was legal.

But for a few organizations and individuals that entered into the cannabis market early, not only has legalization of cannabis been a "green rush," but the participants have been able to create a monopoly position that will keep prices high, and profits enormously high.

Notes to Chapter Eleven

[1] For a review of the various models involved in regulating cannabis, see the very thorough article, "Considering Marijuana Legalization: Insights for Vermont and Other Jurisdictions," by world-leading cannabis researchers, Jonathan P. Caulkins, Beau Kilmer, Mark A. R. Kleiman, Robert J. MacCoun, Gregory Midgette, Pat Oglesby, Rosalie Liccardo Pacula, Peter H. Reuter. Chapter four is especially relevant. Accessed at:

http://www.rand.org/content/dam/rand/pubs/ research_reports/RR800/RR864/RAND_RR864.pdf

CHAPTER 12.

CONCLUSION

The great social theorists—Marx, Weber, Durkheim—as well as a host of other significant social scientists, thought and wrote about the structure of society during times of great transformation and turmoil. It is the chaos, the uncertainty of the current situation, that provides the raw data that leads to inspiration, new analyses, and a re-thinking about what is happening, and why. That is precisely the case with the newly legal cannabis industry in Colorado—it is a first-in-the world legal recreational cannabis market and no one could predict how that market would evolve. Would use of cannabis skyrocket if it were legal? Would crime rates spike upward? Would cartels increase their presence? Would the black market thrive? Would driving under the influence, teenage or youth use increase dramatically? Is wasn't clear what would happen—it was (and is) a social experiment.

So far, none of those negative societal effects have been realized and many of the trends are in the opposite direction from what opponents to legalization predicted. The social consequences of cannabis legalization have mostly been positive, and the impact has been far-reaching. Commercial real estate owners of class C properties have been able to fill vacancies and charge five times the rent of a class A location. Construction workers, security firms, equipment manufacturers, and a wide range of companies offering ancillary services have a new market to sell to. And the list of social impact from legalization of cannabis goes on: 18,000 new jobs created within the cannabis industry in Colorado alone, people have been hired within government to ensure that cannabis companies are compliant, and attorneys, lawyers, accountants, and consultants have new clients in the newly legal cannabis industry. The state of Colorado, since 2014, generated over $681 million in taxes, licenses, and fees that it didn't have before legalization. Communities like Garden City and Log Lane Village generated tax revenues that increase the quality of life for residents and business owners, improve decaying infrastructure, or invest in other worthwhile causes such as programs for youth.

The defining feature of Colorado's legal cannabis industry is one of first-mover advantages, and the advantages went to the existing medical marijuana cultivators, infused product manufacturers, and dispensary owners. They were the first businesses allowed to participate in recreational marijuana, and the opportunities to expand to other parts of the state were nonexistent, and mostly remain that way now, so competition is minimal. Only 23 percent of the jurisdictions in Colorado allow recreational marijuana sales; the other 77 percent either ban sales outright or have moratoria on recreational sales. And even those jurisdictions that did allow recreational marijuana after January 1, 2014, like Aurora, designed a process that severely penalized new entrants from gaining a license. Colorado's cannabis industry has the markings of an oligarchy—it is an industry controlled by a few companies and those companies have successfully thwarted competition from all quarters.

It may seem that the Colorado legislature capitulated to the demands of the cannabis industry given the structure that emerged, but the legislators were working under a very tight time frame—eight months from the passage of Amendment 64 to a July 1 deadline for a full regulatory scheme. That short time frame meant that there was little time to create a completely robust regulatory framework. In addition, everything about the future legal cannabis market was unknown so lawmakers put together the best framework they could. But, it's also true that legislators were operating from a mindset dominated by 80 years of propaganda foisted on the public by the Federal government. The rhetoric of marijuana is all negative despite ample evidence, known for decades, that the cannabis plant has positive benefits. There has been mostly fear surrounding cannabis and a belief that, if it were legalized, society would be far worse off along a number of dimensions, like crime, teenage use, and cartels. Given the near universal one-sided rhetoric of marijuana it is no wonder that the legislature was open to starting legal marijuana with the operators known to them from medical marijuana. But in doing so the legislature helped to create the oligopoly that exists today.

The conditions that existed in Colorado prior to legalization exist in all other states with medical marijuana laws: there is a medical marijuana industry with cultivators, manufacturers of infused products, dispensaries and, in some cases, caregivers. The bifurcated system of Colorado, with an existing medical marijuana regulatory system and a recreational system, wreaked havoc for legislators, and led to gaps, a loosely regulated system, and confusion. Law enforcement didn't have clear-cut directives on what to do if a caregiver had twenty pounds of cannabis in his or her car; they didn't know the constitutionality of searching a home and finding hundreds of plants that belonged to a caregiver. The Colorado Department of Public Health didn't have authority to enforce medical marijuana and their sole role was merely to register patients. The medical marijuana industry fueled the grey market, where a patient could have hundreds of plants assigned to him or her, but regulators had no way to track the plants, and no understanding of how those plants were used, or by whom. Every legislator and regulator that I spoke with said that, if they were to have a second chance to create regulations again, they would either start with recreational marijuana or regulate medical and recreational marijuana at the same time.

Every state with existing medical marijuana regulations is likely to face the same pressures that Colorado did. "Let us take the first bite out of the apple," the medical marijuana industry will say. "We are already doing this, we know the tracking system, the reporting system, and we have trained employees for cultivation and retail sales." And it is very likely that states without medical marijuana regulations will enact them within the next several years. Every national poll indicates that over 90 percent of Americans believe that medical marijuana should be legalized, and the numbers are higher if the question is worded in ways that allow physicians to prescribe medical marijuana. [1]

Most likely, the medical marijuana industry is already active in your state. Eric has relationships with potential partners in Nevada, Illinois, Massachusetts, Florida, and other states, and he is not the only cannabis entrepreneur developing those partnerships. The federal government, regardless of the party affiliation of the president, is unlikely to step in and stop medical marijuana, especially with 90 percent of Americans in favor of it.

But an oligarchy is not a good way to distribute goods and services. Typically, when there are a fixed number of producers of a good or service there is a fight among those producers for market share and usually a company increases market share by lowering price or increasing perceived value. That hasn't happened in the cannabis industry and is unlikely to happen since there isn't true competition, with no new entrants, and because demand is strong. For instance, Eric, the established cannabis operator told me that he could sell all the cannabis he could produce—there was never any leftover product. What industry has the luxury of selling everything they can produce? But, beyond intense demand, there are other forces at work beyond the oligopoly tendencies. For instance, all taxing authorities—state and local—would prefer prices to remain high. Since Colorado collects a 15 percent tax on the sale of wholesale cannabis, a drop in price from $2000 to $1000 would cut those tax revenues in half.

It seems that the market has found an equilibrium—there is flat demand, there are no new entrants, and even if some jurisdictions lift their ban or moratorium, those jurisdictions, like Aurora, could design an entry process that favors existing businesses rather than the start-up business. Marx, of course, would expect that cannabis industry participants would design a system that thwarted competition and kept prices high. It is a mild form of exploitation—mild because cannabis use is a choice, not a necessity, and because Colorado residents have the ability to grow their own cannabis and opt out of the recreational market entirely. But the cannabis industry is likely to remain stagnant, in terms of supply, and that benefits all the existing companies and hurts consumers.

While first-mover advantages define the legal cannabis market so far, that is not the only significant development, and the clash between the black market way of doing business and a corporate way of doing business is another defining characteristic. The black market is characterized by trust, firstly, and dealing with people you know and with whom you have a relationship. This relational and trust-based approach to doing business means that there are no contracts, that conflicts are resolved through negotiation rather than litigation, and most importantly, that a handshake and a person's word is the cement that binds people together. Weber would have immediately recognized the black market way of conducting business as a traditional form of business, although he would have used the term, "traditional authority," to describe it. And he would have recognized the corporate way of doing business with its focus on transactions, efficiencies, and scale, but would have called it "bureaucratic authority." Weber, most likely, would be surprised that traditional authority exists one hundred years after he theorized about it, but traditional authority, what I call a relational and trust-based form, solves problems for people operating illegal goods.

The shift from illegal to legal markets found in the cannabis industry brought into sharp contrast the differences between these two modes of managing a business. Eric, for example, was shocked that he had an agreement with a landlord for a property and the landlord broke his word and rented it to another cannabis business, because that's not done in the traditional cannabis business. Johnny was distraught after every conversation with Derek because he had an agreement with Derek, but Derek would return later with a totally different agreement that always worked in Derek's favor, but not in Johnny's. For people in the corporate world, changing your mind, seeking a better deal, working things to your advantage—those are things that are done in business every day, regardless of prior understanding or agreement. For the people transitioning from the black market, where your word is the bond, dealing with corporate America was a new and alarming experience.

There was unanimous agreement among the people I spoke with that the edibles manufacturers were the deceitful and dishonest operators in the cannabis industry. The manufacturers of edibles resisted control and regulation at every turn, even though people were harmed by using their product—and not just "people," but the most innocent and vulnerable people in our society: the two-, three-, and four-year olds who ingest an edible. *Caveat emptor.* The edibles manufacturers resisted providing information about the dosage and potency of their products. They were unwilling, without a directive from the State of Colorado, to provide child-proof packaging. They resisted labeling their products in a way that would differentiate a cannabis-infused product from one that was not. And they resisted having to tell consumers what constituted a serving size. All the emergency room visits by children involving marijuana were due to a child eating a marijuana-infused product. Every single one.

The ironic thing was, the edibles people were from corporate America, not from the traditional cannabis market. They were MBA's, successful real estate developers, traders, and business people like Patrick and Dave. Their intent was to make as much money as possible and they did that by buying existing candy and spraying it with cannabis oil, making a cannabis-infused edible identical to a non-infused piece of candy. The edibles manufacturers took full advantage of the emergent industry, exploited the ignorance of consumers, and resisted everything that would make their product safer. Unfortunately, the people most harmed so far have been children.

What does the future hold for marijuana? For medical marijuana it appears that more states will develop regulatory frameworks to make medical marijuana available to citizens, despite opposition from Kevin Sabet, SAM, and others. Doug Rosenberg, acting chief of the Drug Enforcement Agency stated, in a question and answer session with reporters, that medical marijuana is a "joke." This sounds like a desperate statement by someone who's power is about to be undermined, since the DEA not only has a mandate to eradicate cannabis, but also controls access to cannabis for research. Although Rosenberg did admit that extracts and other constituent parts show great promise medicinally, "smoking marijuana has never been shown to be safe or effective as a medicine." [2] The American Medical Association would disagree. In an analysis of 79 studies with over 6,000 patients they concluded that there was low-quality evidence that marijuana can be an effective medical treatment—and the "low-quality" evidence is due entirely to DEA restrictions on research.

In addition to the American Medical Association, the 2.6 million registered medical marijuana patients in the United States would also disagree with Rosenberg. There's evidence—anecdotal, of course since medical research has been stymied for decades—that marijuana is effective in treating migraines, epilepsy, Chron's disease, glaucoma, back pain...and 174 other ailments and conditions. Cannabis ought to be put through rigorous, double-blind medical research studies, and that will most likely happen.[3]

For recreational marijuana the future is less certain. Cannabis is the most widely consumed illicit drug in the United States, and it is grown in great quantities throughout the country, in every climate and growing condition. It's here whether you choose to believe that or not. Of course, the medical marijuana industry will advocate for legal recreational cannabis, and lawmakers will be interested in the future tax revenue streams that will result from legalizing marijuana. And as the oldest Americans die off (the people who are most opposed to cannabis legalization at the moment), support for legalizing cannabis will increase. But the structure of new regulatory frameworks may differ radically from Colorado's structure, and we might see government owned and operated cultivation, infused manufacturing, and dispensaries. But what's true in Colorado is true everywhere else in the United States: the smoke is out of the bottle.

Notes to Conclusion

[1] For a list of all state polls and national polls go to: http://medicalmarijuana.procon.org/view.additional-resource.php?resourceID=000149. Polls are listed by date and include the question asked, the sample size, the polling organization, the percentages in favor, don't know or neutral, and opposed.

[2] The Rosenberg comments can be found in a Washington Post article here: https://www.washingtonpost.com/news/wonk/wp/2015/11/10/the-dea-chief-called-medical-marijuana-a-joke-now-patients-are-calling-for-his-resignation/

[3] For a list of the ailments and conditions where marijuana has been reported as an effective treatment, see the United Patient's Group here: http://www.unitedpatientsgroup.com/resources/illnesses-treatable

And to see estimates of the number of medical marijuana patients in the United States, go here: http://medicalmarijuana.procon.org/view.resource.php?resourceID=005889

CHAPTER 13.

EPILOGUE

I started my research on cannabis legalization in June 2014, with little personal knowledge of anything having to do with the reality of cannabis. My beliefs about cannabis were preconceived and based on reports in the media and government information, but I had no direct knowledge of the cannabis subculture that permeates the United States, nor knowledge of the people who cultivate, manufacture, dispense, or use it. I approached the cannabis industry under a veil of ignorance and with an open mind. That perspective drove me to cast a wide net, to speak with as many people as possible involved in the industry, and to understand the perspective of people with strong ideological beliefs (for and against) cannabis legalization. At the time, I didn't have an ideological perspective on cannabis legalization myself, and *Legal Cannabis* details my intellectual journey to learn about the plant, the people involved in its cultivation and distribution, and to understand the social and economic consequences of cannabis legalization.

The cannabis legalization landscape is fast-changing, however, and there are numerous developments since I finished my research. For example, several states have put into motion initiatives to legalize both medical and recreational cannabis; most significantly, California started recreational sales January 1,

2018. As the fifth largest economy in the world, California is poised to generate significant revenues through legalization, as well as push legalization efforts forward.

The federal government, on the other hand, has reversed the policies of the Obama administration, invoking a prior U.S. Attorney General memo from 1980 and the Controlled Substances Act (enacted in 1971) to guide prosecution of marijuana crimes. On January 4, 2018, Attorney General Jefferson Sessions sent a one-page memo to State Attorney Generals stating that the approach to marijuana enforcement from the Trump administration reflects "Congress's determination that marijuana is a dangerous drug and that marijuana activity is a serious crime."[1] Additionally, Sessions rescinded "previous nationwide guidance specific to marijuana enforcement" (the Ogden and Cole memos) effective immediately.

The DEA also cracked down on marijuana and in 2018 made a rule change, initially proposed in 2011, to track marijuana extracts through a new code number. The DEA said that the rule change is administrative, to help medical and scientific researchers correctly categorize what part of the marijuana plant they are researching. Also, the new code number keeps the United States compliant with international treaties that code marijuana and marijuana extracts separately. Extracts from marijuana and hemp, like CBD oil, are used to treat a multitude of medical conditions, including child epilepsy and seizures. However, the new classification defines CBD oils and extracts as Schedule I controlled substances with "a high potential for abuse," and "no currently accepted medical use."[2] The rule change clarifies that any person or organization that manufactures, distributes, or uses marijuana extracts is in violation of federal criminal laws. The DEA effectively expanded the definition of cannabis, providing more control for the organization.

The cannabis industry changed tactics since I first began my research, despite victories in several states. In Colorado and other early cannabis legalization states, the Constitutional

Amendments, laws, and market for legal cannabis was referred to as "recreational marijuana." But the term "recreational" has negative connotations, implying that the people using cannabis are irresponsible, prone to partying, and young. The new term used by the cannabis industry is "adult-use," which implies the opposite: people using cannabis are responsible adults, they use cannabis in a thoughtful way, and the users are not young. The major complaint to legalization by opponents is that legalizing cannabis will trickle down to more use by young people and the semantic change to "adult-use" helps the cannabis industry address that concern and frame the issue closer to alcohol, a widely accepted substance.

UPDATE ON PEOPLE INTERVIEWED

Most of the people I interviewed during the research are doing the same thing when I last spoke with them: Brigitte Mars is still writing about herbs and giving workshops and seminars; Rav Ivker is still practicing medicine; Jonathan Singer is still serving in the Colorado House of Representatives; Governor Hickenlooper is serving out his final term as Governor of Colorado. Rachel O'Bryan is still fighting cannabis legislation and initiatives. Brian Vicente and Christian Sederberg are growing their cannabis law firm, expanding to more states and hiring more attorneys.

But a few people left the industry. Derek, the investor, no longer invests in the cannabis industry and is an executive for a company that revitalizes Colorado's aging pipeline infrastructure. Frank McNulty left the law firm to start a consulting company focused on political strategy, advocacy, and campaigns in Colorado. Andrew Freedman left his position as Director of Marijuana Coordination and started a consulting company to help other jurisdictions regulate cannabis. Pat Steadman took a job in the private sector but is positioning himself to get involved in politics in November 2018. Johnny scuttled his 30,000 s.f. cultivation facility but is still a master grower for the medical dispensary, and still putting together plans for a recreational retail store. Zander and Jack spent an enormous amount of time trying to get investors to provide funding but eventually figured out a way to grow their own marijuana and create extractions. The most surprising change happened to Eric and his partners. Eric once told me that you have to be "incredibly stupid" to go out of business in the marijuana industry. Well, Eric and his partners were incredibly stupid and are now out of the marijuana industry.

MY PERSONAL EXPERIENCE

My purpose in writing *Legal Cannabis* was to look at the emergent cannabis industry objectively, to understand the social and economic consequences of legalization, and to learn about the people involved in producing, consuming, and regulating the plant. My ignorance about the medicinal value of cannabis came to an end during the fall of 2017. I went camping and on the last day woke up with a sore back. It got progressively worse and within several days, I could not move without severe pain and I couldn't sleep more than 15 minutes at a time. Several days after that I lost all strength in my left leg and I couldn't move it—I couldn't even lift my leg an inch off the floor. When I finally went to my physician, she was understandably concerned that I could not move my leg and concerned that there was no precipitating event that led to my condition. She ordered a barrage of tests and prescribed pain medication: hydrocodone acetaminophen, gabapentin, and naproxen.

Gabapentin is a standard drug used to treat epilepsy and neurological conditions; naproxen is a stronger version of Aleve, and hydrocodone acetaminophen is an opioid. Because it's an opioid, I was limited to a 3-day supply. Unfortunately, none of those drugs helped reduce the pain I was in and I suffered for several more weeks before I remembered what Rav Ivker shared with me. He said that every person that he prescribes marijuana to reports back that the pain went away, and they could sleep through the night.

I was desperate for relief and went to a dispensary, described my condition to the budtender, and he suggested two solutions. First, he thought a cannabis infused oil rubbed on my leg would alleviate the pain and second, that eating an edible before bed would help me get to sleep. I was curious about the effects of the edible and asked him how much to use, and what the effects might be.

"Oh, I would start with 10 milligrams, which is one portion, and see how that works."

"And if that doesn't work, is it ok to take more?"

"Sure," he responded. "You could take the whole thing (100 mg) and you would definitely fall asleep, but you'd also wake up super hungry!"

The oil is a 1:1 ratio of CBD to THC so there's no possible side-effect, no way to get "high." The ingredients listed include cannabis infused grapeseed oil, avocado oil, jojoba, sweet almond oil, and a mild blend of essential oils that include peppermint, orange and cedar. And the usage states that it relieves dry skin, sore muscles and joints, speeds healing of injuries, increases circulation and promotes a feeling of relaxation and well-being. I applied the oil and took the edible and within 20 minutes I was relaxed and slept 6 hours for the first time in weeks. And I did the same thing in the middle of the night and slept another 6 hours. I continued with the 2 doses per night for about a week then scaled back to 1 dose per night. Within three weeks I was completely off the cannabis oil and edible since I could sleep through the night and had no pain.

I have empathy for the millions of Americans who are in pain, whether it's mild or severe, and who, because they live in a state with antiquated ideas about cannabis, are prevented from alleviating that pain. The War on Drugs is not really a war on drugs, but a war on people, on U.S. citizens. It's a war on children with epilepsy, on veterans with Post Traumatic Stress Disorder, on people with severe and chronic pain. It prevents people with arthritis, Crohn's disease, or hundreds of other debilitating medical conditions from legally being able get relief.

The so-called War on Drugs is a social construction, devised by powerful men and organizations to advance their self- and economic interests. The interests that drove decisions in 1937 are long gone, and the people who promoted them, deceased. I asked Frank McNulty why cannabis is still a Schedule I drug and he replied that it's not a motivating factor for Congress. That's one way to look at it. The other way is to say that the men and women of Congress lack the courage to change an unjust law. Congress knows that cannabis has potential to positively impact the lives of millions of Americans, but they have no fortitude to change anything, and people suffer. Congress knows that alcohol and tobacco cause far more harm than cannabis, and have real costs to society, but they have no courage to change the status quo.

After speaking with countless people in the cannabis industry, researching the medical benefits, understanding the social and economic impact of legalization, I have come to conclude that a new social construction, a new reality, for cannabis is needed. This new social construction will not come from the President, the Attorney General, or the Drug Enforcement Agency, since those people and organizations also lack courage. It will have to come from Americans, from the will of the people. It will have to come from the power of the people, exercising their free will to vote for a new reality. Until that happens, American society will remain hostage to the values and beliefs of 1937.

Notes to Epilogue

[1]   See   https://www.justice.gov/opa/press-release/file/1022196/download

[2] See https://www.thecannabist.co/2016/12/15/dea-cbd-new-rule-marijuana-extracts/69550/

ACKNOWLEDGEMENTS

Legal Cannabis is the result of a collaborative effort, infused with the ideas, insights, and candid experiences of many people within the cannabis industry, and within state and local government. To all the people who so generously took the time and made the effort to openly share their thoughts with me, I offer sincere gratitude. I also received a thorough reading of my book proposal from Margaret Emerson, Marie Anderson, and Elizabeth Uppman—all talented writers, meticulous readers, and helpful in drawing out and highlighting the salient points of the proposal. The manuscript was improved because of them. Blair Gifford brought his sociological and business acumen to the manuscript, providing helpful comments.

Two anonymous reviewers at the University of Chicago Press read both the proposal and final manuscript and they provided sharp criticism that strengthened the final product. Doug Mitchell, Senior Editor at the University of Chicago Press, was a staunch advocate throughout the review process, championing my manuscript. Ultimately, we decided that *Legal Cannabis* needed a different publishing path, but Doug provided invaluable support and, most importantly, an enthusiasm for the manuscript that propelled me forward.

My parents provided financial support, allowing me to finish the manuscript. My children distracted me when I needed to take a break from writing and gave me space when I needed to focus.

They provided emotional support throughout this long process and they carefully read early drafts, providing me with suggestions that improved the book. For that, I am grateful.

My younger sister, Bente Birkeland, opened all the doors to key policy-makers at the State Capitol. As a public radio reporter for Colorado Public Radio, Bente works closely with state elected officials and government leaders. Her stellar reputation helped me gain access to officials in the highest capacity in the state. The book was improved because of the regulator's perspective, and I am grateful for Bente's help in gaining access to them.

Finally, my wife, Gigi—as always—was steadfast and calm throughout what ended up being a tumultuous project. The writing took longer than I anticipated and came with unforeseen challenges. Her understanding was invaluable. I appreciate Gigi's strength, sunny disposition, and practicality—all of which were needed in full measure during this process, and all of which were immensely helpful in shaping the final book. With love, I am grateful.

REFERENCES

Abbott, Andrew. *Digital Paper: A manual for research and writing with library and internet materials.* Chicago: University of Chicago Press, 2014.

Abel, Ernest L. *Marihuana, the first twelve thousand years.* New York: McGraw-Hill, 1982. http://druglibrary.org/schaffer/hemp/history/first12000/abel.htm (accessed May 29, 2016).

Adler, Patricia. *Wheeling and dealing: An ethnography of an upper-level drug dealing and smuggling community.* New York: Columbia University Press, 1993.

American Civil Liberties Union. *The war on marijuana in black and white.* New York: ACLU, June 2013. https://www.aclu.org/report/war-marijuana-black-and-white?redirect=criminal-law-reform/war-marijuana-black-and-white (accessed May 29, 2016).

——. *Banking on bondage: Private prisons and mass incarceration.* New York: ACLU, November 2011. https://www.aclu.org/files/assets/bankingonbondage_20111102.pdf (accessed May 29, 2016).

Andelman, David A. 1994. *Foreign Affairs* (July / August): 95-108.

Anderson, D. Mark, Benjamin Hansen, and Daniel Rees. 2013.

Medical marijuana laws, traffic fatalities, and alcohol consumption. *Journal of Law and Economics* 56:333-369.

Anderson, Peter. 2006. Global use of alcohol, drugs, and tobacco. *Drug and Alcohol Review* 25:489-502.

Balabanova, Svetlana, S. Parsche, and Wolfgang Pirsig. 1992. First identification of drugs in Egyptian mummies. *Naturwissenschaften* 79(8): 358.

Baum, Dan. 1993. The war on drugs, 12 years later. *ABA Journal* (March): 70-74.

——.1992. The drug war and civil liberties. *Nation,* 29 June.

Becker, Gary S. 1968. Crime and punishment: An economic approach. *Journal of Political Economy* 78:169-217.

Becker, Gary S., and Kevin M. Murphy. 1988. A theory of rational addiction. *Journal of Political Economy* 96:675-700.

Becker, Gary S., Michael Grossman, and Kevin M. Murphy. 2006. The market for illegal goods: The case of drugs. *Journal of Political Economy* 114(11): 38-60.

——. 1994. An empirical analysis of cigarette addiction. *The American Economic Review* 84:396-418.

Becker, Howard S. *Outsiders: Studies in the sociology of deviance.* New York: The Free Press, 1963.

——. 1955. Marijuana use and social control. *Social Problems* 3(1): 35-44.

——. 1953. Becoming a marijuana user. *American Journal of Sociology* 59(3): 35-44.

Benson, Bruce L., David W. Rasmussen, and Iljoong Kim. 1998.

Deterrence and public policy: Trade-offs in the allocation of police resources. *International Review of Law and Economics* 18:77-100.

Bewley-Taylor, David, Martin Elvins, and Peter Reuter. 2008. Rethinking drug markets and societal reactions to them: Contributions in drug policy research. *Contemporary Drug Problems* 35 (Summer / Fall): 205-210.

British Medical Association. *Therapeutic uses of cannabis.* Dordrecht, The Netherlands: Harwood Academic, 1997.

Caputo, Michael R., and Brian J. Ostrom. 1994. Potential tax revenue from a regulated market: A meaningful review source. *Journal of Economics and Sociology* 55(4): 475-490.

Carey, James T. *The college drug scene.* Englewood Cliff, NJ: Prentice-Hall, 1968.

Caulkins, Jonathan P., Beau Kilmer, Mark A.R. Kleiman, Robert J. MacCoun, Gregory Midgette, Pat Oglesby, Rosalie Liccardo Pacula, and Peter H. Reuter. *Considering marijuana legalization: Insights for Vermont and other jurisdictions.* Santa Monica, CA: Rand Corporation, 2015. http://www.rand.org/content/dam/rand/pubs/research_reports/RR800/RR864/RAND_RR864.pdf (accessed May 29, 2016).

Caulkins, Jonathan P., Beau Kilmer, Robert J. MacCoun, Rosalie Liccardo Pacula, and Peter Reuter. 2011. Design considerations for legalizing cannabis: Lessons inspired by analysis of California's Proposition 19. *Addiction* 107:865-871.

Caulkins, Jonathan P., and Nancy Nicosia. 2009. What economics can contribute to the addiction sciences. *Addiction* 105:1156-1163.

Caulkins, Jonathan P., and Eric Sevigny. 2006. How many people does the U.S. imprison for drug use, and who are they? *Contemporary Drug Problems* (Fall): 405-428.

Caulkins, Jonathan P., Bruce Johnson, Angela Taylor, and Lowell Taylor. 1999. What drug dealers tell us about their costs of doing business. *Journal of Drug Issues* 29(2) 323-340.

Caulkins, Jonathan P. and Peter Reuter. 1998. What price data tell us about drug markets. *Journal of Drug Issues* 28:593-612.

Clements, Kenneth W., Yihui Lan, and Xueyan Zhao. 2010. The demand for marijuana, tobacco and alcohol: Inter-commodity interactions with uncertainty. *Empirical Economics* 39:203-239.

Coleman, James S. 1987. Forward to *The organizational state: Social choice in national policy domains* by Edward O. Laumann and David Knoke. Madison: University of Wisconsin Press, 1987.

Colorado Ballot Initiative. November 6, 2012. *Amendment 64: Use and Regulation of Marijuana.* http://www.fcgov.com/mmj/pdf/amendment64.pdf (accessed September 16, 2015).

Colorado Department of Public Health and Environment. 2016. *Medical marijuana statistics and data.* https://www.colorado.gov/pacific/cdphe/medical-marijuana-statistics-and-data (accessed May 29, 2016).

——. 2013. *Healthy Kids Colorado Survey.* https://www.colorado.gov/pacific/cdphe/hkcs (accessed May 29, 2016).

Colorado Department of Revenue, Enforcement Division – Marijuana. 2015. *House Bill 14-1366 Marijuana Edibles Work Group Report.* https://www.colorado.gov/pacific/sites/default/files/HB%201366%20Work%20Group%20Report_FINAL.pdf (accessed June 3, 2016).

Colorado Executive Order B2012-004. 2013. *Task Force Report on the Implementation of Amendment 64.* http://www.colorado.gov/cms/forms/dor-tax/A64TaskForceFinalReport.pdf (accessed June 3, 2016).

Colorado General Assembly. House. 2015. *Concerning Reasonable Restrictions on the Sale of Edible Retail Marijuana Products.* House Bill 14-1366. Second Regular Session, Sixty-ninth General Assembly.

——. 2010. *Concerning Regulation of Medical Marijuana.* House Bill 10-1284. Second Regular Session, Sixty-seventh General Assembly. http://www.leg.state.co.us/clics/clics2010a/csl.nsf/fsbillcont/0C6B6577EC6DB1E8872576A80029D7E2?Open&file=1284_01.pdf (accessed June 3, 2016).

Colorado General Assembly. Senate. 2015. *Concerning Marijuana Issues That Are Not Regulated By The Department Of Revenue And, In Conjunction Therewith, Making Appropriations.* Senate Bill 15-014. First Regular Session, Seventieth General Assembly. https://www.colorado.gov/pacific/sites/default/files/SB_15_014.pdf (accessed June 3, 2016).

Crancer, Alfred. 1969. Comparison of the effects of marijuana and alcohol on simulated driving performance. *Science* 164:851-854.

Cressey, Donald R. *Theft of a nation: The structure and operations of organised crime in America.* New York: Harper and Row, 1969.

Dawkins, Marvin P. 1997. Drug use and violent crime among adolescents. *Adolescence* 32:395-405.

Decorte, Tom. 2010. Small scale domestic cannabis cultivation: An anonymous Web survey among 659 cannabis cultivators in Belgium. *Contemporary Drug Problems* 37(Summer): 341-370.

Denton, Barbara. *Dealing: Women in the drug economy.* Sydney, Australia: University of New South Wales Press, 2001.

DiMarzo, Vincenzo. 2008. CB(1) receptor antagonism: Biological basis for metabolic effects. *Drug Discovery Today* 13(23-24): 1026-1041.

DiNardo, John and Thomas Lemieux. 2001. Alcohol, marijuana and American youth: The unintended consequences of government regulation. *Journal of Health Economics* 20:991-1010.

Duke, Steven B., and Albert C. Gross. *America's longest war: Rethinking our tragic crusade against drugs.* New York: G.P. Putnam's Sons, 1993.

Earleywine, Mitch, ed. *Pot politics: Marijuana and the costs of prohibition.* Oxford: Oxford University Press, 2007.

Fagan, Jeffrey. 1993. Interactions among drugs, alcohol, and violence. *Journal of Health Affairs* 1: 65-79.

Fergusson, David M., Joseph M. Boden, and L. John Horwood. 2006. Cannabis use and other illicit drug use: Testing the cannabis gateway theory. *Addiction* 101:556-569.

Fields, Alan B. 1984. Weedslingers: Young black marijuana dealers. *Urban Life* 13:247-270.

Friedman, Milton. 1972. Prohibition and drugs. *Newsweek,* May 1.

——. 1991. The war we are losing. In *Searching for alternatives: Drug-control policy in the United States,* ed. Melvyn B. Krauss and Edward P. Lazear, 53-67. Stanford, CA: Hoover Institution Press.

Galenianos, Manolis, Rosalie Liccardo Pacula, and Nicola

Perisco. 2012. A search-theoretic model of the retail market for illicit drugs. *Review of Economic Studies* 79:1239-1269.

Gettman, Jon. 2006. Marijuana production in the United States (2006). *The Bulletin of Cannabis Reform* (December).

Goffman, Irving. *Stigma.* Englewood Cliff, NJ: Prentice-Hall, 1963.

Goode, Erich. *The marijuana smokers.* New York: Basic, 1970.

Gray, James P. *Why our drug laws have failed and what we can do about it.* Philadelphia: Temple University Press, 2001.

Green, Bob, David Kavanagh, and Ross Young. 2003. Being stoned: A review of self-reported cannabis effects. *Drug and Alcohol Review* 22:453-460.

Hall, Wayne. 2006. Dissecting the causal anatomy of the link between cannabis and other illegal drugs. *Addiction* 101:472-473.

Hall, Wayne, Nadia Solowij, and Jim Lemon. *The health and psychological consequences of cannabis use.* Canberra: Australia Government Publishing Service, 1994.

Hallstone, Michelle. 2002. Updating Howard Becker's theory of using marijuana for pleasure. *Contemporary Drug Problems* 29(Winter): 821-845.

Harcourt, Bernard E., and Jens Ludwig. 2007. Reefer madness: Broken windows policing and misdemeanor marijuana arrests in New York city, 1989-2000. *Public Policy* 6(1): 165-181.

Harding, Philip, and Richard Jenkins. *The myth of the hidden economy.* Milton Keynes: Open University Press, 1989.

Hazekamp, Arno. 2008-2009. *Cannabis review.* Department of Plant Metabolomics, Leiden University. http://www.oregon.gov/pharmacy/imports/marijuana/staffinfo/cannabisre-view.pdf (accessed October 25, 2015).

Hemphill, John K., Jocelyn C. Turner, and Paul G. Mahlberg. 1980. Cannabinoid content of individual plant organs from different geographical strains of cannabis sativa L. *Journal of Natural Products* 43:112-122.

Henchman, Joseph. 2014. Taxing marijuana: The Washington and Colorado experience. *Tax Foundation Policy Blog* August 25. http://taxfoundation.org/article/taxing-marijuana-washington-and-colorado-experience (accessed December 19, 2014).

Hill, C. Stratton, Jr. 1993. The barriers to adequate pain management with opioid analgesics. *Seminars in Oncology* 20:1-5.

Inciardi, James A., Hilary L. Surratt, and Christine A. Saum. *Cocaine-exposed infants: Social, legal, and public health issues.* Thousand Oaks, California: Sage, 1997.

Institute of Medicine. *Marijuana and medicine: Assessing the science base.* Washington, DC: National Academy Press, 1999.

Jacobson, Mireille. 2003. Drug testing in the trucking industry: The effect on highway safety. *Journal of Law and Economics* 46:131-156.

Johnson, Bruce D. *Marijuana users and drug subcultures.* New York: John Wiley and Sons, 1973.

Kaestner, Robert, and Michael Grossman. 1998. The effects of drug use on workplace accidents. *Labour Economics* 5:267-294.

Kandel, Denise. 1975. Stages in adolescent involvement in drug use. *Science* 190:912-914.

Kandel, Eric R., and Denise B. Kandel. 2014. A molecular basis for nicotine as a gateway drug. *New England Journal of Medicine*

371:932-943. http://www.nejm.org/doi/full/10.1056/
NEJMsa1405092 (accessed May 27, 2016).

Kandel, Denise, Kazuo Yamaguchi, and Laura Cousino Klein.
2006. Testing the gateway hypothesis. *Addiction* 101:470-472.

Kelley, Erin, Shane Darke, and Joanne Ross. 2004. A review of
drug use and driving: Epidemiology, impairment, risk factors
and risk perceptions. *Drug and Alcohol Review* 23:319-344.

King, Rufus. *The drug hang-up: America's fifty-year folly.* New
York: Norton, 1972.

LaGasse, Linda L., Ronald Seifer, and Barry M. Lester. 1999.
Interpreting research on prenatal substance exposure in the
context of multiple confounding factors. *Clinics in Perinatology*
26:39-54.

La Guardia Committee Report. *The Marihuana Problem in the
City of New York.* Prepared for the Mayor's Committee on Marihuana by the New York Academy of Medicine City of New
York, 1944. http://www.druglibrary.org/schaffer/library/stud-
ies/lag/lagmenu.htm (accessed May 30, 2016).

Levine, Harry G. 2002. The secret of worldwide drug prohibition. *Independent Review* 7(2): 165-180.

Levitt, Stephen. 2003. Review of *Drug War Heresies* by MacCoun
and Reuter. *Journal of Economic Literature* 41:540-544.

Lewontin, Richard C. 1995. Sex, lies, and social science. *New
York Review of Books* April 20.

Liguori, Anthony. 2007. Marijuana and driving: Trends, design
issues, and future recommendations. In *Pot politics: Marijuana
and the costs of prohibition,* ed. Mitch Earleywine. Oxford: Oxford
University Press, 2007.

Light, Miles K., Adam Orens, Brian Lewandowski, and Todd Pickton. 2014. *Market size and demand for marijuana in Colorado.* Prepared for Colorado Department of Revenue. https://www.colorado.gov/pacific/sites/default/files/Market%20Size%20and%20Demand%20Study,%20July%209,%202014[1].pdf (accessed September 12, 2014).

Longo, M.C., C.E. Hunger, R.J. Lokan, J.M. White, and M.A. White. 2000. The prevalence of alcohol, cannabinoids, benzodiazepines and stimulants amongst injured drivers and their role in driver culpability: PartII: The relationship between drug prevalence and drug concentration, and driver culpability. *Accident Analysis and Prevention* 32:623-632.

Lukes, Stephen. *Power: A radical view.* London: Macmillan, 1974.

MacCoun, Robert J. 2011. What can we learn from the Dutch cannabis coffeeshop system? *Addiction* 106:1899-1910.

——. 2006. Competing accounts of the gateway hypothesis: The field thins, but still no clear winner. *Addiction* 101:473-474.

MacCoun, Robert J., and Peter Reuter. *Drug war heresies: Learning from other vices, times and places.* Cambridge: Cambridge University Press, 2001.

Marijuana Business Daily. *Marijuana business factbook 2015.* Pawtucket, RI: Anne Holland Ventures, Inc., 2015.

Marx, Karl. 1961. The class struggle. In *Theories of society: Foundations of modern sociological theory,* ed. Talcott Parsons, Edward Shils, Kaspar D. Naegele, and Jesse R. Pitts 2(C): 529-535. New York: The Free Press.

Matsuda, Lisa A., Stephen J. Lolait, Michael J. Brownstein, Alice C. Young, and Tom I. Bonner. 1990. Structure of a cannabinoid receptor and functional expression of the cloned cDNA. *Nature* 346:651-654.

Mehmedic, Zlatko, Suman Chandra, Desmond Slade, Heather Denham, Susan Foster, Amit S. Patel, Samir A. Ross, Ikhlas A. Khan, and Mahmoud A. ElSohly. 2010. Potency trends of Δ9-THC and other cannabinoids in confiscated cannabis preparations from 1993 to 2008. *Journal of Forensic Science* 55(5): 1209-1217. http://home.olemiss.edu/~suman/potancy%20paper%202010.pdf (accessed October 6, 2015).

Mills, Evan. 2012. The carbon footprint of indoor cannabis production. *Energy Policy* 36:56-67. http://evan-mills.com/indoor_files/cannabis-carbon-footprint.pdf (accessed May 28, 2016).

Miron, Jeffrey A. 2006. The market for illegal goods: The case for drugs. *Journal of Political Economy* 114(1): 38-60.

——. *Drug war crimes: The consequences of prohibition.* Independent Institute, 2004.

——. 2003. Do prohibitions raise prices? Evidence from the markets for cocaine and heroin. *Review of Economics and Statistics* 85(3): 522-530.

——. 2001. The economics of drug prohibition and drug legalization. *Social Research* 68(3): 835-855.

Miron, Jeffrey A., and Jeffrey Zwiebel. 1995. The economic case against drug prohibition. *Journal of Economic Perspectives* 9(4): 175-192.

Mishan, E.J. 2001. The staggering costs of drug criminalisation. *Economic Affairs* 21(1): 37-42.

Moeller, Kim. 2012. Estimating drug policy expenditures: Direct costs of policing cannabis in Copenhagen 2000-2009. *Drugs: education, prevention and policy* 19(5): 379-386.

——. 2011. Costs and revenues in street-level cannabis dealing. *Trends in Organized Crime* 15:31-46.

Munro, Sean, Kerrie L. Thomas, and Muna Abu-Shaar. 1993. Molecular characterization of a peripheral receptor for cannabinoids. *Nature* 365(6441): 61-65.

National Commission on Marihuana and Drug Abuse. *Marihuana, A Signal of Misunderstanding.* Commissioned by President Richard M. Nixon March, 1972. http://www.iowamedicalmarijuana.org/documents/nc1contents.aspx (accessed May 30, 2016).

Northrup, David A. 1996. The problem of self-report in survey research. *Institute for Social Research* 11 (Fall) no. 3.

Osbourne, Geraint B., and Curtis Fogel. 2008. Understanding the motivations for recreational marijuana use among adult Canadians. *Substance Use and Misuse* 43:539-572.

Perrone, Dina, Randi Helgesen, and Ryan G. Fischer. 2013. United States drug prohibition and legal highs: How drug testing may lead cannabis users to spice. *Drugs: education, prevention and policy* 20(3): 216-224.

Plant, Martin A., and Charles E. Reeves. 1976. Participant observation as a method of collecting information about drug taking: Conclusions from two English studies. *British Journal of Addiction* 71:155-159.

Redlinger, Lawrence. Dealing in Dope: Market Mechanisms. PhD diss., Northwestern University, Department of Sociology, 1969.

Reinarman, Craig, and Peter Cohen. 2007. Law, culture, and

cannabis: Comparing use patterns in Amsterdam and San Francisco. In *Pot Politics: Marijuana and the Costs of Prohibition,* ed. Mitch Earleywine. Oxford: Oxford University Press.

Reuter, Peter. 2005. What drug policies cost: Estimating government drug policy expenditures. *Society for the Study of Addiction* 101:315-322.

Reuter, Peter, and Mark A.R. Kleiman. 1986. Risks and prices: An economic analysis of drug enforcement. In *Crime and justice: An annual review of research,* ed. M. Tonry and M. Norris, 7:128-179. Chicago: University of Chicago Press.

Richardson, Gale A., Nancy L. Day, and Peggy J. McGauhey. 1993. The impact of prenatal marijuana and cocaine use on the infant and child. *Clinical Obstetrics and Gynecology* 36, no. 2:302-318.

Russo, Ethan B.. 2007. History of cannabis and its preparations in saga, science, and sobriquet. *Chemistry and Biodiversity* 4(8): 1614-1648.

Saniotis, Arthur. 2010. Evolutionary and anthropological approaches toward understanding human need for psychotropic and mood altering substances. *Journal of Psychoactive Drugs* 42(4): 477-183.

Schlosser, Eric. 1994a. Marijuana and the law. *Atlantic Monthly,* September.

——. 1994b. Reefer madness. *Atlantic Monthly,* August.

Sewell, R. Andrew, James Poling, and Mehmet Sofuogla. 2009. The effects of cannabis compared with alcohol on driving. *The American Journal on Addictions* 18(3): 185-193.

Shanahan, Marian, and Alison Ritter. 2013. Confronting the

challenges of conducting a CBA of cannabis policies. *Drugs: education, prevention and policy* 20(3): 175-183.

Shepard, Edward M., and Paul R. Blackley. 2005. Drug enforcement and crime: Recent evidence from New York State. *Social Science Quarterly* 86(2): 323-324.

Smiley, Alison. 1986. Marijuana: On-road and driving simulator studies. *Alcohol, Drugs, and Driving* 2, no. 3-4:121-134.

Turner, Carlton E., Mahmoud A. Elsohly, and Edward G. Boeren. 1980. Constituents of cannabis sativa L. XVII. A review of the natural constituents. *Journal of Natural Products* 43(2): 169-234.

United Nations. *Single Convention on Narcotic Drugs, 1961.* https://www.unodc.org/pdf/convention_1961_en.pdf (accessed May 30, 2016).

United Nations Office on Drugs and Crime. *World Drug Report 2015.* https://www.unodc.org/documents/wdr2015/World_Drug_Report_2015.pdf (accessed May 29, 2016).

U.S. Department of the Treasury, Financial Crimes Enforcement Network. *BSA Expectations Regarding Marijuana-related Businesses.* February 14, 2014. https://www.fincen.gov/statutes_regs/guidance/pdf/FIN-2014-G001.pdf (accessed October 28, 2015).

U.S. Department of Transportation. *Marijuana and Actual Driving Performance.* Washington, DC: U.S. Department of Transportation, 1993.

U.S. Justice Department. *Guidance Regarding Marijuana Related Financial Crimes.* Prepared by James M. Cole, February 14, 2014. https://www.justice.gov/sites/default/files/usao-wdwa/legacy/2014/02/14/DAG%20Memo%20-%20Guidance%20Regarding%20Marijuana%20Related%20Finan-cial%20Crimes%202%2014%2014%20%282%29.pdf (accessed October 28, 2015).

——. *Memorandum for Selected United State Attorneys on Investigations and Prosecutions in States Authorizing the Medical use of Marijuana.* Prepared by David W. Ogden, October 19, 2009. https://www.justice.gov/opa/blog/memorandum-selected-united-state-attorneys-investigations-and-prosecutions-states (accessed October 16, 2015).

Valdez, Avelardo, Charles D. Kaplan, Russell L. Curtis, and Zenong Yin. 1995. Illegal drug use, alcohol and aggressive crime among Mexican-American and White male arrestees in San Antonio. *Journal of Psychoactive Drugs* 27(2): 135-143.

Venkatesh, Sudhir. *Gang leader for a day: A rogue sociologist takes to the streets.* New York: Penguin Books, 2008.

Warf, Barney. 2014. High points: An historical geography of cannabis. *Geographical Review* 104(4): 414-438.

Washington Initiative 502. November 6, 2012. *Initiative Measure No. 502: An Act Relating to Marijuana.* http://sos.wa.gov/_assets/elections/initiatives/i502.pdf (accessed September 16, 2015).

Weber, Max. 1961. The types of authority. In *Theories of society: Foundations of modern sociological theory,* ed. Talcott Parsons, Edward Shils, Kaspar D. Naegele, and Jesse R. Pitts 2(D): 626-632. New York: The Free Press.

Wegman, Jesse. The injustice of marijuana arrests. *New York Times* July 28, 2014.

Whyte, William Foote. *Street Corner Society.* Chicago: University of Chicago Press, 1959.

Wilkins, Chris, and Paul Sweetsur. 2006. Exploring the structure of the illegal cannabis market. *De Economist* 154(4): 547-562.

Wilson, James Q., and George L. Kelling. 1982. Broken windows: The police and neighborhood safety. *The Atlantic,* March.

Yuan, Yuehong, and Jonathan P. Caulkins. 1998. The effect of variation in high-level domestic drug enforcement on variation in drug prices. *Socio-Economic Planning Sciences* 32, no. 4:265.

ABOUT PETER M. BIRKELAND

Peter M. Birkeland received his Ph.D. in sociology from the University of Chicago. He is the author of *Franchising Dreams: The Lure of Entrepreneurship* (University of Chicago Press) and writes about business, entrepreneurship, and society. Peter was named by *Fortune Small Business* as one of the "Top Ten Minds in Business."

He has been featured on national media, including NPR's *Talk of the Nation,* and *To The Best of Our Knowledge,* other national programs (*Voice of America,* Fox Business News) and multiple local and regional radio programs. He has written for *Fortune Small Business, Franchise Times,* and other publications, and has delivered Keynote Addresses at Jimmy John's, Meineke, Harris Private Banking Leadership Conference and other companies. Peter speaks regularly at academic, trade, industry, and government organizations.

He lives in Longmont, Colorado.

To learn more about Peter or connect with him, see www.peterbirkeland.com.

To connect with other readers, read reviews, or buy the book, visit www.greatsocialexperiment.com

www.ingramcontent.com/pod-product-compliance
Lightning Source LLC
Chambersburg PA
CBHW020654270326
41928CB00005B/120